ALARUMS & EXCURSIONS

"Quite simply the most insightful book on Europe's politics today. A unique blend of behind-the-scenes knowledge, compelling ideas and powerful political judgement." Donald Tusk, President of the European Council, 2014–19

"Whatever our future relationship with the EU, our prosperity will be hugely dependent on understanding what it is, how it works, where it might be headed and what crises, beyond Brexit, it is trying to surmount. This book is a truly brilliant guide on all. An extraordinary combination of clear-sighted, forensic and sober analysis." Sir Ivan Rogers, British Ambassador to the EU, 2013–17 and author of the bestselling *9 Lessons in Brexit*

"Refreshing and perceptive ... Van Middelaar is a more thoughtful guide than most, in part because he brings the eye of a political theorist to his years working for the European Council president." Alex Barker, *Financial Times*

"a brilliant series of case studies that illuminate different points in the creation of a new European political theater unscripted by the innumerable treaties and rules that created the EU as we know it today." James McAuley, *New York Review of Books*

"brilliant ... his discussion of the high politics of migration is the best thing yet written on the subject." Christopher Hill, "Book of the Week", *Times Higher Education*

"Van Middelaar, a former adviser to Herman Van Rompuy, is a very fine writer and academic, and has penned the most insightful and original book on this era of European politics." Florian Eder, Politico Brussels Playbook

"Highly recommended if you are interested in understanding present day Europe (and the EU)." Alberto Nardelli, Buzzfeed News

"Part insider memoir and part commentary, this is probably the best analysis yet to appear of how the EU managed its recent crises over refugees, Ukraine, and the euro." Andrew Moravcsik, *Foreign Affairs*

"Van Middelaar writes succinctly and elegantly, moving seamlessly between Machiavelli and the nitty-gritty of daily EU politics ... should be required reading for scholars, practitioners and interested members of the public alike." Leonard Schuette, *International Affairs*

"One of the most thoughtful and uncompromising books to appear on the EU in recent years. It should be widely read by EU specialists and used as a core text for EU studies in advanced graduate seminars." Mark Gilbert, *Journal of Common Market Studies*

"With his fluid style and sharp eye for detail and context, Luuk van Middelaar has captured many of the critical themes with which Europe must grapple over the coming years ... I found his observations rewarding as they often provided new insights and valuable distillations of complicated issues." Anthony Gardner, US Ambassador to the EU, 2014–17

"Elegantly-written ... combines the inside knowledge of a participant in the theatre of European politics with the critical distance of the political theorist. It is neither a partisan defence of the European Union nor a pessimistic prophecy of doom, but a cool analysis of the role of European institutional structures and of key personalities." Bruno De Witte, Professor of European Law, Maastricht University and European University Institute

"This splendid new volume, written by perhaps the ultimate 'insider' ... will become perhaps one of the most important texts for students, teachers and would-be reformers for many years to come." Derek Hawes, *Journal of Contemporary European Studies*

"Lively and well-informed ... offers thought-provoking insights into the European Union, its ways of working its many challenges, both historical and contemporary." Professor Dame Helen Wallace FBA

"a fascinating take on events in recent European history." Matthew Partridge, *MoneyWeek*

"an elegant and magisterial follow-up to his 2013 study, *The Passage to Europe* ... Van Middelaar writes in a literary style which is immensely pleasurable to read and lards the texts with insights from classical philosophers and strategists which further enhance the pleasure." Martin Westlake, *European Political Science Review*

"While it reads like a thriller, this book provides one of the most lucid and profound analyses of European politics in recent years. ... This perspicuous, arresting, and insightful book on Europe is a must-read for every practitioner, student and scholar interested in the Union." Johann Justus Vasel, *European Journal of International Law*

ALARUMS & EXCURSIONS

Improvising Politics on the European Stage

LUUK VAN MIDDELAAR

Translated by Liz Waters

agenda
publishing

English translation © Agenda Publishing Ltd 2019, 2020

Translated by Liz Waters

First published as *De nieuwe politiek van Europa*
by Historische Uitgeverij, Groningen

© Luuk van Middelaar 2017, 2019, 2020

The publisher gratefully acknowledges the support of the
Europa Instituut of Leiden University and the
Dutch Foundation for Literature.

N ederlands
letterenfonds
dutch foundation
for literature

First English-language edition published in 2019
by Agenda Publishing

First paperback edition 2020

Agenda Publishing Limited
The Core
Bath Lane
Newcastle Helix
Newcastle upon Tyne
NE4 5TF

www.agendapub.com

ISBN 978-1-78821-172-7 (hardback)
ISBN 978-1-78821-277-9 (paperback)

British Library Cataloguing-in-Publication Data
A catalogue record for this book is available from the British Library

Typeset in Nocturne by Patty Rennie

Printed and bound in the UK by TJ International

Contents

Preface

I'll play it first and tell you what it is later.

Miles Davis

During 70 years of peace and prosperity, the political debate in Europe revolved around issues of growth and redistribution, education and health-care, freedom and identity. Far less was said about state and authority, strategy and war, security and the border, citizenship and opposition. The preconditions for the miracle play that is a free society disappeared from view. A succession of wars, civil wars, dictatorships and military conflicts in other places should have reminded us that Europe's democratic paradise cannot be taken for granted, but we managed to reason away all those warnings. The rest of the world had yet to achieve our level of civilization: we had arrived at world history's end. Then suddenly the crises came: banks collapsed, the euro wobbled, Russia attacked Ukraine and annexed Crimea, vast numbers of desperate people attempted to cross into Europe, and in Washington a new president, Donald Trump, pulled the US security rug from underneath the European continent. And so the realization dawned that our order is fragile, our future no smooth highway. Politics matters. "History is back".[1] We live in a world of conflict and rivalry, of force and counterforce. A reorientation has become a bitter necessity.

It is difficult for today's politicians to find or recall suitable language and gestures for this situation, certainly for those in the European arena. Historically the European Union's model of cooperation has relied on imagining politics away. The Brussels institutions, working methods and ways of thinking are designed to smother political passions with a web of rules: depoliticization. This is a strength when building a market, when regulating cucumbers and bananas (and the web is powerful, enmeshing as well as connecting, as few things demonstrate better than Britain's divisive attempt to extricate itself). But depoliticization quickly turns into weakness when there is a need to act and to respond to events, as has been clear almost daily since the financial crisis of 2008.

When danger arises and sudden threats emerge, when stark decisions must be taken and the public persuaded to endorse those choices, other political qualities are needed: speed and determination, a keen judgement of the situation, visible gestures and authoritative words; leadership, in sum. Under the pressure of recent events, often in violation of their own deeply held beliefs, European leaders – in Berlin, Paris, Brussels and elsewhere – have been improvising this new politics, in order to save their Union. It was never going to be a straightforward process, and it has indeed featured serious mishaps and bitter disputes, with rival visions of the future set out in the open in front of disgruntled voters. The Brussels backroom rule-making factory is giving way to political drama played out on a continent-wide stage: a sign of Europe's political maturity. After ten years of improvisations it is time to reflect on what we have seen.

Conveying the feverish mood when action becomes imminent, *Alarums and Excursions* tells the inside story of Europe's political metamorphosis and deciphers its consequences for political actors and the public alike. "Alarums and excursions" is an Elizabethan stage direction used to prepare the actors for an onstage skirmish or to make the noise of battle. It refers to tumultuous activity and clamour, so it captures the response to the crises that the European actors have faced. The theatre metaphor also points to the voters and their relationship to that political drama: as an audience they stand outside looking in, even though in principle they can change the cast. Their participation is limited, but observation and scrutiny are essential, as the European grand plan has gone from being a backstage activity to one played out in full view.

Almost ten years ago I published a book that was later translated into English as *The Passage to Europe*. Is this book a sequel? Yes, in the sense that *The Passage* laid the groundwork for an understanding of the EU and its prospects. Many of its main themes are further pursued here and the book has proven its worth as a conceptual toolkit for developments that to some extent had yet to occur. But at the same time, no, because *Alarums and Excursions* is not a book that starts where its forerunner ended, nor is it a chronicle of the years 2009–18. In order to understand the frenzied present and shape the open future, a fresh look at the past is indispensable.

The scrutability of political activity is of vital importance to democracy. Incomprehension is the gateway to mistrust, and mistrust opens the door to indifference, despondency or revolt. The aim of this book is therefore to provide insight. Not final verdicts, easy solutions or academic polemics but interpretation and analysis in the form of stories, images and concepts that make readers better able to judge for themselves – and to act accordingly.

For this book, more than for *The Passage*, I have been able to draw upon personal experience at the very heart of the European Union. From early 2010 to early 2015 I worked as speechwriter for the first permanent president of the European Council, Herman Van Rompuy.[2] I watched from close proximity at nocturnal summits as the 28 heads of state and government battled with the markets and with each other to save the euro, or responded to the Arab uprisings and the Russian invasion of Crimea. As a speechwriter I experienced first-hand how difficult it is to tell a convincing common story, how this one "Europe" from Dublin to Sofia and from Madrid to Helsinki forms a continually changing projection screen for national desires and fears. To France, "Europe" meant the hope of rebirth, to Germany the hope of redemption, to Belgium the glue of national unity, to Spain the return to democracy, to Poland a return to the free West and to Britain the advantages of a market. More than 25 national experiences come together in the Union – an essential plurality. Which made it all the more striking to discover that in Brussels entirely normal words, such as power, national interest or cultural difference, are beyond the boundaries of what can be said.

Now, once again, I stand outside the melee, and as an academic, author and columnist I have regained my intellectual and analytical detachment. New events have fed into my thinking: it was only in 2017 – the year of Trump – that we saw Europe's new politics rise to its full height, not just improvising and taking shape despite itself but acquiring self-knowledge and vitality. And it was in 2018 and 2019 – with the Brexit plot further unfolding – that we saw the European public at large decide not to leave the theatre but to demand a better performance.

One clear conclusion this book arrives at is that the European Union is not moving towards a "United States of Europe", a federal state with a single EU government above the national governments. Yet the pressure of events is such that Europe's nations are working ever more closely together and will continue to do so. The Union does not face a fateful choice between federalism and disintegration. That is a false dichotomy, which only impedes public understanding and feeds distrust.

This is all the more regrettable since public support for joint decisions is indispensable if the nations on the European continent – economically privileged and strategically vulnerable as they are – are to defend their interests, values and way of life in between Africa, the Middle East, Russia, China and the United States in the twenty-first century. With the US retreating and the Europeans' Atlantic security guarantee put in doubt by the American and French presidents, an increased sense of weakness could trigger new responses. As the pages that follow make clear, such common action may sometimes take shape impromptu, but it would be unwise to be too quick to dismiss Europe's vitality.

Acknowledgements

Although it is impossible to name all those who shared their insights or voiced their reactions in conversations that in some cases began more than 15 years ago, at Brussels workplaces, in public debates, or between friends, I should like to mention explicitly Pierre de Boissieu (Paris), Hugo Brady (Brussels), Tom Eijsbouts (Amsterdam), Matthias Krupa (Hamburg), Alice Richard (Brussels), Undine Ruge (Berlin) and Stephen Wall (London).

I would also like to thank Philippe Van Parijs for working with me on a project and a book in which, in 2013–15, we tried to get a dialogue going between the closed political cast and the engaged intellectual class, a book that took me back to my writing desk.* Thanks too to my colleagues Stefaan Van den Bogaert (Leiden University) and Bernard Coulie and Vincent Dujardin (UCLouvain) for allowing me the freedom to work on this book.

For their comments on parts of the manuscript I thank Maryem van den Heuvel, Nanda Kelly, Sarah Nelen, Ton Nijhuis, Coen Simon and Martin Westlake. Five readers read everything, sometimes more than once, and I am very grateful: Hans Kribbe, Brussels expert and political philosopher; Vestert Borger, discerning lawyer; Pieter van den Blink, who managed with relentless tact to shorten the text; Patrick Everard, empathetic and sharp-witted publisher, master of the right word; and my wife, Manon de Boer, lucid reader, without whom this book would not exist. For their heartening dedication to this English translation, I thank my translator Liz Waters and editor Alison Howson. Thanks too to Julius, for enjoying his play while I wrote.

---

*   Luuk van Middelaar and Philippe Van Parijs (eds), *After the Storm: How to Save Democracy in Europe* (Tielt: Lannoo, 2015), with contributions from Rémi Brague, Maurizio Ferrera, Dieter Grimm, Jürgen Habermas, Turkuler Isiksel, Ivan Krastev, Koen Lenaerts, David Miller, Dani Rodrik, Pierre Rosanvallon, Fritz Scharpf, Paul Scheffer, Amartya Sen, Larry Siedentop, Frank Vandenbroucke and Herman Van Rompuy.

Dramatis personae

AMERICAN PRESIDENT

Commander in chief, living in the White House; from 1950 to 2016, an enthusiast of European integration, provided the continent's security remains dependent on US armed forces; since 2017, the European Union's self-declared foe.

Barack H. Obama (2009–17): uber-cool headteacher; orders Europeans to save the euro, but leads from behind in Syria, Libya and Ukraine.

Donald J. Trump (2017–): global disrupter and agent provocateur; gravedigger of the "transatlantic order"; supporter of anti-EU forces in Europe.

BRITISH PRIME MINISTER

Resident of "Number 10"; party leader, who is generally elected by the people; mission is to further the national interest by either advancing or thwarting continental unity.

David Cameron (2010–16): standoffish spectator in Europe's crises; chooses party over country by calling the referendum on EU membership.

Theresa May (2016–19): vows to "deliver" Brexit but gets trapped in her own mantras and red lines.

Boris Johnson (2019–): former London Mayor, disgraced foreign minister, who promises to "get Brexit done".

COMMISSION

Driver of EU integration thanks to its right to propose legislation, represent certain common positions (as in trade) abroad, manage programmes and oversee respect of rules; consists of a 32,000-staff bureaucracy and is formally steered by a "College" of commissioners but in practice by its president.

COMMISSION PRESIDENT

Boss of the "Berlaymont", the EU's Brussels headquarters; proposed by national leaders and elected by European Parliament; as steerer of the European project, relentlessly compared to local hero Jacques Delors (1985–95).

José Manuel Barroso (2004–14): former Portuguese PM; after a firm start, loses authority among protagonists during the banking crisis, never to fully regain it.

Jean-Claude Juncker (2014–19): former Luxembourg PM; euro veteran with an unmistakable knack for politics; becomes Brexit's bogeyman and overplays his hand during the refugee crisis.

COUNCIL OF MINISTERS

Officially the "Council of the European Union": body where ministers of all member states take decisions in various configurations (agriculture, finance, and so on); co-legislator with the European Parliament; its six-monthly presidency rotates among member states so as to guarantee low visibility; it frequently meets in Luxembourg for the same reason.

COURT OF JUSTICE OF THE EUROPEAN UNION

The Union's highest court, based in Luxembourg and composed of 28 judges; it habitually pushes for greater economic integration; in recent crises-related judgments it has also begun interfering in EU "events-politics".

ECB PRESIDENT

Head of arguably the strongest EU institution, the Frankfurt-based European Central Bank, which decides the euro's monetary policy and now also supervises banks; the president chairs the ECB's Governing Council, which is composed of the 6-person Executive Board, together with the eurozone's 19 national bank governors.

Jean-Claude Trichet (2003–11): former president of French Central Bank, widely respected professional, but warns once too often against looming financial disaster.

Mario Draghi (2011–19): former president of Italian Central Bank and former investment banker; earns nickname "super Mario" by out-bluffing anti-euro speculators.

EUROGROUP

Body in which the 19 finance ministers from euro states meet to decide on Economic and Monetary Union matters, such as budgetary rules, or bailouts and other crisis measures; its chair has been held by Juncker (2005–13), Jeroen Dijsselbloem (2013–18) and Mário Centeno (2018–); the Eurogroup's harsh approach to the bailouts of Greece and other euro states provokes a public backlash.

EUROPEAN COUNCIL

The summits where the presidents and prime ministers gather to set the Union's political course; as the Union's highest political authority, indispensable for crisis management.

EUROPEAN COUNCIL PRESIDENT

Summit chair, who, since 2009, is appointed by national leaders for a 2.5-year term, renewable once; without direct electoral mandate, the president's agenda-setting power relies on personal trust and moral authority; convenes 8–10 times a year, mostly in the Europa building in Brussels.

Herman Van Rompuy (2009–14): former Belgian PM, cautious philosopher-economist, uncomfortable in the limelight, shrewd negotiator during the euro crisis.

Donald Tusk (2014–19): former Polish PM, liberal realist, outspoken on Brexit and Trump, forces the EU to focus on border control in the refugee crisis.

EUROPEAN PARLIAMENT

Directly elected every five years with seats in Strasbourg and Brussels, composed of 751 MEPs from 28 member states (705 once the UK leaves), divided into "groups" of national parties; the centrist block composed of Christian Democrats, Social Democrats and Liberals has recently been challenged by anti-EU MEPs such as Marine Le Pen and Nigel Farage. Since 2009 enhanced with powers greater than many national parliaments, but frustrated when EU crisis management takes place outside its reach.

FINANCE MINISTERS

The EU's finance ministers meet in a Council configuration called ECOFIN under a rotating chair to decide on economic policy, banking supervision and taxation. For their inner circle of euro ministers, see "Eurogroup".

FOREIGN MINISTERS

The EU's foreign ministers meet in their own Council configuration to deal with foreign crises, sanctions and military or humanitarian missions; the meeting is chaired by the "EU High Representative for Foreign Affairs and Security Policy", an office held by Catherine Ashton (2009–14) and Federica Mogherini (2014–19).

FRENCH PRESIDENT

Since Charles de Gaulle, a directly elected head of state with the mandate to act in crises; at home in the Elysée palace; mission is to project France's interests onto Europe.

Nicolas Sarkozy (2007–12): enjoys improvisation, fully exploits the Union's potential when at the helm for six months in 2008.

François Hollande (2012–17): self-declared "normal president" who overdoes being "normal" and ends up an indecisive and weak actor in both Paris and Brussels.

Emmanuel Macron (2017–): stormed onto the stage from nowhere with a newly founded party and waving an EU flag; encounters more resistance, at home and in Europe, than he expected.

GERMAN CONSTITUTIONAL COURT

Karlsruhe-based body of nine judges which, like the US Supreme Court, takes decisions that pertain to the German Basic Law; in EU matters, authoritative defender of the rights of German voters and taxpayers against Brussels centralization, with a reputation for barking, not biting.

GERMAN FEDERAL CHANCELLOR

Governing from the *Bundeskanzleramt*, powerful figure as head of the EU's economically strongest and most populous country, encountering many checks and balances at home; mission is to embed Germany's interests in Europe.

Angela Merkel (2005–): prudent anchor of Europe's crisis politics; her preferred step-by-step method, at work in the euro crisis, does not preclude bold measures at other times, as in the refugee crisis; Europe's pre-eminent leader, now in her final years in power.

GERMAN FINANCE MINISTER

Given Germany's economic weight, informally Europe's finance minister in chief.

Wolfgang Schäuble (2009–17): respected "European" who becomes a hate figure for his EU austerity policies in Southern Europe.

GREEK PRIME MINISTER

Giorgos Papandreou (2009–11): unleashes the euro storm by announcing his country's true debt when he enters office, then goes under.

Alexis Tsipras (2015–19): the hope of Europe's radical left upon his election as leader of "Syriza"; wins the battle of the dramatic 2015 euro referendum, but loses the war on austerity policies; now widely respected by centrists across Europe.

HUNGARIAN PRIME MINISTER

Viktor Orbán (2010–): crusader against Muslim migrants, European "opposition" leader on issues of migration and identity; cements domestic power in an authoritarian, "illiberal" drift, bound to clash with EU rule of law.

ITALIAN PRIME MINISTER

Resides in Rome's Palazzo Chigi; head of a fragile coalition government; desperate to play in the league of the "Big Three" – France, Germany and the UK – but rarely does.

Silvio Berlusconi (2001–06; 2008–11): media magnate regarded in rest of Europe as a clown; loses last shreds of his credibility in the euro crisis.

Mario Monti (2011–13): former EU commissioner, technocrat with a short-lived career in high office, more popular in Brussels and Berlin than in Rome.

Matteo Renzi (2014–16): "Berlusconi of the left", forty years younger.

NATIONAL PARLIAMENTS

Embodiments of national democracy and public opinion; collectively, they ratify treaties, budgets and certain crisis measures; individually, they control national leaders and ministers in the European Council and the Council of Ministers; their renewal in national elections is followed intensely across Europe. The German Bundestag and the UK's House of Commons stand out as legislators with a strong grip on their executive.

RUSSIAN PRESIDENT

Sits in the Kremlin; in the footsteps of the Tsars, one of Europe's most powerful and feared rulers; claims special ties with Slav and Orthodox countries; border issues are bound to arise; black sheep of Europe's family, but family nevertheless.

Vladimir V. Putin (2000–08; 2012–): restorer of domestic order; master of geopolitical chess; undercuts Ukrainian and Georgian territorial integrity and Europe's normative cohesion.

TROIKA

Born during the euro crisis as ad hoc body for creditors composed of experts from the Commission, European Central Bank and IMF, which provide funding for bailouts; symbol of hated austerity and technocratic overreach.

TURKISH HEAD OF GOVERNMENT

Successor to the Ottoman Sultan, sovereign ruler to Europe's immediate southeast, with special interests in the Balkans and the Black Sea region, and nurturing close ties with Turkish communities in Europe.

Recep Tayyip Erdoğan (prime minister, 2003–14; president, 2014–): strongman at home; defiant suitor in Europe, as head of what is formally still a "candidate country"; Europe's saviour in the migrant crisis.

Prologue

The *polis*, properly speaking, is not the city-state in its physical location; it is the organization of the people as it arises out of acting and speaking together, and its true space lies between people living together for this purpose, no matter where they are.

Hannah Arendt[1]

The truth is that the Europeans do not know what they have built.

Marcel Gauchet[2]

Crises and metamorphosis

Banks on the point of collapse, a currency on the edge of the abyss, wars flaring on the continent's periphery, internal borders closed, a member stuck halfway out of the door – a series of dramas has played out before us in recent years. If a crisis is indeed a moment of truth and if tribulations can bring self-knowledge, then the European Union should have learnt a great deal about itself in a short time.

The first lesson is that when the unity of the Union or peace in the region is at stake, political motives for being together prevail over purely economic interests. In abnormal situations the underlying politics, rarely visible under normal circumstances, actively comes to the fore.

This was a striking feature of the Brexit negotiations. It was brilliantly illuminated when, in late 2017, the then British Brexit secretary David Davis gave a speech in Berlin to an audience of German business leaders, as part of

1

a London charm offensive aimed at securing favourable terms in the withdrawal agreement. Davis warned Germany and other European member states to beware of harming their own economies in the Brexit talks, advising them not to put "politics above prosperity". His audience greeted these words with laughter and disbelief. The encounter reveals the depth of mutual misunderstanding. German business leaders see the Brexit referendum as an irresponsible political act, a case of economic hara-kiri. How could a leading Brexiteer, of all people, tell them not to put politics above prosperity? The British minister, using a pragmatic win-win argument in the best Brussels tradition, failed to grasp the extent to which his country's exit from the European order is experienced by Germany and other EU member states as an existential political attack on the foundations of the Union, to be withstood at all costs.

This small misunderstanding foreshadowed the more fundamental deadlock in the autumn of 2018 over the avoidance of a future "hard border" between the Republic of Ireland and Northern Ireland, in order to preserve the fragile peace in the north. That issue pitted the territorial sovereignty of the United Kingdom against the European Union's determination to defend its integrity, expressed on the one hand by Prime Minister May's solemn promise to party and nation not to "break up my country" (by accepting a customs border in the Irish Sea as a way out of the dilemma) and on the other by the EU's resolve since the Brexit vote not to let the UK "have its cake and eat it too", for fear of encouraging further exits. In sum: politics above prosperity on both sides (albeit with far lower relative costs for the remaining 27 members).

That politics trumps economics when the stakes are high should not have come as a surprise to those who had followed the Greek crisis. In 2010 it was indeed financial prudence that dictated the outcome: the stronger eurozone members, not least France and Germany, helped Greece with money and built firewalls, in order to avoid the kind of "financial contagion" that would put their own banks and economies at risk. At later stages, however, once the firewalls had been shown to work and the European Central Bank had stepped up its efforts, the calculation was less clear cut. From 2012, and again when the radical left-wing party Syriza came to power in Athens in early 2015, the German and Dutch finance ministers started quietly to plead for a "Grexit", as a less costly option in the long run. But the gathered government leaders, whose ultimate decision it was, looked beyond their coffers. In their political cost–benefit analysis they took account of a different type of risk, perhaps unquantifiable but nevertheless real. What cascade of events might be triggered by a Greek exit? Instability in the Balkans, Russian influence on a weakened Athens, tension in Franco-German relations, the disintegration of the internal market or even of the European Union? American and British eurozone doomsayers always underestimated this political logic.[3] Greece remained.

Greek voters, who in a breathtaking referendum in summer 2015 massively backed their prime minister's defiant rejection of the EU aid on offer, likewise did so not out of any desire to return to the drachma but to make a political point. They wanted to be treated with respect by the rest of Europe: "better dignified poverty than a future as Europe's penal colony". (When their prime minister lost his gamble, executed a U-turn and then called a snap election, the Greek voters still backed him; their point had been made.) In future monetary turmoil, perhaps involving Italy, politics will again intervene.

The crises brought a second realization: if we as Europeans are to safeguard our way of life, then Europe as a whole must think more strategically and be able to engage in power-play among the other players. It must step out of the shadows, throw off the regulatory straitjacket within which it deals with cucumbers and bananas, and appear on the global stage as a supporting actor or even as a protagonist. But leaving the know-it-all sphere of technocracy for a truly political stage will mean, as the ancient Greek playwrights tell us, entering the realm of tragic dilemmas and hard choices. In that respect, the kind of tough decisions Europe faced during the migrant crisis of 2015–16 and the Ukraine crisis a year earlier entailed a loss of innocence.

In Brussels' image of itself, two fundamental ideas have become entwined: Europe as peace project and Europe as power project. As a peace project its task is to dissolve the nations, to breach state sovereignty, to take the first step towards world peace, as Europe. As a power project it is to bind the nations into a single whole, to combine their capacity to act and thereby defend their common interests in the world. As a peace project, Europe is "above all a moral act",[4] requiring idealism and openness to reconciliation. As a power project, Europe is a political act, requiring a redefinition of self-interest, political will and decisiveness.

To stem the flow of refugees from Syria into Greece, European leaders concluded an ethically and legally questionable deal with President Erdogan's Turkey, in the name of higher political interests. To help end the war between Ukraine and Russia – the most dangerous outbreak of violence on the continent since the Yugoslav Wars – Chancellor Merkel and President Hollande brokered a compromise between Ukrainian President Petro Poroshenko and his Russian colleague Vladimir Putin, prioritizing the chances of peace and sparing human lives above a rigorous enforcement of international law. In the future, too, the Union will continually have to choose between doing justice to what have traditionally been our most cherished values and guaranteeing our security.

A third truth that the crises have driven home is that rules and legislation cannot anticipate all new situations. What, after all, is a crisis? An event that previously remained beyond the horizon of the conceivable (or was kept there). Greece's imminent bankruptcy, in the spring of 2010, was a stark case in point. Among eurozone countries, this was simply not supposed to happen. The EU Treaty lacked tools to curb the emergency; worse, it banned the other member states from stepping in to avoid Greece's financial collapse. In this situation, applying the rulebook to the letter would have been politically irresponsible. Which explains why European leaders, if with some hesitation, decided to circumvent the Treaty and take action to save the euro.

There have been other such situations. What if a nearby dictator massacres his people? What if hundreds of thousands of refugees turn up at our borders? What if a fellow member of the club suddenly walks out? No prescriptions can be written in advance for such twists of fate. Historically, treaties and established rules were the Union's greatest achievement, but they do not offer an adequate basis for effective joint action in all unforeseen circumstances. Since Europe is more than a market, for which rules can patiently be agreed, now that it has become involved with a currency, a border and foreign policy, such situations are bound to arise ever more frequently.

Crises, therefore, demand a different political capacity to act than can be provided by the traditional Brussels structures. Rather than the application of norms, they require decision-making. At moments when rules cannot provide answers, it becomes evident who has the authority to jump in, the power to act. The Commission, the European Council, the Parliament? France, Germany, the two together? Is that even allowed?

Under the pressure of events, a new Union is taking shape. After ten years in which we breathlessly raced to keep up with developments, from one crisis to the next, while commentators and experts kept pasting outdated concepts onto a shifting reality, it is time to step back and assess the unsuspected strengths of Europe's new politics. The politicians who have captured the stage to deal with events have at least as much need of a new perspective, in my experience, as the European citizens watching from the public gallery. Hence this book.

Creating the performance space

The European institutional structure that came into being over six decades in Brussels, Luxembourg, Strasbourg and Frankfurt appears inscrutable. The founding states all aimed to improve prosperity and security for their populations by working more closely together, but they never agreed on the best means to achieve this. There was no single plan. Europe was created through constant interplay and rivalry – between France and Germany, between large and small states, between national capitals and central institutions – and finds itself in a state of permanent evolution.

If we think of political life as playing out in a theatre – with its actors and audience, its frontstage and backstage, its scripts and directors – then we could say, simplifying in the extreme, that, virtually from the beginning, three dramaturgical approaches were used. Each proposed a specific relationship with the audience of European citizens and proffered a specific institutional set design to achieve it. Remarkably, all three have remained in operation and they continue to work away side by side: depoliticization, parliamentarization and summitry.

The first question faced by the "founders of Europe" was whether they should provide a visible political stage at all. Their initial answer was clear: "Rather not; let's start with a backstage operation". This initial approach to creating Europe, dominant for many years, amounts to depoliticization through law. Dedramatization, in other words, in response to a surfeit of political drama during and immediately after the Second World War. Only the anonymous force of Law would enable six European states to undertake something new that could unite peoples divided by almost everything, without a language, history or culture in common. In concrete terms, the participating states restricted each other's freedom, by treaty, in a limited number of fields, farming out their means of action to some extent to shared institutions and installing neutral judicial supervision.

Three EU institutions were essential to this backstage approach: the Commission, the Court of Justice and the Council of Ministers. In Brussels the European Commission was given the task of making proposals, performing certain executive functions and serving as "guardian of the treaties". It is a collegiate body of commissioners, originally appointed by their own governments but more recently also subject to approval by the EU Parliament, that relies on a bureaucratic apparatus comparable to that of a medium-sized city. The Commission lies at the origins of the success of the common market from the 1960s onwards and later of the internal market of 1992. From Luxembourg, the powerful Court of Justice watches over the Treaty, which soon became regarded as a sacred text, and doggedly defends the EU legal order. This European judicial space is also a space for economic negotiations among the members. After all, before a rule can do its depoliticizing work, it has to be laid down, a political step that was taken solely by the Council of Ministers, the forum in which the governments come together at ministerial level in various constellations (as a Council of finance ministers, of agriculture ministers, and so on).[5] The Council of Ministers emerged as the first centre of decision-making, a key link between EU decision-making and national bureaucracies.

Initially, all this happened behind the scenes. The technocratic approach allowed the bureaucracy in Brussels and the capitals to flourish. The forging of compromises and the interweaving of interests works best when conducted out of public view. In the words of an anonymous national negotiator, "If you want smooth decision-making in Europe, you must keep it away from the politicians". Away from the voters too, therefore. Questions of accountability and representation were not on the agenda; for public support the backstage approach did not bet on democratic input but on practical results.

Yet from the 1960s onwards two other institutional projects attempted to bring politics and the people of Europe back into this depoliticized structure, over time empowering two new institutions: the European Parliament and the European Council of heads of state or government. Starting out with rival visions of political engagement, they both sought to offer Europe a performance space, a stage on which political actors could engage with each other under the scrutiny of an audience of voters. The disagreement among them concerned how best to reach out to the public and, as a consequence, to whom to allocate the leading roles. The first project aspired to create a new, single audience of citizens who saw themselves, over and above their national identities, as Europeans. It sought to upgrade the existing parliamentary body, still composed of national parliamentarians and its powers still limited, by establishing direct elections; the Parliament was expected to attract more public attention and become a truly European, "supranational" choir that would back the Brussels-based cast of the Commission. The second project was intended to draw in the old, plural audience of national voters. It advocated summitry for national leaders – who during the early years had been carefully held at a distance – to unite the member states at the highest political level and thereby create a visible forum for interaction and decision-making, in what would become the European Council of heads of state or government.

These rival visions of the future had lasting repercussions for the development of Europe, but not initially. Ideological distrust between the two camps resulted in an impasse. The first camp, with representatives in Italy, West Germany and Benelux, regarded the depoliticized marketplace as a first step towards a European federation, with the Parliament-backed Commission as future protagonist. The other camp, dominant in the France of De Gaulle, believed that Brussels regulatory techniques suited only the market, and that collaboration in domains affecting core state powers would need to take a different shape and have stronger backing from national voters; Paris even threatened to set up a whole new decision-making centre.[6] As long as the two sides battling for the political stage held each other in check, no changes could be introduced and the curtain of Europe's theatre remained down.

In December 1974, French President Valéry Giscard d'Estaing notched up an important theatrical success. He forced through the commitment to regular summit meetings that France wanted, thereby establishing the European Council. The new institution was butted up against the existing structure and formally kept outside the Treaty. For the sake of balance, the Belgians, Germans and Italians achieved the direct elections to the European Parliament they so fervently desired. It was now finally given its own base in the form of a Europe-wide electorate; since 1979 elections have been held every five years. This dual breakthrough enabled Europe's institutions to remain united while giving access to Europe's citizenry. In a single move, two groups of politicians became attached to the project: national government leaders (generally in closer contact with voters than their ministers) and Euro-parliamentarians or MEPs (a group that previously did not exist and would want to prove its usefulness). As so often in Europe when two oppos- ing desires collide, a way was eventually found to satisfy both. An identical institutional compromise was reached with the treaties of Maastricht (1992) and Lisbon (2007). On each occasion, Germany asked for more powers for the Parliament, the institution in which it can dominate because of its demo- graphic preponderance and the financial clout of its political parties, while France stressed the importance of the European Council, the Union's highest political authority and the forum in which each French president in turn has a chance to shine.

The three dramaturgical styles for Europe's theatre – backstage depolit- icization, frontstage parliamentarization and frontstage summitry – do not necessarily result in coherent performances. This is obvious when we look at the roles the Commission is expected to play. Roughly speaking, in the depoliticization model the institution makes proposals in the name of the common interest, plays the "honest broker" during negotiations and oversees adherence to the rules – mostly behind the scenes. According to the parlia- mentary politicization model, the Commission must prepare to assume the lead role and gradually turn into a kind of European government, dependent on a majority coalition in the Parliament. In the politicization plan of the government leaders it must remain in a supporting role, acting as a general secretariat at the service of the European Council. These three directions, of course, cannot all be followed at the same time.

Hence the friction caused by Commission president Jean-Claude Juncker with his desire to lead a "political Commission". Of the three styles, Juncker resolutely opted for parliamentary politicization, at the expense of both strained relations with national governments and loss of neutrality for the Commission. For the first few years, in Parliament he leant on a two-party "grand coalition" of centre-right and centre-left after the German model, while at the same time self-consciously presenting proposals that met with considerable resistance in the national capitals, such as the compulsory quotas for asylum seekers in 2015, and showing a willingness, from time to time, to interpret the rules in their broadest sense; "because it's France", Juncker once said to explain his leniency with regard to the French budget deficit, provoking predictable annoyance in Berlin and The Hague. Amid a torrent of crises and other events, the tension is growing between the political ambitions of the Commission and its role as guardian of the regulatory framework, between its desire to step onstage and the need to provide essential services in the wings.

Europe's theatre is therefore the product of three competing styles, and the resulting political performances can easily be misread. When the actors themselves do not understand their parts, it is no wonder if the public is confused.

This triptych of styles may be difficult to grasp for anyone who has traditionally regarded the Union's institutional battle as taking place between two governmental strategies, namely "supranationalism" and "intergovernmentalism". After all, who gets ownership, the European institutions or the national capitals? The presumed contest between the two is the yardstick for the Brussels doctrine – taken up by countless lawyers and political scientists – used to measure every extension to the European structure. This binary perspective, however, not only ignores the preliminary question of whether a political stage is desirable or not, it has never been consistent with the way things work. Immediately after the Second World War, when there was a need to create from scratch, the three styles existed in their purest form. They were labelled federalism (parliamentarization), confederalism (summitry) and functionalism (depoliticization). While the federalist movement's battle for a "United States of Europe" proved a bridge too far and the confederalists' push for cooperation between governments ran into the sand of veto issues, the step-by-step approach of the functionalists achieved a breakthrough with the 1951 Coal and Steel Community.[7]

The dichotomy "supranational versus intergovernmental" is misleading. "Supranationalism" includes both parliamentarization and depoliticization, or a future European federation coupled with a technocratic rule-making factory. "Intergovernmentalism" includes both the involvement of government leaders and (again) depoliticization – highly visible these days as the summit circus, in which leaders bring cameras and public opinion in their wake, but not without involving the technocrats, with national cabinet ministers and civil servants brought in to help draw up the rules.

The triptych therefore makes the character of the ongoing battle within the European Union far easier to understand and can help the audience to make its voice heard. This is all the more important now that the curtain across Europe's stage has been permanently raised and the dramas played out on it are there for all to see.

The politics of rules and the politics of events

Besides the distinction between the three styles and their views on staging Europe, there is another categorization that can be extremely helpful in making sense of developments in the European Union.

In a September 2015 masterclass for mid-career officials working for the EU institutions in Brussels, I asked participants to compare the internal market created under Commission president Jacques Delors from 1985 onwards – for most of them the great success story of the years of their studies or recruitment – with Europe's major challenge of that autumn, the stream of refugees entering the Union over land and sea from Turkey. It seemed obvious to me that, 30 years on, Europe now found itself in a different world. From the perspective of Brussels, this proved difficult to see. There was surely a difference between patiently drawing up market rules and acting at the external borders, between predictable conflicts of interest and sudden shocks, between commentary in professional journals and screaming headlines – but at least half of the course participants were unconvinced. They reduced the issue to fit their own box of tricks: sharing pain, smoothing away conflicts of interest, depoliticization. When I drove the point home, doubts arose; a handful of younger participants responded eagerly, but two or three old hands failed to see the difference between fish quotas and the relocation of 160,000 refugees according to asylum quotas forced through by majority vote.

What was lacking here in my view was an awareness of the metamorphosis Europe has been through under the pressure of crises, the transition from a system based purely on the politics of rules to a system that can also engage in the politics of events. Traditionally the institutions of the European Union were equipped simply to construct and run a market. This rules-politics is an ingenious mechanism that produces consensus and results, but it can work only within a certain set-up, by dint of the fiction that history runs along predictable lines. In events-politics, by contrast, what matters is getting a grip on unforeseen events. This form of political action is not played out within a specific framework; it occurs when that framework itself is put to the test, in the most extreme case by a war or disaster. In 2008 the disaster was the credit crisis, when the economy refused to continue behaving according to forecasting models. The solution to an unforeseen situation may of course lie in the creation of a new regulatory framework (we then see an interplay between events-politics and rules-politics), but certain political decisions can be translated only into one-off acts (in the military domain, for example).

The politics of rules requires a politician with the temperament and expertise to participate in a balancing act. The public values honesty and dependability, but in our highly regulated welfare states it cannot always see the difference between a politician and an expert. The politics of events, by contrast, requires politicians who can improvise. They need to convince parliament and the public with a narrative that reveals why this or that decision is necessary. Authority is won by the individual who, judging the situation correctly, displays initiative, courage and incisiveness at the right moment.

A system built for rules-politics cannot be transmogrified for use in events-politics. The choices and dilemmas involved can be seen more clearly if expressed in a diagram showing the characteristics of the rule-making factory and of political action (see figure on page 13). One question concerns the novelty or uniqueness of the decision to be taken. Does the matter at hand fit within existing rules and frameworks or is it completely unexpected, entirely contingent, or extremely sensitive? A fundamental question for every political order. The distinction is rarely black-and-white; the institutionally embedded politics of rules and the surprise-intercepting politics of events

11

exist along a graduated scale.[8] For instance, setting up a common market for scrap metal back in 1952 required more action than running it and supervising it, but given that its establishment flowed from the desire to form a Coal and Steel Community, ratified by a treaty – and it was not therefore decided upon in a vacuum – we might nevertheless say that it took place within the sphere of rules-politics.[9] Conversely, the establishment of the European Coal and Steel Community itself (the initiative taken by French foreign minister Robert Schuman with the prompt agreement of German Chancellor Konrad Adenauer) can definitely be regarded as a political act. This was the creative deed, a profound intervention in the postwar European order, demanding courage and a sense of timing.

The other question is: which type of players are involved, officials or elected politicians? The answer determines the type of authority a decision acquires. Was it taken based on earlier agreements, procedures and expertise, or on public support expressed in a parliamentary majority or an election result? This distinction too is graduated, from administrative executors, experts and those who apply the rules, via players on the boundary between the technical and the political (such as ministers or European commissioners) to presidents and prime ministers in the public gaze. We can also speak of a transition from "governance" to "government", from anonymous, multi-layered administration to the undisguised, visible authority of a government, or from the sphere of judicial or bureaucratic competences to that of political responsibility and authority.

If we now place a situation's degree of newness or sensitivity on an X axis, running from supervision and implementation within a given framework (left) to political action in an unfamiliar situation (right) and cross this with a Y axis for the institutional players and the basis of their authority, running from officialdom (bottom) to government (top), then we have four squares. At the lower left, in the square for implementation and officialdom, we find the politics of rules, with the market for scrap metal and other examples from the Brussels rule-making factory, while in the upper right, in the square for political action and government, we find the politics of events, like the impromptu negotiations for a ceasefire between Russia and Georgia in 2008.*

---

* For this episode, with Nicolas Sarkozy in the main role, see Chapter 2.

If Europe wants to transform itself into a system that, as well as regulating, can also act, then diagonal movement is required, since the transformation needs to be accompanied by a simultaneous appeal to a different type of authority. Only by this route can the Union, starting off from the cherished rule-making factory at the bottom left, reach the square of events-politics at the top right.

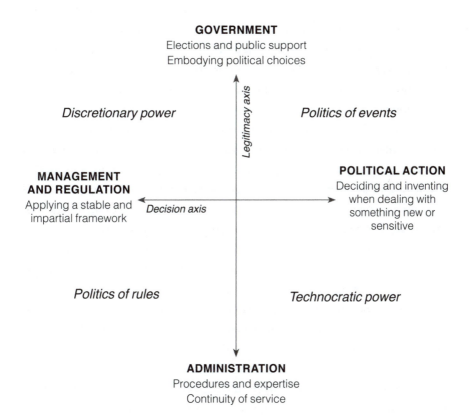

What about the other two squares? What happens there? Here we find several particular and less successful forms of engagement in politics. The square at the top left provides room for the combination of implementation and government, activities such as regulation with supervision, not however exercised with an appeal to expertise, mandates or procedures but based on political decisions. This is the domain of discretionary power, in which politicians with governmental authority interfere in neutral or independent procedures. One notorious case dates from 2003, when, under Franco-German pressure and to the fury of the Commission, the finance ministers disregarded the budgetary rules of the Stability and Growth Pact (without having a public mandate to rewrite those rules). Political intervention also occurs in response to public indignation about the effects of blindly abiding by the rules; the press can make a story out of that and put pressure on elected politicians (far more so than on civil servants), after which an exception may be made after all. When such an intervention is legitimate, the term "discretionary power" becomes appropriate. But politicization of implementation can sometimes be dubious or unlawful: corruption and nepotism also belong in this square.

The Brussels rule-making factory has procedurally armed itself against abuse by discretionary power. It is proud of this, and in general it is best left that way. In doing so, however, it fails to recognize that what for the politics of rules are vices (haste, willpower or visibility, for example) are virtues when it comes to getting to grips with events. So it falls into another trap, that of the square at the bottom right. Here the engineers of rules-politics move into the domain of events-politics, but armed only with regulatory tools. Here too, accidents can occur, in an ethical sense not as bad as corruption perhaps, but no less disastrous in their consequences. This square, the mirror image of discretionary power, is that of technocratic power, of the exercise of bureaucratic competences on the terrain of events, without adequate public support. Recent European crises have been played out in this domain. It is here that we need to focus our attention; this is the trap we should worry about. Because yes, controlling an influx of refugees requires more than merely the application of fish-quota techniques. And yes, forming close ties with Ukraine and other neighbours of Putin's Russia demands more strategic insight than can be learnt through the economic tick-box approach of WTO guidelines. There are plenty more examples of bureaucratic hubris by which Europe, through either overconfidence or insouciance, set off on the path of events-politics without the proper toolkit. After ten years of crises, Europe can no longer claim the innocence of inexperience.

14

Agreeing the script

In a speech at a university in Paris several years ago, German finance minister Wolfgang Schäuble argued that responsibility for explaining European politics did not lie with politicians alone: "Everyone ought to ask themselves how they speak about Europe and what effect their discourse has on public opinion".[10] For this veteran politician it was obvious that our use of language not only shapes our thinking but determines political reality.

In politics words are not innocent. It was with this conviction that I opened my book *The Passage to Europe* (2013) with a cartography of European words and discourses. Even apparently descriptive terms like "integration", "construction", "unification" and "cooperation" each have their own resonance and force. Integration refers to a shock-free process that ends in complete fusion. Construction evokes a building project on an empty plot. Unification leaves open the question as to whether it takes place voluntarily or by force. Cooperation stresses the continuing independence of member states. The choice of words reveals something about the type of analysis.

One way of escaping such connotations is to bring a new word into play or to give a new connotation to an existing one (as *The Passage to Europe* did, for example, with the concepts "sphere" and "passage"). Another way is to investigate which vocabulary is used and with what motives – a fairly common approach in intellectual history.[11] To quote Michel Foucault, "Discourse is no mere verbalisation of conflicts or systems of domination but the very thing for which and with which one fights, the power one is aiming to seize".[12]

The history of the European Union features many battles over words. To take one example, it was not until 1987 that the European Parliament was permitted to call itself a "Parliament", although the earliest attempts to throw off the unassuming name "Assembly" date from the 1950s.[13] Now again, old words and habits of thought stand in the way of a recognition that the Union is governed, that forms of executive power are unfolding before our eyes. Time to bring the terms into line with reality: another reason for writing this book.

The European Union is having obvious difficulty with the public battle of words now raging. Opponents of the Union – nationalists and populists of every stripe – are monopolizing the conversation, while its supporters remain silent or sound overblown. In the European referendums since 2015 – not just in Britain but in Greece, Denmark, the Netherlands and Hungary, with more promised or already announced – it repeatedly becomes clear that the pro-European "yes" camp is no match for the "no" camp. Too late the Union realized that if a word prompts a riposte you had better not hold your peace.

European politics has lost the capacity and natural ability to address the public by telling convincing stories. Economic and judicial depoliticization since the days of Jean Monnet has effectively removed convictions and fundamental political motives from sight. In the euro crisis it turned out that only when the system stands on the edge of the abyss is the underlying politics brought to the surface. (Chancellor Angela Merkel demonstrated this in May 2010 in the Bundestag with her statement "If the euro fails, Europe fails".) The political rationales are no longer heard, partly because they are no longer interpreted. There is no adequate language in which to put them. The spokespersons have withdrawn into their shells. As integration went on, the right to speak was taken over by economists, by lawyers and EU ideologues. With their jargon, acronyms and self-congratulation, they drove even interested members of the public to despair.

If it is to survive, therefore, the Union must not merely increase its capacity to act and to protect, it must win a battle of words. Shortly before Emmanuel Macron was inaugurated as French president, in May 2017, summit chair Donald Tusk visited him at the Elysée Palace. Tusk said that precisely because he was a patriot he was convinced of the importance of a "united and sovereign" Europe. He went on: "Words such as security, protection, dignity and pride must return to our political dictionary. There is no reason why, in public debate, extremists and populists should have a monopoly on these terms. Today they are cynically taking advantage of social fears and uncertainty, building their own model of security on prejudice, authoritarianism and organized hatred. Our response must be clear and decisive."[14] A response that must come in both deeds and words.

An open stage

This book is not about Brussels rules-politics, even though that remains an unrivalled pacifier and creator of prosperity, and even though Brexit is revealing to the public at large just how difficult it is to escape its clutches. In contrast to 1950 or 1985, in 2019 it is no longer the site of development and renewal.

Europe's events-politics, the subject of this book, is accompanied by quarrels, failures and tensions. Yet under the pressure of crises, leadership is being improvised, new political players are appearing onstage and forms of governmental power are emerging. The Union turns out to have a supreme authority at its disposal, which in times of need can show decisiveness and mobilize the capacity to act – although, so far, almost only then.

This book is also about how its search for responses to events makes the Union into a single noisy public space. We hear about elections in neighbouring countries because they affect us too. In 2015 the whole of news-conscious Europe was familiar with the Greek finance minister and his German adversary. On Twitter people discuss the strongmen of Hungary and Poland, or the poker face of the president of the European Central Bank. Whether the subject is the euro, Greece, Ukraine or Schengen, the public senses intuitively that governments and institutions take decisions every day about Europe's shared fate, decisions that cannot now remain hidden behind an economic rationale or a technocratic smokescreen. The old Europe of a market and a mania for rules encountered indifference or mild ridicule from its population, but that did not stand in the way of its progress. The new Europe of currency, power and borders sets loose larger public forces and counterforces, higher expectations and deeper distrust. In this new Europe, decisions are taken that are no longer always based on treaties or expertise but instead are a joint response to the needs of the moment, born out of a clash of opinions. Precisely for that reason they require public justification and scrutability and have to be fought out on an open political stage.

In the pages ahead we will see how the dramatic episodes of recent years have played out, not first and foremost in the parliamentary arena but rather in the forum of Europe's presidents and prime ministers. It is another sign that the European Union is not moving towards a "United States of Europe". Notwithstanding the indispensable central institutions they created, member states are also finding other ways to decide on issues that concern them all. This is why the Union does not face a fateful choice between "superstate" and irrelevance. More than by such ideological debates, Europe is being shaped by events that have forced its leaders to improvise a new politics on a public stage. The public has known and expected it all along. Time to raise the curtain.

PART I

Acts and scenes

To act, in its most general sense, means to take an initiative, to begin (as the Greek word *archein*, 'to begin', 'to lead', and eventually 'to rule' indicates), to set something into motion (which is the original meaning of the Latin *agere*). Because they are *initium*, newcomers and beginners by virtue of birth, men take initiative, are prompted into action.

Hannah Arendt[1]

1

Improvising:
the euro crisis

What theory of the duties of an orator is there which permits him to ignore such sudden issues? What will happen when he has to reply to his opponent? For often the expected arguments to which we have written a reply fail us and the whole aspect of the case undergoes a sudden change; consequently the variation to which cases are liable makes it as necessary for us to change our methods as it is for a pilot to change his course before the oncoming storm. [...] I do not ask him to prefer to speak extempore, but merely that he should be able to do so.

Quintilian[2]

No toolkit

When the euro crisis hit, no one knew what to do. Given the chorus of commentators who claimed with hindsight to have predicted everything, it can do no harm to remember that. No one had contemplated a crisis spreading from one eurozone country to another, the risk that drove the subsequent financial turmoil.

What do you do when you find yourself in an emergency and existing habits, rules and agreements prove useless? You have to improvise. Improvising can have the negative connotation of a botched response or a lack of preparedness, but it can also suggest something positive and creative, as in jazz music or the debating chamber, where the best improviser is typically the hero of the hour. A host who serves unanticipated guests an "improvised meal" – certain ingredients not in the fridge, more diners than expected – is unlikely to venture to say beforehand how it will turn out. Here "improvisation" can be negative if you ought to have known better and have failed to prepare, ignoring experience. But if you are forced to act and think on your feet when an unexpected challenge arises, then the ability to improvise becomes a special quality, a gift.

A capacity to improvise is an essential part of decision-making in general. Every major choice in life involves uncertainties: what will you study at college, with whom will you share your life, whom do you trust? Of course, you can try to exclude uncertainty – by making preparations, feeling things out, calculating – but there will always be a crack through which unintended consequences, unexpected reactions or unforeseen developments can squeeze. Fortunately. The openness of the future is not a burden, not a banana skin, rather it provides space for freedom of action. It brings out the best in us. If everything is predetermined, we are nothing more than the puppets of fate.

Seven crucial decisions taken during the euro storm show how European political leaders operate in an emergency, when there is nothing to hold onto. Each of these episodes falls under the ambiguous moniker of improvisation. The situation was unprecedented. No solutions were available. Surprises came thick and fast. Of course from the start there were critics who believed the solution was perfectly simple, if the eurozone would only do this or that. But no expert had anticipated the risk of financial contagion, the crucial factor. No one had understood the degree to which eurozone member states were financially interwoven, as were the states and the banks. Monetary reports, from the Werner Plan (1970) to the Delors Report (1989), had made no mention of centralized banking supervision as part of a currency union; in the negotiations that led to its creation in 1990–91, the idea was discussed, but it was regarded as unnecessary, even as undesirable by some. The idea of a "banking union", which proved decisive in controlling the crisis in 2012, did not arise until late 2011. It is important to realize this when judging political action during the euro crisis. It makes the difference between improvisation as art and as neglect.

Even more importantly, there were no instruments for jointly tackling a crisis in the currency union. In fact there was not even a toolkit. In Maastricht (1992) it had been solemnly decided that the new monetary union required rules alone and there was no need to anticipate joint action. In this respect the crisis forced a volte-face, reluctantly entered into in many cases. There was something else, too. In the chaos of the moment – and for want of collective instruments – national players fell back on old reflexes, based on their own financial interests, historical experiences, or beliefs about debt or inflation. Without a shared melody, if all the band members improvised at the same time on their own initiative, there would be mere cacophony.

Germany, the strongest player, was devoted to the founding contract and looked upon shifts in the monetary union with deep concern. It was France that in the historic weeks after the fall of the Berlin Wall (1989) successfully pushed for the creation of a European currency, but after that major concession, Germany was able to determine what it would look like – otherwise it would refuse to join. Bonn wanted a currency with the stability of the Deutschmark, with low inflation and without mutual financial liability, so it needed to be kept at a safe distance from political arbitrariness, laced up in a confidence-inspiring corset of rules. Hence the outsourcing of monetary policy to a competent and independent Central Bank; hence the embedding of budgetary policy in strict regulation; hence too the ban on financing each other's debts. All this was designed to prevent national governments from indulging in extravagant spending and transferring their debts to the Union, or at least to the stronger economies ("moral hazard"). The German and Dutch preference for a depoliticized currency and price stability fitted wonderfully well with Brussels thinking. Reports presented the single currency as a technical "solution" to fluctuating exchange rates. For Brussels experts, monetary union was not an unprecedented historical and political leap but a logical next step in the successful economic integration of the European single market, which had included the free movement of capital for some years already. As a Commission report from 1990 succinctly puts it: "One market, one currency". So the euro came into the world under the auspices of the old politics of rules. In an initiative that fell somewhere between visionary statesmanship and technocratic overreach, it was left to the future to determine who would shape euro-politics.

Member states with other ideas, such as France, resigned themselves in Maastricht to the German vision, because they had little choice and because they believed that through future treaty changes (and before then in everyday practice) they could steer things in the direction they desired. Paris made no secret of its wish for a "more political" euro: greater budgetary flexibility and discretionary decision-making power, political influence over the European Central Bank and overt guidance by unambiguously named *"gouvernement économique"* meetings of government leaders. Paris would also have liked an expansion of the European budget as a tool of political will. These French preferences arose in part out of a tendency towards political opportunism and a desire to be able to make exceptions for themselves at any moment, against which German aversion and suspicion continually had to be mobilized (lest Germany end up contributing even more money to the shared coffers than it already did). It also arose from the realization that at times of crisis you have to be inventive, flexible and in a position to act; a corset of rules can pinch too tightly. Nevertheless, the French did not succeed in reopening the debate on substantive matters after Maastricht. Germany kept that door firmly shut, and because the euro seemed to be functioning satisfactorily, reconsideration seemed superfluous. The three changes to the Union treaty after 1991 – the last of them signed by the heads of state and government in late 2007 in Lisbon – did not provide a toolkit for managing the currency union.

The test was already approaching. The financial crisis that erupted in the summer of 2007 was the overture to the euro crisis. In substance, the former lay at the origins of the downward spiral of weak banks and weak state finances that were to bring the monetary union close to collapse. In form, it demonstrated the power of national reflexes in emergency situations, especially when there are neither forums nor frameworks for joint engagement in events-politics.

For America and Europe the banking crisis was the most profound economic shock since the Great Depression of the 1930s. The collapse of Lehman Brothers in September 2008 was like an infarction, stopping the blood flow of Western economies. The states had to rescue their banks with taxpayers' money and stimulate their economies with additional spending. While the US government rapidly intervened with such measures, European governments did not manage to draw themselves up in battle array. There was a "coordinated" stimulus package (many governments were perfectly happy to be able to spend more than EU rules allowed) and the European Central Bank injected billions into the banking system, but when it came to failing banks, everything fell apart. The stronger member states felt responsible for their own savers only – a natural tendency that was nevertheless incompatible with the European internal market for capital. Who was responsible when banks that operated across borders went bankrupt? There was no clear answer. A few banks – such as the Belgian-Dutch ING – were broken up along national lines. A French plan from October 2008 for joint guarantees for the banking system encountered German opposition. *"Chacun sa merde"* – each his own shit – the French president summed up the German attitude after a fruitless consultation.[3] (Without batting an eyelid, spokespersons for the chancellor claimed that she had in fact been referring to a quote from Goethe, according to which every citizen has a duty to sweep the pavement outside their own house.)[4]

The banking crisis was a harsh but instructive experience. It transpired that arrogant global "flash capitalism" cannot do without the order provided by states. In an emergency, political power became visible again. States had to rescue the banks, not out of any love for bankers but to safeguard their citizens from economic and social catastrophe. This gave politicians renewed self-confidence. But Europe learnt something else too in the crisis: there was a disparity between the level of threat and that of the political response. In the face of the borderless internal market for financial services, no integrated political system existed. This disparity was not eliminated during the banking crisis but (provisionally) resolved by means of laborious coordination, the task of a new banking agency headquartered in London.

This experience gave pause for thought about the single currency. If the multitude of transnational European banks could no longer be carved up along national lines in times of crisis and therefore a capacity for joint action was required, what about the European single currency? Did that not also require a capacity to act? You could not simply slice up the euro. Moreover, amid all the uncertainty, one thing was now plainly predictable: at some point some sort of crisis would hit the monetary union. The Maastricht model of pure rules-politics would then be put to the test. There would be no evading the question as to the relationship between the currency and governmental power, so carefully separated when the euro came into being.

When in the course of 2009 Greek public finances reached an alarming state, the moment drew closer when this question would have to be answered. In an end-of-year essay about the economic crisis for Dutch news-paper *NRC Handelsblad*, I wrote:

> Plenty of shared rules, but they are all being trampled underfoot. Unprecedented treasury deficits threaten monetary stability. The ques-tion arises: where does political authority in Euroland lie? Who is able, in times of crisis, outside the rules, to address unforeseen threats to prosperity? Or is the euro a pleasure craft without a captain, for good weather only?

I found it striking that, earlier the same month, in a speech to her party in Bonn, Angela Merkel had suggested the Union should take upon itself part of the fiscal burden of those member states with unmanageable debts, and in that context she said the states "share responsibility for the euro" in times of crisis. I concluded: "By using those words, the chancellor crossed a boundary. Anyone who starts talking about responsibility recognizes that the euro needs more than established rules alone. [...] Responsibility is demanded in all situ-ations where the rules laid down do not work, where we are empty-handed."[5]

That analysis dates back to 29 December 2009. Three days later I joined the private office of the first permanent president of the European Council, a man in a new role.[6] The newspaper article encompassed in part a task I had set myself. For the time being I would put down the pen of the independent writer, but I would keep my eyes and ears open. And I knew where I wanted to focus my attention. In the months and years that followed, events unfolded before me in all their intensity.

Seven episodes

"SHARED RESPONSIBILITY": 11 FEBRUARY 2010

It was snowing that morning. Several of the participants' flights were delayed. The media were informed that the European Council would begin late. That suited its chair, who needed time for a pressing problem. Crisis was in the air: Greece was teetering on the verge of state bankruptcy. But the snow did not offer endless postponement. When the last of the government leaders entered the building, Herman Van Rompuy had to choose between two roles. As host it would be impolite to make more than 20 national leaders wait, especially for the first summit since he took up his new post. But as chair it would be irresponsible to break off preparatory talks and risk indecisive division in the plenary session; that would send a disastrous signal to the outside world. He opted for responsibility over courtesy.

It was Thursday 11 February 2010. The meeting, arranged weeks before, had been intended as an informal brainstorming session between the 27 heads of state and government* about Europe's structural economic growth. Events decided otherwise. The Greek situation demanded urgent decisions. As a result of astonishing revelations about statistical fraud – uncovered by the incoming government after the parliamentary elections of October 2009 – and because of a budget deficit that was steadily approaching 15 per cent, capital markets were losing confidence that the country could pay its debts. Athens was in danger of being cut off from the markets, a dramatic moment for Greece and its citizens, with results impossible to predict.

But this was about more than just Greece. Speculators were starting to bet billions on "a eurozone debt crisis", the *Financial Times* reported that week.[7] During the summit the other 26 leaders came to realize that a Greek bankruptcy would have severe repercussions for the eurozone, for the entire Union and consequently for their own countries. Their much-praised economic interdependence had a downside, they now discovered, without immediately grasping its implications.

That Thursday morning the heads of government needed above all to ward off an acute crisis. In doing so they could have no recourse to shared rules; they would have to invent something from scratch. The EU Treaty explicitly bans member states from taking on each other's financial obligations.[8] This no-bailout clause is a fundamental principle of the monetary union, a pillar of the politics of rules without which neither Germany nor the Netherlands would have agreed to enter into the monetary adventure in 1991. For some the judicial obstacle corresponded with a political aversion

---

* Croatia, the 28th member state, joined the Union in 2013.

to saving a country that had violated all the agreed rules. Other leaders felt it would disgrace Europe if one of them had to go cap in hand to the International Monetary Fund in Washington. This left little room for manoeuvre. Meanwhile the Greek prime minister – not himself responsible for the mess he faced – had made clear by phone the evening before that he needed a sign of confidence to calm the markets.

The president of the European Council and his staff hurriedly put together a new draft declaration to be signed by all the leaders. It would take the Union into virgin territory, so it was best to reach agreement with the key players beforehand. That morning, in various combinations, Van Rompuy received the Greek prime minister, the French president, the German chancellor and the presidents of the Commission, the rotating Council, the European Central Bank and the Eurogroup (the euro's finance ministers). The crucial meeting was with the first three: Giorgos Papandreou, Nicolas Sarkozy and Angela Merkel.

The statement began in an orthodox manner: "All euro area members must conduct sound national policies in line with the agreed rules". Immediately after that came the crux: "They have a shared responsibility for the economic and financial stability in the area". Shared responsibility was the principle for which Van Rompuy was hoping to gain Merkel's assent; she had already spoken of it in late 2009, but only now did he get her (and the others) to commit to it. It was given concrete significance by the concluding lines, "Euro area Member states will take determined and coordinated action, if needed, to safeguard financial stability in the euro area as a whole".[9]

Without explicitly saying that the other member states would lend Athens money, this text rubbed up against the boundary of the no-bailout clause. Only if a Greek bankruptcy threatened the stability of the eurozone would the member states take action. It was an important nuance: they would do so not for the sake of solidarity with Greece (the word "solidarity" does not appear in the text) but for the sake of the stability of the currency, a rather more German parameter. The motto was not "help Greece" but "save the euro" – a distinction with major strategic consequences, since from then on Greece could be helped only if the euro was in danger.

The statement was carefully composed with a conditional clause. In February 2010 the discussion was all about general principles, not about paying out money the following day. As a result of Greek semantic sensitivities the original wording "if necessary" was replaced by "if needed". (When this was not immediately changed in a subsequent version, a mini-crisis broke out among advisers in the corridors.) In the meeting, Papandreou said repeatedly that he was not asking for money. The others paid little attention to this assertion from the almost-bankrupt premier. But Van Rompuy – who as the former prime minister of a perpetually negotiating Belgian five-party government had his ears permanently cocked for innovative solutions – suggested adding a line: "The Greek government has not requested any financial support". This additional sentence, the very last in the statement, sealed the deal. Both the Greek prime minister and the German chancellor now found it easier to agree, while the French president was already itching to go to the press. The full European Council could finally begin. The meeting changed only a few details. Most government leaders were happy simply to have an agreement that respected everyone's sensitivities.

When the government planes took off from Brussels again that afternoon, many questions remained. Who would do what and when to secure financial stability? The markets were groping in the dark. The statement offered no answer to those questions. The breakthrough of 11 February lay in the principle of "shared responsibility" for eurozone stability. By using that term the leaders were acknowledging that monetary union, which up to that point had relied on rules alone, could necessitate joint political action. They were breaking through the dogma of depoliticization and organized impotence. The statement said: we, the eurozone leaders, don't yet know what we are going to do, but if the worst comes to the worst we will do it together. It expressed a form of political solidarity, the purport of which no one understood on the eve of the euro storm.

With this seemingly innocent yet historic closing statement, balances in the currency union started to shift. On that one sentence all the later bailout mechanisms rested. More politics was allowed in. It was no accident that this was an outstanding example of an accord that emerged from the "intermediate sphere" of European politics, the space where member states discover they share more than merely Treaty rules and common institutions since they also occupy, as a club, their own sphere – a world hovering in between the fully Europeanized "inner sphere" and the purely national "outer sphere".[10]

After all, the two obvious paths out of the crisis were blocked. The path of the treaty-bound "inner sphere" was shut off, because of the no-bailout clause and Germany's attachment to it; without a treaty mandate the EU institutions could not act (quite apart from the fact that the prohibition also placed judicial restrictions on member states). The path of the diplomatic "outer sphere" of the sovereign states – embodied in the monetary field by the IMF – was politically impassable. The French president and the presidents of the Commission and the Eurogroup regarded an appeal to the Washington-based body as humiliating for Europe, while the European Central Bank and the German finance minister saw it as legally dubious.

Lawyers might think that if neither is possible, nothing is possible. This is a mistake. What is possible is that the member states, despite clauses in the Treaty that require almost the opposite, can take political responsibility together. Shared responsibility trumps the rules in such cases – which is why such responsibility is best assumed in the intermediate sphere, outside the Treaty, by the leaders in the European Council.

In EU jargon, "political responsibility" is not a term frequently used. Lawyers and civil servants speak and think in terms of "competences": Why does an institution act? Because it has the competence to do so. But an unprecedented crisis demands a degree of authority and power to act that goes beyond limited competences and requires concentrated political responsibility. It is a matter of addressing a situation with full personal authority, not randomly but specifically in response (the etymology is relevant) to a circumstance, a disaster, a question from real life. Although taking responsibility undoubtedly involves a sense of moral duty – as becomes particularly clear when it is not taken – ultimately it is a voluntary act.* Strictly speaking no one can be forced into it.[11]

In the Union the European Council is the obvious place for assuming shared responsibility, for mobilizing the personal political authority called for by events-politics. On 11 February 2010 the European Council was acting in its role of "shaper". To be more precise, its members acted in their capacity as "heads of state or government of the European Union" (as they called

---

* We therefore need to distinguish between this creative, political responsibility and "responsibility as self-discipline", a concept frequently used in Brussels that lies in the sphere of individual adherence to self-imposed rules.

themselves in their closing statement). The same gathering, in short, but not meeting as a formal EU institution called the European Council but rather as an informal circle of national leaders. This allowed them to tread on territory the Treaty had not mapped, while still acting jointly as members of the club. On this occasion they left the concrete outcome to others: they gave precise tasks to the Greek government (to reduce the deficit), to the Commission, the European Central Bank and the Council of finance ministers (to exercise supervision) and finally to themselves, too, as member states, in case in the end intervention were to be needed.

This represented a political breakthrough, but its communication to the public foundered. After the agreement on principle had been made, six protagonists left Herman Van Rompuy's offices for the plenary session: the leaders of France, Germany and Greece and the presidents of the European Council, the Commission and the European Central Bank. In the corridor they ran into journalists angling for news. For a moment there was confusion. Who would speak? Merkel and Sarkozy prompted the ill-at-ease "Herman", the linchpin of their meetings, to announce the existence of an accord. The text itself could not yet be made public. Not until all 27 leaders had agreed to it was the shared responsibility real and ready to be made visible.

The announcement flopped. In the snow of the Leopold Park in Brussels – to mark the beginning of his presidency with an unusual venue, the host had chosen the nearby Solvay library instead of the Council building – the two EU presidents Van Rompuy and José Manuel Barroso stood in front of a video camera that someone had rigged up. There was no European flag, no lectern, no microphone stand, nothing: only snow and wind. One man floundered through a page while the other stood next to him in silence, head tilted to see how much longer it was going to take. To make matters worse, they thought it was a video recording, but it was a live feed to a packed Brussels press room. To the hilarity of hundreds of journalists, Van Rompuy had to read the statement twice; the first time he had been standing too far from the mike. In sum, the significance of the 11 February accord escaped both the markets and the media. There were hardly any positive reactions.

This too was virgin territory. A stable monetary union demands not just concerted political action but convincing public speaking. The one-act play for two men in a park was based on a logistical misunderstanding, certainly, but as a lapse it is revealing. It cannot be a coincidence that at the very moment when rules-politics lost its Maastricht monopoly on the steward-ship of the monetary union, when the leaders jointly acknowledged for the first time that, for the stability of the currency, events-politics is required – precisely at that moment, the importance of public communication and the need for persuasiveness made themselves felt.

"THE FULL RANGE OF MEANS AVAILABLE": 7–10 MAY 2010

In early May 2010 the euro was exposed to virtually ungovernable forces. The spectre of Greece as "the next Lehman" stalked the continent. The world-wide tidal wave caused by the fall of the investment bank in the autumn of 2008 was still a fresh memory; politicians, central bankers and policymakers on both sides of the Atlantic did not want to experience anything like that a second time. When Moody's credit rating agency said on Thursday 6 May that the Greek debt crisis might spread to Spain, Portugal, Ireland, Italy and Britain, concern increased in America and the rest of the world. A flash crash on Wall Street that same day, later blamed on a technical fault, triggered panic. Europe's central bankers, gathered in Lisbon, feared that their luke-warm response to the crisis was a contributory factor and had no idea what to make of it all. Politicians spoke of an "organized worldwide attack against the euro".[12] Early on Friday 7 May, President Obama rang Merkel and Sarkozy. The message was clear: save the euro.

Greece was no longer the problem. Prime Minister Papandreou had asked for support on 23 April after all, and an accord was signed on 2 May detail-ing a rescue package of €110 billion, which would shelter the country from the capital markets until 2013. That the operation had taken so much time was problematic, however. The European approach looked hesitant, messy and risky. It was improvised, of course, since no instruments had been to hand; there was no difficulty in explaining that. But why did it have to take place under such high pressure? Not just because Athens dawdled for so long before asking for help but also because – faithful to the Statement of 11 February 2010 – the stability of the eurozone needed to be in danger first.[13] Only when the blaze threatened to spread could the flames be extinguished. For such an approach a rescuer cannot expect applause, especially since to most members of the public a self-imposed handicap was incomprehensible. (Was a delay to firefighting really the best way to convince the neighbours of the risk of conflagration?) Investors had no confidence in this kind of crisis management. For Spain and Portugal too, interest rates shot up. Spanish Prime Minister José-Luis Zapatero therefore wanted to see political resolve confirmed at the highest level. At the end of April, president Van Rompuy announced a summit for the eurozone "on 10 May at the latest", at which the leaders could give their final blessing to the Greek bailout and look ahead.

Fixing a date proved difficult. Angela Merkel was keen to wait until after the elections of Sunday 9 May in North Rhine–Westphalia, the largest of the German states. Her CDU party was facing losses, the German electorate had been irritated by the support for Greece – "just sell the Parthenon" was the mood in *Bild Zeitung* – and she was in danger of losing her coalition majority in the Bundesrat. But in that first week of May the seas became so rough that it was no longer possible to wait until Monday 10 May. Commemorations were due to take place in Moscow on Sunday, the day before, to mark 65 years since the end of the Second World War. So that day was also impossible, as a German chancellor could not be absent. Eventually the only option was a working dinner on Friday 7 May. It heralded the hectic marathon series of meetings now known as the "trillion-dollar weekend". (Although all the talks were in euro, converting the final figure of €750 billion in rescue funds into such a big and beautiful round number of US dollars proved irresistible to EU spokespersons eager to impress the markets, and to the media.)

At the opening on the Friday evening, ECB governor Jean-Claude Trichet immediately demonstrated to the 16 eurozone leaders, by means of stark diagrams, how closely the panic in the markets and the contraction of interbank lending resembled what had happened after "Lehman" in September 2008. Action was needed, or soon there would no longer be a euro. "Couldn't we wait a few days?" asked the president of Cyprus. No, Merkel now agreed. When the Asian markets opened on Monday morning the response would have to be ready. That gave them just over 48 hours.

But what to do? There was no toolkit and this was an emergency. The meeting was therefore tumultuous. Could the European Central Bank not step in by buying up government bonds? That would put downward pressure on interest rates and restore market confidence, declared the leaders of

France, Italy, Spain and Portugal one after the other. To the fury of Sarkozy, ECB president Trichet (snarled at as *citoyen français* by his Président de la République) said over and over again that he could not promise anything: the credibility of the Bank rested on its independence from political pressure. Merkel and others supported Trichet; she had reason to expect that the Bank would do what was necessary.

Yet the political leaders realized that they too would have to pull out all the stops to save the euro. In a concluding statement they reaffirmed their commitment to use "the full range of means available".[14] This was unusually strong language. Their plans can be grouped under the headings of legislation, separate action and joint action. To take legislation first, the leaders wanted better regulation of the financial markets and credit rating agencies, and to get on with the work that had recently begun on stricter budgetary controls and economic oversight. The realization was dawning that government deficits, such as those of Greece, were not the only risk. Ireland was vulnerable because of a banking bubble and Spain because of a housing bubble, even though both countries had had relatively small deficits and debts as recently as 2009. Such preventative work was important for the future, but emergencies cannot be tackled by legislation. Decisive action was needed. Which is why, secondly, under the heading of separate action, the leaders declared that "each one of us is ready, depending on the situation of his country, to take the necessary measures" to reduce budget deficits according to agreed norms and with precise commitments. Good intentions count for nothing when it comes to winning back confidence. Individual member states under pressure from the markets would have to introduce cuts and reforms. Everyone was thinking above all of Spain, including Prime Minister Zapatero himself. Thirdly, the most urgent point: joint action. A massive protective umbrella was needed to scare off speculators. The Commission had a plan for a fund of around €60 billion, based on the EU budget. It was a start, but hardly impressive, given the sums that Athens alone had needed the month before. The leaders asked the Commission to come up with a proposal for a "stabilization mechanism" quickly, so that the 27 finance ministers could take a decision on it on the Sunday.[15]

Saturday and Sunday brought a succession of meetings, marathon phone calls and theatrical intrigues. In the Commission offices a proposal was thrashed out. Lawyers sought "hooks" in the treaty that could take the weight of the emergency fund. In Spain Zapatero set to work on his budget. Sarkozy and Silvio Berlusconi cancelled their trips to the Moscow parade to coordinate the crisis response from Paris and Rome. Today's "war against the markets" surely took precedence over yesterday's war against the Nazis. This put Merkel, who did set off for Red Square that Saturday evening (where she brought the alarmed Chinese president up to date on the euro) at a disadvantage. Her minister would have to win back lost ground on the Sunday afternoon. On arrival in Brussels, however, Wolfgang Schäuble was taken to hospital after suffering an allergic reaction. The German chancellor called in her confidant Thomas de Maizière, minister of the interior. He was summoned from a Sunday woodland walk with his wife in Saxony and whisked off to Brussels in a government plane; towards 8.30pm he entered the meeting room. By then the ballot boxes in North Rhine–Westphalia had closed. There were just over five hours left before the stock market in Tokyo opened.

The meeting found itself at an impasse. All that was settled was the size of the pot of cash, which Sarkozy and Merkel had agreed on the Saturday evening by phone. On top of the €60 billion covered by the EU budget (which Commission president Barroso had proposed on the Friday evening), another €440 billion would come from the member nations. The IMF would add another €250 billion, a sum that IMF boss Dominique Strauss-Kahn had promised French minister Christine Lagarde. Early misgivings about the involvement of the Washington-based body had disappeared; Berlin and The Hague had pushed for the IMF's expertise around the table while other capitals welcomed the extra money it would contribute. In total it came to enough for a three-year protective umbrella over Spain, Portugal and Ireland. Sarkozy was content: "Angela" was at last thinking big; this would surprise the markets. But Merkel did have three small points: the emergency fund must be temporary, there must be IMF involvement, and each rescue must be decided upon unanimously, so that the Bundestag had a veto. This was precisely the opposite of what Paris wanted and what the Commission had put on the table on Sunday, namely a permanent, purely European €500-billion emergency fund, decided upon by majority vote, in control of both Friday evening's €60 billion and the €440 billion from the member states. There was more. While the Commission claimed the emergency fund was compatible with the Treaty, Berlin regarded it as in conflict with the no-bailout clause. To sweep the Commission's plan off the table, the Germans brandished the fault-findings of their Constitutional Court in Karlsruhe; in play under the surface was their refusal to entrust the pot to Brussels bureaucrats. Now the ministers began tinkering themselves. De Maizière was not in favour of a joint fund but wanted bilateral loans between eurozone countries instead. At midnight, when the meeting almost collapsed, Merkel told him, "Stay firm. We still have two hours to negotiate".[16] At the last moment a Dutch civil servant thought up an ingenious trick, whereby the eurozone countries could stand surety pro rata for a "special purpose vehicle" to be set up under private law in Luxembourg that could raise €440 billion on the markets. The French and Italians agreed to it and pulled Germany across the line, just a few minutes before the Japanese stock market opened.

Although the ministers were putting together a rescue vehicle, the operation remained a *Chefsache* (a matter for the top brass) right to the last moment. Immediately after agreement was reached, at 2.00am, Sarkozy rang Trichet. Like Merkel that evening with De Maizière, Zapatero in Madrid kept in contact with his minister in the room, Elena Salgado. The Spaniard, untroubled for a long time, had been shaken awake that Friday and he now responded with the biggest cuts to the welfare state since the Franco era; Salgado negotiated with her colleagues in Brussels on how to add up the austerity measures to reach a 1.5 per cent extra reduction to the Spanish deficit. After that Zapatero could not sleep for nerves, as he told *El País* later: how would the Nikkei index react to the European decisions?[17] He realized that the cuts would probably finish him politically, but he wanted to spare his country humiliation and to avoid having the collapse of the euro on his conscience.

In the early hours of Monday 10 May, the European Central Bank also issued a statement. It would buy government bonds, not over the counter from the member states but on the secondary market. With these, to use the jargon, "non-standard measures" it was entering unknown territory. In the banking crisis of 2008–09 the Bank had adopted emergency measures, but doing so now in the debt crisis took it further along its adventurous path. It meant breaking a taboo of German monetary thinking, according to which buying government bonds counted as a fatal step towards "printing money" for the benefit of profligate governments. (The president of the German

Bundesbank, Axel Weber, voted against the decision of 10 May; he was out-voted in the ECB governing council by his fellow European Bank presidents.) In its statement the Bank quoted with approval the 7 May commitment by the government leaders that they would "take all measures needed to meet [their] fiscal targets this year and the years ahead in line with excessive deficit procedures".[18] Later it leaked out that the decision to buy bonds had been taken on principle during the flash-crash confusion of 6 May in Lisbon, but Trichet kept his mouth shut the following evening. The monetary authorities wanted to maintain the pressure on the political leaders and avoid doing all the dirty work of crisis control themselves.

The weekend of 7–10 May 2010 was a formidable tour de force. The European Council, meeting for only the second time ever in euro-formation, performed as rarely before in its role as crisis tamer.[19] In an absolute emergency it mobilized "the full range of means available" on the Friday. Thanks to its dual capacity (with members of the European Council also being leaders of their countries) and with the president of the Commission among them, the body of heads of state and government could get two Union institutions, namely the Commission and the Council of finance ministers, as well as their separate governments, all moving in the same direction. Only the independent European Central Bank refused to be told what to do, but it did it all the same. Necessity knows no law.

Thus the Union woke on Monday morning 10 May with a Central Bank that turned out to have a greater willingness to act than had been thought possible a few days before. The eurozone countries had also given themselves what looked like a "European monetary fund", later christened the European Financial Stability Facility. This was judicial jerry-building, but it worked. The markets were surprised in a positive sense this time. The situation stabilized. The improvisation was a success.

Yet not everyone applauded. With these decisions the Maastricht monetary union unmistakably changed its shape. The terms of the founding contract were shifting, which the keepers of the temple found hard to take – or in fact the keepers of two temples. First there was strong criticism from monetary orthodoxy in Germany and the Netherlands. It was felt that the Bank had exceeded its mandate and that the rescue mechanisms violated the no–bailout clause, with all the risks of moral hazard and inflation this entailed. The euro was losing its shine, looking less and less like the strong D-Mark or Guilder of days gone by. This criticism found its most important institutional spokespersons in the German Bundesbank and the German Constitutional Court; it led to notorious cases for that same Court, which, based on its Maastricht Judgment (1993), could even have led to Germany's exit from the eurozone.[20] At its heart the reasoning went: if the criteria from Maastricht were straightforwardly complied with – or were to be complied with in the future – then there would be no need to alter the currency union. All its legal niceties notwithstanding, this argument comes down to saying that as long as no one plays with fire, there is no need for a fire brigade. It reasons in terms of competences in a situation that calls for responsibility.

Secondly there was criticism from the institutional orthodoxy in Brussels circles. The emergency fund of €440 billion could not become a treaty-based Union institution in the early hours of 10 May, since the German, Dutch and other euro governments wanted to retain authority over the billions of national fiscal resources that were going into the emergency pot (and also because the British and other non-euro governments did not wish to participate). To their frustration the European Parliament and the Commission were therefore largely side-lined. An essential pillar of the monetary union took shape in a sphere out of their reach. So amid all the relief that a catastrophe had been averted it was nevertheless a "black Monday" for true believers. The European Parliament in particular, in the name of democracy and transparency, set itself up as the voice of an aborted pure-Brussels solution.

This dual criticism needs to be seen as a single whole. The political response to the threat to the currency was a mobilization of public resources, of taxpayers' money. But which taxpayers would foot the bill? Or, to be more precise, taxpayers in which capacity? That was where the battle lines lay. The general mobilization of 7 May 2010 showed unerringly the boundaries of what each was able or willing to contribute. First €60 billion, based on the EU budget, was put on the table. Here we encounter the taxpayers in their capacity as EU citizens, represented by the Parliament and the Commission. But that Brussels pot was too small to calm the financial storm. Of necessity the eurozone member states then called upon their national taxpayers collectively. The emergency fund of €440 billion was made up of German, French, Italian, Spanish, Dutch, Belgian, Austrian, Greek, Portuguese, Finnish, Irish,

Slovakian, Slovenian, Luxembourgian, Cypriot and Maltese tax revenue; the sums ranged from almost €120 billion from Germany to €0.4 billion from Malta. Together that too was a European fund – not one that was raised in the Brussels "inner sphere", but a joint fund nonetheless.

The tough question as to who ends up footing the bill always lays bare constitutional and democratic relationships. (The American revolutionaries understood this very well, as is clear from their 1776 slogan "No taxation without representation".) In this light the dual criticism of the Bundesbank and the European Parliament is easier to understand. The Bundesbank was speaking unambiguously on behalf of specific bodies of national taxpayers. It gave voice – in the language of the existing rules – to a "northern" distrust of the emergency measures as a disguised "southern" cash grab. The European Parliament by contrast claimed to speak for the "European" taxpayer. But it had a handicap: the latter is above all a promise. For one thing there are no direct EU taxes (to the regret of the Parliament) and for another the EU budget accounts for no more than about 1 per cent of European wealth, whereas the national budgets added together account for around 45–50 per cent. In short, the Bundesbank speaks on behalf of the northern, national public that does not want to pay the bill, while the Parliament speaks on behalf of an incipient European public that cannot (yet, at any rate) pay.

In this apparent impasse a way out opened up. Which political representatives would speak in the name of the group of national taxpayers that could and must pay? Who could transform the "against our will" of necessity into a free and welcomed choice? Such a choice would mean that the governments of the eurozone countries would be saying to their citizens that the euro belongs to us all and we're saving the currency not just out of financial self-interest but as a collective response to events. This is indeed what they did. The temporary emergency fund was a successful improvisation, a collective act in between necessity and free will. But they said it only in dribs and drabs. Political communication with the public faltered.

There was one exception. On Thursday 13 May Angela Merkel gave a speech in the former imperial city of Aachen, at the presentation of the Charlemagne Prize to the then Polish Prime Minister Donald Tusk. Perhaps it was a sense of relief that the elections in North Rhine–Westphalia were over and the euro situation had calmed, or perhaps the solemn occasion inspired a deeper historical dimension. In any case she spoke for the first time in months with real animation: "So why save Greece, why save the euro, why spend countless days and nights to achieve a common goal after difficult, sometimes tough, negotiations? Because we sense that if the euro fails, it is not just the currency that fails [...] It means Europe fails, the idea of European unification fails".[21] Here she discovered the free choice argument, a more principled reason for doing what was necessary. She repeated it a few days later in the Bundestag debate about the emergency measures: "If the euro fails, Europe fails".[22]

That sentence, which became a mantra, offered something to hold onto in the storm. It appealed to a stronger compass and ensured that the rules would not have the last word. "Europe" trumped the treaty. Its seemingly naive wording conceals a rarely noticed truth: essentially the states had committed themselves at the Union's foundation not only to adherence to Union law but to the continued existence of the Union as such. In emergency situations, therefore, breaking with the rules could actually equate to being true to the contract.[23] For that reason too, the spokespersons for one orthodoxy or the other proved no match for the political leaders of the European club, who represented not just the established law but Europe's constituent power.

The chancellor's uttering of that sentence heralded the rise of Germany's power in Europe.

"ADEQUATE PARTICIPATION BY THE PRIVATE SECTOR": DEAUVILLE, 18 OCTOBER 2010

A wide panorama, the autumn sun low over the sea, two leaders in warm conversation: the images are irresistible. One afternoon in late October, Nicolas Sarkozy and Angela Merkel took a walk along the beach at Deauville. They discussed the state of the euro and confirmed a deal. A meeting with their Russian colleague Dmitri Medvedev, right after their stroll, was the reason for their coming together at the Normandy seaside resort, but Sarkozy wanted to make full use of his *moment à deux* with "Angela". No sooner said than done; the president's staff outfoxed their Berlin colleagues and as five o'clock approached they issued a Franco-German statement about the eurozone.

Both France and Germany had a problem with the continual work needed to make the eurozone crisis-proof. In the Deauville declaration they each agreed to the other's wishes. Paris had assented to stricter budgetary rules in the Stability and Growth Pact – a ministerial working group chaired by the president of the European Council was busy drawing them up – but would like to avoid "automatic" sanctions. It wanted to preserve a space for political discretion and therefore the chance of escape (not least for itself). The chancellor for her part wanted to give a solid basis to the ad hoc emergency fund of May 2010 that some countries simply wanted to extend. Improvisation in a crisis is one thing, she thought, but a permanent emergency fund needed to be anchored in the law, preferably by treaty change. This would also be an opportunity to agree that if taxpayers keep a eurozone country on its feet, private investors must share the pain; that could perhaps quell voters' sense of injustice and their anger towards the bankers. In the beach agreement each conceded to the other their point.

The presentation and timing of the declaration caused consternation. That same 18 October 2010 in Luxembourg the Van Rompuy task force was finalizing a eurozone report with the EU's 27 finance ministers, ECB president Trichet, the then Eurogroup chair Jean-Claude Juncker and commissioner Olli Rehn. In March that year the government leaders had asked Van Rompuy for plans for a more robust currency union; the report's authors were dealing with the same issues as Sarkozy and Merkel. The news from Deauville was a bombshell. It cut across procedures and brushed aside sensitivities. The dazzling beach walk in Normandy demoted those working in Luxembourg to mere extras. That did not worry the French president; his aim was to show the public that two countries led the eurozone, not just one.

The content compounded the affront. In Luxembourg the indignation was focused on the "French" side of the Deauville deal, the weakening of the proposed budgetary supervision. No one was surprised that the French had tried this, but they were astonished that the Germans had given in. The Netherlands, Finland, Sweden, the Commission, the European Central Bank: all the advocates of strict budgetary discipline felt betrayed by Berlin. The rules designed to prevent a future crisis had in their view lost all credibility. They were so upset by this, and the press so focused on it, that practically no one paid any attention to 11 far-reaching little words the declaration also contained.

Only ECB president Trichet realized it at once. He spotted the real danger on the "German" side of the Deauville deal. He regarded the idea that investors would help to pay for bailouts from 2013 onwards, as Merkel blithely proposed laying down, as downright dangerous. "You're going to destroy the euro", he said in dismay.[24] But the politicians ignored the bit about the emergency fund, so shocked were they by the main thrust: Berlin wants treaty change! Among diplomats alarm bells sounded. Would the hard-fought Lisbon Treaty, in force for less than a year, have to be broken open already, with the risk of referendums and other horrors? So the Deauville bombshell, after the whole carry-on over the budget, left another smokescreen behind it that concealed the provision that made Trichet shudder. And anyhow, he was exaggerating, wasn't he?

The Summit of 28–29 October 2010 would have to decide the matter. The ECB president repeated to the government leaders his worries about the proposed private sector involvement. But Trichet was no longer effective. Since 2008 he had all too often warned the political leaders of financial armageddon. Merkel listened to him politely and then laid out her standpoint again. Sarkozy by contrast exploded: "You're trying to convince the world that you saved the euro but we, heads of state and government, took the vital decisions. You may be able to talk to bankers like that, but we have to deal with voters".[25] Since Deauville the chancellor had lobbied her 25 other colleagues. On this occasion they were happy to help her. So the European Council decided on "limited treaty change" to set up a permanent crisis mechanism. In preparatory work on the subject, "i.a. the role of the private sector" would be included.[26]

Yet doubts soon arose as to whether this was manageable and sensible. After Deauville and after the European Council, interest rates on the public debt of the weaker euro economies jumped. Investors understood that from 2013 onwards they would have to help pay for a state bankruptcy in the eurozone and they immediately adjusted their risk assessments. For the past two years Ireland had been struggling with the banking crisis. Now it went under; it sought support from the emergency fund and on 27 November 2010 it signed up for a bailout of €85 billion. The sequence of events did not look good. Merkel backed down. The future emergency fund would act "in line with IMF practices" (which meant that private participation would take place only after a sustainability analysis of the debt position) and moreover, existing debt would not be the subject of private participation, even after 2013. This compromise put forward by the euro ministers on Sunday 28th – and negotiated earlier by video conference between Van Rompuy, Merkel, Sarkozy, Barroso, Trichet and Juncker – did not reassure the markets. On Monday 29 November interest rates in Spain also rose. The *Financial Times* spoke of a "Merkel crash".[27] After Ireland it was Portugal's turn to collapse and in February 2011 it too asked for support. Despite all the good work of May 2010 the storm blew up again.

Deauville was a scene best forgotten. The Franco-German performance had been brusque and careless. In the "improvisation" category it was an error by trial.

The French side of the deal held until July 2011. In the shadow of yet another crisis summit, after a long campaign by the ECB and the European Parliament, Sarkozy silently assented to "automatic sanctions" for budgetary transgressors. After the summit of December 2011 even less remained of the German side, which had already been rapidly weakened by agreeing to make the private contribution "in line with IMF practices" (although a reference made it into the preamble to the treaty establishing the European Stability Mechanism). The romantic beach scene reinforced the image of a Franco-German pair imposing its will on the rest, just as the French president had in mind. But from October 2011 onwards an ironic nickname for the intimate couple made clear once again who was boss: "Merkozy".

Despite this complete failure, in Deauville Merkel had in fact touched upon a fundamental problem. Leaders felt trapped between the interests of investors and those of their voters. If foreign investors no longer invested in the eurozone, economic growth would stagnate. But why should taxpayers in strong economies foot the bill for risks taken by, say, American investors in Greece or Ireland? The banking crisis had cast the financial sector in a bad light. Politicians who wanted to take on the banks were popular. It was no accident that the Social Democrat opposition in both Germany and the Netherlands supported the proposal wholeheartedly. Merkel wanted to make the rescue mechanisms, which ran counter to the German view of the terms of the monetary union, easier for her voters to swallow. On the side of the debtors, that of the "grasshoppers" from Aesops fable, living beyond their means,

Merkel had managed to combat moral hazard by means of "conditionality".[28] For every cent that went to Greece, the country had to make cuts and introduce reforms. Now, with private sector involvement, she also wanted to combat the moral hazard on the side of the creditors, the irresponsible lenders. But these financial "locusts", as they have often been called in Germany, proved a formidable opponent.[29]

"A UNIQUE SOLUTION": 21 JULY 2011

On a warm summer's day in 2011 the leaders of the eurozone came together in sombre mood on the top floor of the European Council building in Brussels. For the first time since May 2010 there was a prevailing fear that the eurozone might collapse. It was 21 July, a national holiday in Belgium, with the traditional military parade. To the surprise of those present, at the start of the summit ear-shattering jets flew low over the meeting room.

Inside, too, they were thinking in terms of attack and defence. Europe's leaders felt besieged by the markets. *Si vis pacem para bellum*, would have been the advice from military science: "He who wants peace must prepare for war". Transposed to their own situation: the firepower of the temporary emergency fund would have to be increased. Greece needed support again as well. The leaders were calling upon joint national tax money once more.

Slovakian Prime Minister Iveta Radicová – her country was poorer than Greece, yet would nevertheless have to contribute – was under extreme pressure. She was trapped between her European colleagues in the room and her coalition partners in Bratislava on the phone. She took a dramatic decision and personally gave her word that Slovakia would support the increase in firepower to save the euro. In return she promised her home front early elections, which she knew she would lose: the greatest sacrifice a politician can make. Just as Zapatero had held off the markets and an emergency programme in May 2010 with reforms at the cost of his re-election, so Radicová became the first leader on the creditor side to throw in their lot with the European expression of solidarity of February 2010. This meant all 17 leaders in the eurozone were on board.* In future the temporary emergency fund could

---

* Estonia had joined the eurozone on 1 January 2011, bringing the membership to 17 (Latvia and Lithuania having joined since, membership now stands at 19).

provide loans for recapitalization to banks "without a programme" (which meant Spain and Italy) and intervene in certain situations in the secondary market for government bonds (a task the European Central Bank performed only with great reluctance).

The other matter the leaders addressed on 21 July was Greece. The country's economy was deteriorating rapidly. Even optimists recognized that the bailout of May 2010 was insufficient to get the country through the storm. The likelihood of bankruptcy was increasing, and with it nervousness in Frankfurt, London, Washington and New York. The government leaders held out to Papandreou the prospect of a second bailout to the value of €109 billion. Private investors would help pay for it. This was new. It was an attempt to channel the unrest that had arisen after "Deauville". The private contribution agreed on that occasion would not begin until 2013 (as part of the permanent emergency fund agreement) and it would not be applicable to pre-existing debt, but nevertheless the markets behaved towards Greece as if they were already having to take their losses. So the bailout might as well be made right away. There was something else, too. To avert the danger of contagion, leaders were content to ease Greek debt, but several refused simply to present their taxpayers with the bill again. They could not keep pushing for more. They broke the taboo on debt restructuring for a eurozone country, with immediate effect. In long and intense consultations with Merkel and Sarkozy in Berlin the evening before, ECB president Trichet – flown over from Frankfurt specially during their meeting – had made both leaders promise that private sector involvement in the case of Greece would remain "an exceptional and unique solution". So it is described in the conclusions of the summit, and so everyone said repeatedly at press conferences.[30]

But the markets were not convinced. After all, had the government leaders not declared months before that the same rule would apply to all bailouts from 2013 onwards? And, incidentally, who was to say that even this assertion would not be tampered with under pressure from voters? Once again an announcement made things worse; this time interest on Italian and Spanish government debt rose within hours.

HUMAN RESOURCE MANAGEMENT BY SMILE:
23 OCTOBER–13 NOVEMBER 2011

The leaders had to change tack. But what ways and means did they still have of keeping events in check?

In July 2011 attention turned to Italy. No one could allow the third largest eurozone economy, with the world's fourth largest public debt, to go bankrupt; that would be the end of the euro. Italy was struggling with a lack of credibility. Undertakings by Italy's political leadership to introduce measures to stimulate economic growth and reduce the deficit were no longer believed – not by the eurozone partners, not by the markets, not by Italians themselves. Those that the electorate do not believe lose the political capacity to shape the future, and therefore power. The problem lay at the top. Prime Minister Silvio Berlusconi, media magnate and multimillionaire, embroiled in corruption allegations and sex scandals – even the quality newspapers were lapping up stories of "bunga bunga parties" in his mansions – was living in a state of denial. His peace was rudely disturbed that summer and autumn.

On 5 August the Italian premier received a letter from Frankfurt/Rome: "Urgent action by the Italian authorities is needed to restore the confidence of investors". It was signed by Jean-Claude Trichet and Mario Draghi. The sitting president of the European Central Bank and his successor (still in his job as governor of the Italian central bank) reminded Berlusconi of his promise of 21 July, along with that of the other euro leaders, to honour his sovereign signature under Italy's debt obligations with "inflexible determination".[31] They spelt out a detailed reform agenda, from liberalization of the labour market to pension reform. This unprecedented interference in national economic policy would inevitably raise the question of what mandate the ECB had for its actions. The letter was therefore confidential. It functioned as an internal "insurance policy" for the Bank to be able to purchase Italian government debt, which it announced on 7 August it was going to do.[32] Yet the text leaked out a few weeks later in the Italian newspaper, *Corriere della Sera*.[33] To get the reforms through the Chamber of Deputies and the Senate, Berlusconi weakened them on several points. The *Cavaliere* appeared to be going back on his word, as given to Trichet and Draghi. This caused resentment and endangered the credibility of the ECB (which could not stop buying up debt without losing face but could not continue either). Was it again mere cosmetics and *belle parole*? Now that even pressure from Frankfurt was not working, his fellow eurozone leaders increasingly saw the opportunistic Italian leader as a threat to the monetary union as a whole. They were running out of patience.

For a long time there was nothing more than mumbling and whispering in the corridors of Brussels, Rome, Berlin, Paris and Frankfurt – that is until 23 October 2011. During a press conference after another European Council meeting, a journalist asked Chancellor Merkel and President Sarkozy for their evaluation of the reforms by their colleague Berlusconi. The smile exchanged by the pair is etched on the Italian soul. Both leaders looked from their own lecterns into the room full of journalists. On hearing the name Berlusconi, Merkel smiled slightly, to herself and without looking sideways; she then suppressed the smile and turned, straight-faced, to Sarkozy. He had not been able to see her brief smile but he turned towards Merkel grinning, thereby giving her permission to smile "officially". It was the Frenchman's grimace that opened the flood gates: let's not take each other for fools; we have a problem.[34] The journalists laughed with them. It was infectious.* No one listened to the carefully calibrated words that followed; the dam had burst. Now the public too could see that his colleagues did not trust Berlusconi. The irony: impatience with *belle parole* found its deadliest expression in a wordless grimace.

Ten days later in the French resort of Cannes, a G20 meeting began, with Sarkozy as host. The meeting of the world's largest economies brought the European politicians to a new low. The conversation was dominated not by the scheduled themes of banking regulation, global growth and food security but by the fate of the eurozone. On 3 November Sarkozy and Merkel put Berlusconi under heavy pressure to accept an IMF support package of €45 billion in exchange for reforms; true, the sum was modest in light of Italy's government debt of €1,900 billion, but the operation would give IMF experts in Rome a foot in the door of parliamentary procedures. To the surprise of several of those present, US President Barack Obama took the helm at a private meeting of the eurozone leaders attending the G20 (the leaders of France, Germany, Italy and Spain and both EU presidents). When it became clear that

---

* In hundreds of newspaper reports of the scene, not a single reporter mentioned that the press laughed as well. A telling silence by the media, as ever ignoring their own role in the political theatre.

the Italian was resisting the Franco-German diktat, supported in doing so by Van Rompuy and Barroso, Obama tried a different tack. Ingenious American and French financial experts in Washington had figured out a plan that would increase the size of the European emergency fund. They wanted to achieve increased firepower by means of "special drawing rights", or financial conjuring tricks. Suddenly the pressure was on Merkel. She refused to endorse the plan; officially it was for the Bundesbank to decide on this form of financing. To the astonishment of Obama and Sarkozy, bank governor Jens Weidmann in Frankfurt, on the phone, proved unshakable: Germany is devoted to price stability and does not rush to participate in ill-considered schemes. Both presidents increased the pressure on Merkel even further – failing to appreciate the degree to which in Germany the Bundesbank's word is law – until in despair she declared that in that case the foreign powers that occupied her country after 1945 ought to have given it a different constitution (meaning: less balanced, with more power for the executive to overrule other institutional players). When the chancellor's eyes filled with tears as she told them "I'm not going to commit suicide", Obama realized he had gone too far. By the next morning, Friday 4 November, the storm had passed. No one was any longer talking about "special drawing rights"; Italy was given a monitoring programme without a bailout.[35] Buoyed by bravura, Berlusconi said at the closing press conference: "Italy is rich, the planes are full, the restaurants are full".

Italy's prime minster left Cannes battered but intact. Yet his end was not slow in coming. Within a few days the difference in interest rates between Italian and German ten-year government bonds had climbed above seven per cent. On Tuesday 8 November Berlusconi promised to step down to get a parliamentary majority behind the "Stability Law". On 12 November, that vote out of the way, he tendered his resignation, becoming the latest prime minister to fall victim to the euro crisis. The next day Italian President Giorgio Napolitano asked former European commissioner Mario Monti to put together a cabinet of technocrats. The response from the markets and the European partners was positive: they found Monti credible.

Meanwhile, in Athens, a similar drama played out. Back in the city after the series of European summits of 23–26 October, Prime Minister Papandreou and his close circle decided on a referendum concerning the cuts entailed by the support package that had been decided upon in July and had just been made definitive. It was partly a way to commit the conservative opposition to the programme and enforce national unity. His move came as a shock, to his own party and to his fellow European leaders. In hours of discussion the week before, he had said not a word about it.

A furious Sarkozy summoned Papandreou to Cannes. The initial reaction of the eurozone leaders was: this is insanely dangerous; we must talk Giorgos out of holding a referendum. Then an adviser reminded the French president that his esteemed predecessor De Gaulle held the plebiscite in high regard as a democratic instrument. Sarkozy showed himself sensitive to this, but the gathering did force Papandreou to change the question. It was not the package of cuts that would be at stake in the referendum, but Greek membership of the eurozone.

Some still had doubts. Commission president Barroso, who feared the turbulence of a weeks-long referendum campaign, was in touch with the Greek conservative opposition leader outside the room, and he whispered to Papandreou's finance minister and old party rival Evangelos Venizelos as he left, "We have to kill this referendum".[36] Venizelos did not need to be told twice. When he arrived back from Cannes that night he stabbed his prime minister in the back. Even before leaving Athens airport he issued a statement saying that euro membership was too important an issue for a referendum. Exit Papandreou. Yet the traitor did not win power. On Friday 11 November 2011 Greek President Karolos Papoulias asked economist Lucas Papademos, former governor of the Greek central bank and former member of the board of the European Central Bank, to put together a new government of national unity.

These two simultaneous episodes left a bitter aftertaste. Although the new Italian and Greek governments rested on parliamentary majorities, Brussels, Berlin and Paris had signalled a desire to lodge political leadership with technocrats, men who would be regarded as credible by the capital markets. To make matters worse, "Europe" – and Germany in particular – was seen to be interfering in the domestic politics of sovereign democracies. Nevertheless, political leaders and markets stood together this time, facing the electorate. The Italians were not given fresh parliamentary elections (those followed only in 2013); the Greeks did not get a referendum on the support package (even if that was an internal decision and a referendum did take place in 2015). The tension between national democracy and membership of a monetary union became painfully palpable.

In the autumn of 2011 the eurozone experimented with a tough form of crisis politics: the replacement of weak governments. Not via the ballot box but by means of political and financial pressure that was beyond the reach of the public. That smile by Merkel and Sarkozy grew into a perfidious key moment in this period. It made clear for an instant how in this debt crisis power lay with whomsoever could pronounce the verdict "credible" – and therefore "creditworthy". In fact, in that scene the duo adopted the role of the credit rating agencies they so despised. They gave Berlusconi a downgrade.

In contrast to the six other episodes outlined in this chapter, their staffing policy was not the result of a formal "decision". It was no joint act. Berlusconi's fall looked more like the perfect murder. Unsurprisingly, it led to conspiracy theories. Who had done this to Italy? When more than two years later it turned out that, from the summer of 2011 onwards, serious discussions had taken place between President Napolitano and Mario Monti, there was further tumult.[37]

In three other eurozone countries in crisis, voters proved more than capable of changing their political leadership. On 21 November 2011, within ten days of the changes of government in Athens and Rome, the opposition took power in Spain. In scheduled parliamentary elections, the conservatives won a majority, gaining 186 of the 350 seats, which left the governing socialists – Prime Minister Zapatero had left the battlefield to a successor – far behind. In Ireland, which had requested European emergency relief in 2010, the ruling party was defeated in early elections in February 2011 by the centre-right opposition. The same scenario was repeated in the Portuguese elections of June 2011, which Prime Minister José Socrates lost to Pedro Passos Coelho.

Such changes of regime as a result of shifts in the public mood are immensely useful, as Machiavelli knew. In his *Discourses on Livy* the Florentine wrote, "Thus, there is nothing that makes a republic so stable and steady as organizing it in such a way that the variability of those humours that agitate the republic has a means of release that is instituted by the laws".[38] Voters in all three eurozone countries punished governments that had been forced to ask for humiliating bailouts (Ireland and Portugal) or had escaped them by a whisker (Spain); they placed their trust in the established opposition, for the time being at least. The democratic machinery was still functioning. It was beginning to rattle and squeak, however. The musical chairs played by centrist parties, all criticized as tarred with the same brush, opened up space for populist challengers on the flanks – on the far left in the case of Spain and Greece.

In Italy there was a loss of confidence not merely in one or other party but in the entirety of political institutions and practices, which frustrated every change. In 2011 a segment of the Italian population secretly welcomed the tough European intervention from outside as a reality check, while another segment placed its trust in the outspoken outsider-comic Beppe Grillo. For want of better, voters resorted to external anchors in order to restore the credibility of Italy's political word.

"CONSIDERING THE ABSENCE OF UNANIMITY": 8–9 DECEMBER 2011

Almost two years after the Greek crisis broke, the situation was still not under control. Everyone was racing from the latest "moment of truth" to the next "last-chance summit". While in November 2011 new governments in Athens, Rome and Madrid set to work and the Commission in Brussels produced proposals for even stricter budgetary rules, the need for a systemic approach to the crisis was growing again. The eurozone must be reformed. But how? Right from the start the focus had been on the states and their budgets. Although there was a feeling in November 2011 that the crisis was fuelled by more than public debt alone, that remained the first trail to be pursued.

On 2 December Angela Merkel said in the Bundestag that the EU institutions must be given the power to overrule governments in order to punish "without reservation" the breaching of budgetary thresholds.[39] For his part, Sarkozy had appealed the previous day in Toulon for a political "refoundation" of Europe and a "government of the eurozone", made up of the heads of state and government. Without naming the Commission, he said, "A Europe on automatic pilot, simply applying the rules of competition and free trade blindly, is a Europe that cannot cope with a crisis".[40]

Both approaches – the Europe of rules and that of the capacity to act

– came together in a German–French letter to Van Rompuy of 7 December. In it the chancellor and the president asked on the one hand for more strongly binding rules and obligations for eurozone countries and on the other for six-monthly summits of eurozone leaders (even monthly for as long as the crisis lasted).[41] They wanted to include such an agreement in the Union Treaty and if that was not possible in a separate eurozone treaty. The letter arrived just ahead of a decisive summit.

The meeting of 8–9 December was angry and unpredictable. The leaders quickly agreed on the content, the what: the eurozone needs stronger debt rules. But as so often in the Union – built on treaties, rules and protocols – it was more difficult to decide on the judicial form, the how. Prime Minister David Cameron refused to accept a formal change to the Treaty, or rather he would accept it only if in return his partners guaranteed the position of London as the UK's financial centre. A resolute Sarkozy said, "David, we will not pay you to save the euro". Van Rompuy tried a lighter version: no full treaty change with parliamentary ratifications and the whole caboodle, but utilize instead a legal hook from a treaty protocol.[42] It was a method Merkel rejected as not authoritative enough for the markets and the public; her spokesman had spoken a few days before of "Brussels tricks". It could certainly count on the assent of most of the other leaders, however. Cameron refused to lower his price, which decided the matter. At four in the morning the Council president concluded, "considering the absence of unanimity",[43] that the content required a different form. The 17 eurozone members decided to put their budgetary agreements in a treaty under international law, open to the others. Of the ten non-eurozone countries, eight participated. The UK stayed out, as did the Czech Republic, whose prime minister felt steamrollered that night;[44] Hungary, which at first said no, came on board at dawn. David Cameron, although de facto unable to stop anything, was hailed as a hero in his own country on account of his "veto".

When it was all over there was considerable confusion, both among those involved and in the media. Everyone had the feeling something important had happened, but it was very unclear what. According to some, the Union had been "refounded" by the Fiscal Stability Treaty, while for others all it had erected was a "façade". It is worth taking the architectonic imagery seriously for a moment and comparing Europe – always, after all, a mixture of structure and conviction – with a Gothic cathedral. Just like Gothic architecture in its time, the Union had recourse to innovative building methods.[45]

During the night of 8–9 December, the UK used the blackmail that the unanimity principle provides for to oblige its European partners to seek salvation – an urgent solution to a vital problem of budgetary credibility – outside the European treaties. It is rather as if this time, instead of the faithful chasing the moneychangers out of the temple, the moneychangers chased out the faithful. Thus Britain prevented the Union from deploying its usual construction method, namely building separate little chapels inside the cathedral for the more pious member states who wanted to do more good works together (e.g. the euro, Schengen and other forms of cooperation). The British veto having barred them from using the Union Treaty, the eurozone countries and their followers had no option but to put their decisions on budgetary discipline and economic policy into a separate treaty, outside it.

To stay with the architectonic imagery: the heads of state and government, obstructed in their work inside the cathedral, decided to go on building on the outside. Much as the master builders of the Gothic period, frustrated in their efforts to make the nave of the cathedral higher and higher, invented the flying buttress, a structure that was not part of the building but made the edifice stronger, lighter and higher than the heavy walls of the Romanesque style.

What conditions did this important architectural renovation have to satisfy? There were two. In order to fulfil its function the flying buttress needed to be in contact with the wall of the cathedral, which is to say form a single whole with it. At the same time, for reasons of harmony and cohesion, it needed to be made of the same material and in the same style as the main building. Translated back into the Fiscal Treaty, negotiated within a few weeks and signed on 2 March 2012 by 25 national leaders, it was to be seen not as a threat to the existing structure or as a completely separate element but as an extension of the established treaties and cohesive with them. It was therefore striking that the Fiscal Treaty (just like the temporary and permanent emergency funds that preceded it) gave a role to the European Court and the Commission, and that the intention of the signatories was to integrate it in due course into the main building.

All this was not immediately clear after the long, hard night of negotiation on 8–9 December. Improvisation stretched out into elementary logistics. The next day there was no room for doubt that 25 countries would conclude a new treaty, outside the European Union, but where were they to gather to draft it? In an official Union building, as the secretary-general of the Council proposed? For several days the frustrated British threatened to lodge an appeal with the Court of Justice against the use of the EU institutions, indeed even against the use of EU buildings by a budding non-EU institution (the costs! the rent! the heating! the translators!). Until they realized they were being unreasonable. To save their skin the eurozone countries were unable to use the Treaty, but they were soon granted a meeting room, and then the institutions as such. The British had been out-vetoed. Within weeks David Cameron began to contemplate bringing a more dangerous political tool into the game, to cement his country's position: a referendum.[46]

"BREAK THE VICIOUS CIRCLE": 28–29 JUNE 2012

On 13 January 2012 France lost its triple-A status. That highest credit rating was retained only by Germany, the Netherlands, Finland and Austria – but for how much longer? The crisis had now gone to the heart of the eurozone. The fall of the Greek government, in February, set off a new chain of breathtaking events. That spring, worries about the Spanish banking sector also surfaced. In Italy it was the combination of a weak economy and high public debt that disturbed investors and drove up the interest rate.

Gradually the government leaders – including those of creditor countries – began to realize that the crisis ran deeper than a series of nations that had "not done their homework" and that the Fiscal Treaty was therefore less than adequate. There was obviously a shared problem too. Confidence in the eurozone as such had been lost. That spring the governors of the European Central Bank advocated a long-term vision. Their argument was pragmatic. All the eurozone governments were looking for investors to buy up ten-year government bonds. Those investors were quite reasonably wondering what the eurozone would look like in ten years' time. Would it be more than a monetary system built purely on rules and fixed exchange rates? In the uncertainty of the moment, knowing that their visions and interests conflicted, the leaders hesitated to answer that question.

To achieve a breakthrough, Van Rompuy invited them for an open debate. Several of the controversial ideas that were doing the rounds in think tanks and academic circles – such as euro bonds, new banking supervision and binding agreements on economic reforms – had yet to reach the leaders' desks. At the end of May 2012 came the first summit since the election of François Hollande, the man who had defeated Nicolas Sarkozy. "No taboos" was the motto of the meeting.[47] Thus the president of the European Council used his specific role as key player in between national government leaders and the Brussels institutions to encourage everyone to think outside the usual framework, and thereby to increase the shared capacity for improvisation.

Van Rompuy had prepared conclusions in his capacity as chair, so it was not a text that would be formally endorsed by all 27 leaders. One passage suggested giving the presidents of the Commission, the European Central Bank, the Eurogroup and the European Council a mandate to write a report about how to set right the architecture of the eurozone. Everyone was in agreement. This decision created the necessary political opening. Five weeks later, a few days before the summit of 28–29 June, the requested report was ready. "Towards a Genuine Economic and Monetary Union" it was called. Its core message was simple. National economic policy cannot be determined in complete isolation if the consequences affect the whole of the eurozone. Europeans should draw lessons from their interdependencies in the fields of financial policy, budgetary policy and economic policy. This was a far-reaching road map.

Yet it was not the long-term perspective but the immediate crisis that dominated the last weeks of June. On Sunday 17 June the eurozone heaved a sigh of relief, when the second round of Greek parliamentary elections ended with a majority for parties that wanted to keep the euro. This did not ease the worries about Spain and Italy. As in Cannes the year before, a G20 meeting – this time on 18–19 June in Los Cabos, Mexico – became the theatre of European crisis talks. The Italian Prime Minister Mario Monti, who believed the markets were treating his country disrespectfully, wanted the European Central Bank to buy up government debt "automatically" if the interest rate of a member state that had complied with the rules rose above a certain threshold. That was unacceptable to the Bank and to the German chancellor; the fact that Monti had tried to get Obama behind the idea was not appreciated by Merkel either. Spanish premier Mariano Rajoy had a different problem: the Spanish banking sector was on the point of collapse. After long hesitation – his predecessor Zapatero had refused a bailout deal in Cannes[48] – Rajoy asked for help in restructuring Spain's banks.

Since the fall of Lehman Brothers in 2008 a vicious circle had formed between banks in difficulties and weak public finances. If a bank collapsed, taxpayers would foot the bill, thereby increasing the country's public debt. If in a subsequent phase the capacity of the government to pay off its debt was called into question, the entire national banking sector would suffer. Ireland was the textbook example of this vicious circle or "doom loop", but in the spring of 2012 Spain was the most dangerously exposed to it. There was a realization that this dynamic had to be curtailed.

After the G20 meeting there was continual political consultation. On 22 June, during a meeting in Rome of the leaders of Germany, France, Spain and Italy, Merkel repeated her opposition to Monti's plan for the unconditional purchase of government debt. She did show a willingness to help Rajoy with his banks, as long as a balance was found between solidarity and financial responsibility. The four agreed that their finance ministers would work on some ideas in Paris on 26 June. At that Paris meeting, which senior Brussels civil servants attended as well as the four large eurozone countries, German minister Wolfgang Schäuble proposed allowing direct recapitalization of banks from the permanent European emergency fund on condition that centralized European banking supervision was put in place. Both points were new. Until then the emergency fund was supposed to lend only to states; banks could be recapitalized only "indirectly" (via a state that channelled funds to them, and by doing so saw its own debt position worsen). The other element was no less remarkable: central banking supervision. Germany had strongly resisted it even when the financial crisis was at its peak, in 2009. Now, a deal seemed within reach.

The leaders came to the decisive summit in Brussels on 28 June with different priorities. François Hollande was intent upon announcing measures for growth and employment, a key promise to voters in the French election six weeks before. Mariano Rajoy and Mario Monti, concerned about their banks and government debt, had obviously coordinated their positions. Angela Merkel and other "northern" leaders wanted to prevent moral hazard arising from additional financial support without conditions attached. To the delight of the 2,000 journalists in attendance, the working dinner on Thursday evening coincided with the semi-final between Germany and Italy in the European football championships. (When not needed in the meeting room, Mario Draghi joined the catering staff to watch Italy win thanks to two goals from that other "super Mario" – Balotelli.)

It was a long night. The discussion was focused on the banks. By the time the draft text reached the leaders around midnight their advisers had spent six hours negotiating. The tension quickly mounted. Everyone was now in agreement that the rescue fund could inject capital into insolvent banks as soon as there was ECB supervision, but what was to be done in the meantime? It might take years to set up such a thing, and Spain had a problem right now. The draft text spoke of "interim solutions" but for Merkel and her Dutch and Finnish allies that was not acceptable; the order must be: first supervision and then money, not the other way around. Then Mario Draghi said that if the eurozone leaders showed they were making serious work of banking supervision, the capital markets would immediately take that into account. Merkel jumped in and proposed giving the legislative institutions a firm deadline; "before the end of 2012" it must be clear how supervision would work. By EU standards this was an unprecedentedly rapid procedure. The leaders also made explicit that banking supervision must fall to the European Central Bank, not to the Commission or a new institution. They agreed that it was "imperative to break the vicious circle between banks and sovereigns".[49]

Those were the words the markets were waiting for. At an improvised press conference as dawn broke, Van Rompuy read out the concluding statement to the exhausted journalists. The statement was unexpected, even at its source (the Council's own press staff had been sent to bed at around 3.00am when a final decision no longer seemed on the cards). Within ten minutes the message got through to the markets.

A few hours later that Friday, just before the start of the last working session, Mario Draghi entered Van Rompuy's office. Ever since coming to power he had been living under extreme pressure. The entire world wanted his bank to act decisively, but it was in too tight a straitjacket to be able to do so. Now he looked relieved. "Herman," he said, "do you realize yourself what you all achieved last night? It's the game changer we need." The decision by the

European leaders to establish central European banking supervision created the opening *he* needed to give his institution a greater role in containing the crisis.[50]

On 6 September the European Central Bank in Frankfurt promised "unlimited but conditional" support to countries that were under pressure from the financial markets. The announcement of this intervention – by Draghi in London in late July ("and believe me, it will be enough") – had been a warning shot. On 12 September the Constitutional Court in Karlsruhe ruled that the permanent emergency fund was not in conflict with the German constitution. That same evening parliamentary elections in the Netherlands brought defeat for the anti-Europe party of national populists. Ireland was successfully preparing itself to go to the markets. In the early autumn of 2012 many people began to realize that the euro was there to stay. Even the ever cautious philosopher-economist Herman Van Rompuy felt sufficiently sure of his ground on 25 October 2012 to state for the first time in public, in front of a business audience in London, that "the eurozone is no longer in 'existential threat' mode".

The first test came in the spring of 2013, when in Cyprus the banking system – a pillar of the island's economy – was in danger of collapsing. The ECB set a strict deadline for measures to be taken. After a chaotic start, a vigorous but controlled reorganization was forced through by eurozone leaders on 24 March 2013, in a summit meeting with the Cypriot president.[51] The country would need to close one large bank, accept an emergency programme and impose controls on the free movement of capital. Yet the Cyprus crisis did not at any point lead to a fear of financial panic beyond the island. The eurozone as such was no longer in danger.

However, something else happened after that. Although the fear of "financial contagion" had receded, fear of "political contagion" now made its entrance.[52] This became clear in 2015 when the crisis flared up again in Greece, after the left-wing populist Syriza party took power. Turbulent months of negotiations between the Tsipras government and its eurozone partners about a third bailout ended with the Greek referendum of 5 July 2015 and a Euro Summit a week later. These events held all of Europe spellbound, but the markets saw no financial risk for the rest of the eurozone this time. Political passions, however, ran far higher than in 2010–12. The drama resonated well beyond Greece in a European debate about debt and solidarity, democracy and (German) leadership. This had its effect. Decision-making and analyses were dominated not by the expected reaction of the markets but by the anticipated response of voters in the other eurozone countries. The Spanish conservative premier Rajoy, who was facing elections that autumn, feared that concessions to Athens would undermine the credibility of his own narrative about Spain having to tighten its belt, thereby energizing Syriza's Spanish sister party Podemos (the Greek 2015 episode is discussed in Chapter 7).

For the umpteenth time since 2008, political leaders found themselves faced with conflicting demands: they needed to maintain the trust of investors without losing the trust of their voters. This problem is so profoundly bound up with the functioning of the European democratic welfare states that it will not go away.

Balancing discipline and empathy

The monetary union has undoubtedly gained institutional solidity, but in the years to come the euro storm will almost certainly rise again in new forms and the uncertainty will have to be parried in new ways. It will then be highly relevant to look back at the efforts, failures and successes of the years 2010–12. Some things worked, a few did not. So, for the sake of future crisis management it is important to know whether there is a pattern here. Is it possible to make a meaningful distinction beforehand between a promising improvisation and a predictable fiasco? The best starting point is to investigate how success was achieved in the end.

The first striking thing about the banking agreement of June 2012 that brought the final breakthrough for the currency union is that the leaders credibly linked a decision in the short term to a perspective for the long term. For two years they had tackled the problem step by step. In the fog of the crisis this was not unwise in itself (although each step was criticized as "one day late and one dollar short"), but after two years more was needed. Markets and the public did not actually expect the eurozone to produce fully worked out scenarios for the future so much as to demonstrate the self-confidence needed to look ahead, and to take the firm decision that a joint future was seriously intended. This combination of short and long term was provided by the banking agreement of 28–29 June. The leaders gave the green light for work on a "banking union" – a project for the coming years the outlines of which were sketched by Van Rompuy & Co in the eurozone report of 26 June – and immediately took the first concrete step with the appointment of one supervisor for all eurozone banks.* They thereby showed, in the words of Hannah Arendt, "the capacity to dispose of the future as though it were the present", and thus miraculously expanded the domain in which power was effective.[53] They showed the "will to form", the first precondition of successful improvisation.

Contrast this with the weakest improvisations, the decisions in 2010 and 2011 on the private involvement of investors in the future settlement of government debt. Deauville (October 2010) went wrong immediately because two players spoke prematurely on behalf of the entire club, reducing the others, in theatrical terms, to a chorus. This was an infringement of the mores of unity and shared responsibility that Europe's events-politics demands, the second precondition of successful improvisation. But the Deauville agreement did not comply with the first condition any more than the second, because even when protocol was restored and the Merkel–Sarkozy deal was given the blessing of all members at a summit ten days later, the problem of its content remained. The suggestion that from 2013 onwards public debt could be restructured saw to it that after Greece, Ireland too fell into the abyss. As French economist Pisani-Ferry has written: "While logic would dictate that the creditors of yesterday are made to pay for their carelessness and those of tomorrow are reassured, the effect was precisely the opposite: the announcement of the agreement increased the tension instead of mitigating it."[54] More than six months later, at the Euro Summit of July 2011, the club made a comparable mistake. The taboo on debt relief for Greece was immediately broken without the agreement relieving the country's debt sufficiently to ward off further misfortune. This improvisation too failed in its handling

---

* The deadline of the end of 2012 for the establishment of the supervisory mechanism was met. The steps that were to follow, also announced at the June 2012 summit, such as the establishment of a "single resolution mechanism" to deal with failing banks, were also taken according to plan. Although creditor countries were reluctant to allow joint financing of the resolution funds and consistently dragged their feet, the banking union acquired so much authority as a remedy intended to prevent the future flaring up of the euro crisis that no member state could risk allowing it to fail.

of time and did not gain a grip on the future. In short the decisions of October 2010 and July 2011 demonstrated division (the first, initially) and impotence (both, almost immediately) – two transgressions on the improvisation stage that the banking resolution managed to avoid.

So far little cause for surprise perhaps, but that is not all. As well as proof of the "will to form" and a show of unity, successful improvisation needs to fulfil a third condition: to avoid opportunistic arbitrariness, or, positively formulated, to seek a connection with historical values and concepts that find resonance with the public. In musical terms we might speak of root melodies.

The banking decision of 2012 linked solidarity and responsibility, or empathy and discipline.* The "southern" states insisted on the solidarity of members with the entity as a whole, while the priority of the "northern" states lay with everyone's responsibility for healthy budgets and banks. Such a situation leads in many cases to an impasse, a double "no". But in the night of 28–29 June 2012 the leaders decided to do both at the same time. They linked two political decisions: ECB supervision (in the name of responsibility) and the option of capital injections from the rescue funds for ailing banks (in the name of solidarity). This was a double "yes": more responsibility and more solidarity.

There was reciprocity throughout the eurocrisis between these two values. A balance was repeatedly sought. Emergency support for Greece, Ireland and Portugal was a matter of credit (solidarity) in return for reforms (responsibility). The renovation of the eurozone as a whole was a matter of balance between the emergency funds set up from May 2010 onwards (solidarity) and stricter budgetary rules for eurozone countries (responsibility). The two remarkable agreements in which both those reforms were contained, the Stability Mechanism Treaty and the Fiscal Treaty, were once called by Van Rompuy, guardian of this political equilibrium, the "Solidarity Treaty" and the "Responsibility Treaty".[55] The two treaties are closely interlinked. Only those who have signed the Fiscal Compact Treaty can call upon the emergency fund. In the Irish, Italian and German parliaments this interplay became visible through simultaneous parliamentary scrutiny and voting.[56] In

---

* This individual "responsibility-as-discipline" is distinct from the "shared responsibility" of the statement of February 2010, which is about taking responsibility, being called upon to act, as an answer to a question posed by reality.

France, by contrast, the dialectic was not appreciated; the emergency funds were welcomed as a natural correction to the original monetary union project, whereas the Fiscal Compact Treaty, as a commitment thought up by the Germans, encountered strong parliamentary opposition. Mario Draghi's bond purchase programme of September 2012, to many observers the remedy that did most to temper the crisis, was likewise a miraculous mixture of solidarity and responsibility. By introducing it, the European Central Bank made itself, as the markets wanted it to, a "lender of last resort" for the eurozone as a whole (solidarity), but with built-in conditionality for any member state that made an appeal to the programme (responsibility).

It was precisely the simultaneous linking of solidarity and responsibility that made the dual deal of summer 2012 (the "banking union" decision by the European Council including the bond purchase decision by the Bank) superior to earlier improvisations. The improvisation brought about by the emergency funds, initially in an ad hoc form (May 2010) and later anchored in the Union Treaty, was also a success but not of the same calibre. The emergency funds brought welcome changes, but for the northern public, despite the built-in conditionality, they leaned too heavily on the first principle, while the Fiscal Compact Treaty (December 2011) came too late and leaned purely on the second. This temporal imbalance contributed to the fact that the eurozone remained focused for too long on government debt; in autumn 2011 Germany still wanted to use the Fiscal Treaty to get back in fiscal discipline what it had earlier, through the emergency funds, given away in solidarity. Not until the summer of 2012 was the right balance struck. At that point improvisation succeeded.

Why were both values, solidarity and responsibility, so important? Why did so many political players – Merkel, Sarkozy, Hollande, Van Rompuy, Barroso, Draghi and Monti – take rhetorical refuge in them countless times? In a situation in which existing rules fall short and action is urgently needed, a politician must have reasons with which to convince the public of decisions. Effective improvisation is never arbitrary. In Europe the public has long been receptive to stories that invoke values and virtues, from Christian, humanist, classical, traditional or other sources. Out of this amalgam of values the improvising politicians derived the root melodies that they then further elaborated upon, the themes on which their practical decisions could be variations. They were then able to give their decisions meaning that went beyond mere caprice and have them accepted as free and responsible choices.

In this game, "responsibility" and "solidarity" resonated best, not just because a particular interest and a vision of the future could be attached to each one, but because a meaningful relationship developed between them. Solidarity and responsibility are in the same dynamic balance as pairs like "the whole and the parts" or "unity and diversity". Their interplay provides a language in which a union of member states can understand itself as a mobile entity and with which it can capture – in one new balance after another, improvising all the time – the events the open future brings.

Yet something else was missing, which still needs fixing. For a successful improvisation the three elements – the unity of the group that acts, evidence of the will to give shape to the future and an appeal to root melodies – are not enough. The best improvisation creates a bond with the public. As jazz musician Chick Corea once said, "The fact that an artist is experiencing the joy of creation makes me feel like we're in it together". Improvisation creates a bond between players, and between them and the audience. The "Save the Euro" show certainly captivated the European public for more than two years, but it was mostly played out above their heads. Many had the feeling they were looking at a failed series, whereas in fact the sequence, as improvisation, got the very best out of the players.

In the euro crisis the political leaders were themselves overwhelmed by the show in which they found themselves; they engaged in the events-politics that the situation demanded of them uneasily, sometimes reluctantly. Perhaps that was why they failed to notice they had stepped onto a new stage. After all, they did not yet know what we know now: that in the currency union they were playing not just for their own home audiences but for an entirely new European public sphere, created precisely by and through those events. Perhaps this should in fact have been the moment to create a bond with that new public sphere, because finally a broad and plural public had poured in, one that felt concerned and actually demanded a direct say. But the public too needed time to get used to such an unwritten new role, to muster resounding cheers and jeers in response to the more or less successful improvisations of the ensemble on offer.

2

Negotiating:
the Ukraine crisis

The connotation of courage, which we now feel to be an indispensable quality of the hero, is in fact already present in a willingness to act and speak at all, to insert one's own self into the world and begin a story of one's own.

Hannah Arendt[1]

The magnet and the border

When the Cold War ended, Western Europeans took their leave of History with a capital H. As capitalist democracies, we had attained the ultimate historical goal, as proclaimed by Fukuyama, and no longer faced an ideological rival. It was merely a matter of waiting for the rest of humanity – in Eastern Europe; in Africa; in Asia and the Middle East – to achieve its own salvation. Our task was to help everyone become just like us, through development aid and trade agreements, and by exporting our market rules and democratic values. This became the essence of the Union's foreign policy: an extension of the politics of rules, an expansive trade policy under the banner of our best values – freedom, equality and prosperity. Rampant good intentions.

In that post-communist climate, Europe acted as a magnet to the outside world, exerting a positive influence on its surroundings. Our model had magnetic force, was perhaps even "sexy" – after all, who would not want to become like us? A flattering thought. Political scientists provided the accompanying theory of "soft power": the ability to mobilize others in support of one's own values, culture or reputation, as distinct from the "hard power" that relies on power-politics or military force.[2] While the United States wielded both soft and hard power worldwide, the European Union commanded only the former. In self-conscious Brussels this was not counted as a deficiency but regarded as evidence of our progress and civilization.

This firmly buttressed self-image had one great merit: it stabilized the continent after the shock of 1989. None of the popular uprisings in Central and Eastern Europe ended with a Cromwell, Robespierre or Khomeini, instead they each opened passages to democracy. The prospect of Union membership, offered in 1993, spurred impressive transformations. From Warsaw and Budapest to Riga and Sofia, constitutions were rewritten, market rules introduced, human rights recognized, boundary disputes set aside – whatever it took to be allowed in. Since the forces of reform worked in its favour, the Union could impose conditions, set deadlines, steer the process. After 40 years of dictatorship and planned economies, the candidates were only too willing – mostly out of conviction, sometimes pro forma – to be disciplined by the politics of rules. This process was called "Europeanization". The same method was used to stabilize former Yugoslavia after the conflicts of the 1990s. Slovenia and Croatia have since become member states, while Serbia and three of its neighbours are in the waiting room and another two have been granted a "European vocation". To this day the Union's power of attraction has prevented the Balkans from slipping back into intractable armed conflict. No mean achievement.

For a long time the European Union was fixated on the magnetic success of expansion by attraction. A successful formula in a specific situation was declared a universal remedy. In 2003, with the first Central and Eastern European accession states at the threshold, Commission president Romano Prodi dreamed of a wider positive aura. He envisaged a "ring of friends" stretching from Morocco in the south-west via Egypt and the Caucasus to Ukraine in the east.[3] If you could bring those countries too into the sphere of markets and values, it would be to the benefit of all. "Wider Europe" was the maxim of this spatial policy. Geopolitics using a pair of compasses: take a map of the world, stick the spike into Brussels and draw a broad semi-circle to the south and east – those are your friends. Thus the Neighbourhood Policy was born.[4] When Prodi presented this vision in Washington, a rather alert George W.

Bush said, "Sounds like the Roman Empire, Romano".[5] An ominous warning. It seems outsiders immediately grasped that the Union's high-sounding dream also pointed to an ambition of territorial expansion.

The magnet model's knack is to influence the behaviour of countries that want something from the European Union. This is known as "normative power". You can come to the party if you trim your nails and promise not to drink too much. To make greater demands, the appeal needs to be stronger. If you are required to buy an expensive outfit, then you will want to be assured of a truly unforgettably night out.

The Union was unaware – or acted as if it were unaware – of the extent to which the pull of the magnet relied on the promise of membership. That was the main prize. According to the Treaty, however, only "European states" qualify (without being specific about which states they are[6]), so after the many post-1989 accessions a mere dozen potential members remain, most on the edge of the continent. For one of these borderline cases, Turkey, the question arises as to whether the Union really wants to make good on its promise, or whether it will choose to renege; for his part, Turkey's President Recep Tayyip Erdogan is preparing his people to take their leave of the European prospect. To other countries, in North Africa for example, the Union has no membership to offer, only the consolation prizes of market access for their products or visas for their citizens. Important, yes, but not existential. For non-European countries, therefore, the EU magnet has little pulling power.

The magnetic force of the Union, with all its ambiguous borderline cases, can be felt even out in the wings, as I discovered in small and penniless Moldova in May 2014. As one of the staff of the president of the European Council, I travelled to three eastern neighbours for political discussions about their future in between Europe and Russia. In Kiev we commemorated the victims of Maidan, in Tbilisi we saw the snow-capped Caucasus in the distance and in Chișinău we drank the local wine. In the Moldovan capital, "European president" Van Rompuy was received on arrival as the figurehead of a superpower, with the sort of respect that in Western European capitals is reserved for the president of the United States: public life at a standstill, a military parade, choirs of schoolchildren and a thousand-strong audience in a theatre.

A few days earlier, after a visit to the pro-Russian enclave of Transnistria (officially Moldovan territory), the Russian defence minister had been denied access to Romanian airspace on the return journey because of Western sanctions. Half-jokingly he tweeted that he would come in a TU-160 next time: a bomber. Such worries did not get in the way of practical considerations on the part of our host. Could Brussels perhaps provide extra money to help dissuade the teaching unions from going over to the pro-Russian communist side? Here Europe's power of attraction became thoroughly concrete for a moment.

In my role as speechwriter I experienced in Chișinău an entire forcefield of existential expectations. In the big closing speech of the visit, the audience in the immense Palace of the Republic would no doubt have liked nothing better than to be told Moldova could join the Union. This made it tempting to rouse the hall to great heights of emotion with a few well-targeted phrases and thereby enable the speaker to triumph; a manifest temptation, to which it was easy to succumb. In the wording of the speech I laid Moldova's "Europeanness" on thick – historical ties, neighbours, values, freedom and prosperity – and briefly the magnet seemed to pull the country on board, but the anti-climax of the agreed formula from the Brussels repertoire was as unavoidable as it was disappointing. "The European Union recognizes the European aspirations of Moldova and welcomes its European choice." The door was not opened, but neither was it shut. This game of hard-to-get did not elicit the kind of old-fashioned applause for which the soviet-era theatre had been built.

While the ambiguities of the accession promise will in due course be clarified, a second miscalculation of magnet-thinking remains: the power of attraction is passive and does not presuppose any capacity to act. How to deal with magnetism-immune foreign players? How to influence superpowers or the malevolent? What if the resulting movement causes instability or clashes? You then need a foreign-policy toolkit with different instruments altogether. Yet that necessity was brushed aside. One well-known "soft power" theoretician claimed, unabashed, in 2002: "The most important factor shaping the international role of the EU is not what it does or what it says, but what it is".[7] Europe did not need to do anything; its very existence sufficed. Rather than being a player jostling with the rest, it would rise high above the field of play, at once affable and haughty, a shining example.

Strategic insouciance went hand in hand with geopolitical inaction. The

European magnet let loose unanticipated forces, at which everyone stared in astonishment. It was this, in part, that led to two crises that have recently put the Union to the test, the Ukraine crisis (2013–15) and the refugee crisis (2015–16). It is no accident that both concerned the delineation or control of a border: the territorial eastern border, and the physical southern and south-eastern borders.

While in the Maidan revolt of winter 2014 Europe saw itself as a well-meaning, passive magnet, the Kremlin regarded it as a hypocritical actor, shifting its external border eastwards. While Brussels applauded the Ukrainians for freely opting for European values, Moscow descried a coup with foreign interference. These irreconcilable narratives produced deadlock. In the refugee crisis the Union made a discovery of a different kind: it was exerting a gravitational force not just on states but on people. It could keep its door shut to neighbouring countries, but it turns out that people can simply walk across the border, in their hundreds of thousands. Everything "happened to" the Union, which was helpless for months. Europe's magnetic power became a fatal attraction, for several parties.

In their spatial effects, a magnet and a border are opposing forces. A magnet sets things in motion; a border calls a halt to them. A magnet's pull reaches out; a border marks a limit. A magnet makes no distinction; a border creates a distinction.

The subject of the external border was taboo for many years. Where did the Union stop? That could not be spoken about. After 1950 the Brussels institutions had found their calling in the removal of internal borders: civilized ideal and practical law-making combined. Borders seemed like a relic of a bygone world of sovereign states. But after 1989 the slogan "Europe without borders" no longer chimed with the situation. The removal of internal borders did not presage the disappearance of external borders. On the contrary, in the Union Treaty (1992) the member states laid down that together they wished to play a role on the world stage, "to safeguard the common values, fundamental interests and independence of the Union".[8] Inherent in that wish was a trial of strength with other players, a feeling out of spheres of influence, including geographical boundaries: old-fashioned power-politics as it was in the days of the European concert of nations. But the Union thought it had left these realities behind, and so the language for this geopolitical shift never took shape. Typical was the Brussels concern in the early 2000s that any eastern demarcation of the Union would amount to "a new Iron Curtain", and therefore the reincarnation of evil. The name for the approach to the region in those days, "wider Europe", was telling: it was as if the border problem was being avoided by pushing it further out. Although everyone understood that eastward expansion could not continue all the way to Japan, even to contemplate the drawing of a line was forbidden. Brussels thinking placed itself outside space and time, above geography and history.

This geopolitical myopia becomes a little less surprising when we consider how diplomatic competences are distributed between the Union and its member states. To exaggerate a little, the Union does values: human rights, democracy, foreign aid, trade-driven prosperity – the soft power. This mainly means acting according to the law and humanitarian principles, in which the Commission can take the lead (funding included) and national governments can relatively quickly reach agreement. The member states, by contrast, have assigned to themselves the domain of strategic interests: classical diplomacy, geopolitical choices, issues concerning borders, war and peace – the hard power. They have given the Union competences including a common security and foreign policy, but these are limited. Moreover, control lies mainly with the governments, jointly, in the European Council and the Council of Ministers, usually with a veto for each of them. The assumption is that national interests inevitably conflict and lead to disunity, because of differences in geographical location, historical experience or political culture.

This division of labour generates separate practices and fields of responsibility, separate official and diplomatic structures, roughly overlapping with the distinction between (Brussels) rules-politics and (national) events-politics. Shared values on one side, national interests on the other: what seemed to be painfully lacking was a forum that could determine the shared strategic interests of the Union as a club of member states in the world. The crises of recent years forced a breakthrough and made plain that this forum already potentially exists in the form of the European Council of heads of state or government. It repeatedly took upon itself the role of an authoritative strategist that, with regard to both Russia and Turkey, bundled all its interests to form a united front. That it is indeed a forum of this kind gradually dawned on all parties, including members of the European Council themselves.

Public awareness of common interests is meagre. Even the European diplomatic service, set up in 2009 to bridge the gap between the resources of Brussels and those of national diplomatic services, has done little to change the fact. It proved incapable of expressing those interests in an appropriate strategic definition. After 18 months of work and consultation, in 2016 High Representative Federica Mogherini produced 60 pages of amiable prose that avoided many awkward questions.[9] It perfectly illustrated an earlier verdict by a respected diplomat on Brussels strategies:

> They are not real strategies, since there is no significant geopolitical analysis. Therefore the Eastern Partnership carefully avoids the issue of relations with Russia; policy regarding our Mediterranean neighbours is void of any in-depth thought about the type of dialogue that should be developed with the region's main actors (Egypt, Algeria, Morocco, etc.). Procedures are put forward (association agreement monitoring), principles are announced (differentiation), instruments are developed (simplified action plans) but all of this gives the impression of floating in a political and strategic vacuum from which all power dynamics, antagonisms and lines of division between nations have been sucked out.[10]

What do border problems do? They define us as a club in relation to the rest of the world. They starkly bring home to the European public that it shares not just values but interests. Border problems make us feel that the Union is a political body in space and time. The border can do this so effectively because it has two sides: even if "we" on this side deny that political body's existence or declare it taboo, "they" on the other side of the border need not pay the slightest attention. It is those others, therefore, who show us our European political identity and responsibility. Not because they hold up a mirror but because they break the windows – windows we had not previously noticed. Experience is more instructive than theory. Thus in the conflict with Russia, all the member states and national publics discovered that Ukraine is a neighbour of the Union as a whole, not just of Poland, Slovakia and Hungary. The conflict with Moscow is therefore about Ukraine's place in the continental order, about the issue of whether it will ever become a member of the Union, and therefore about the Union's external border and identity. A discovery of a similar kind was made during the refugee crisis. Syrian asylum seekers arriving on Lesbos or Lampedusa felt they were stepping not onto Greek or Italian soil but onto European soil (on their way to Germany or Sweden). Moreover, the sheer numbers involved inevitably made the movement of people a shared problem, requiring a shared acceptance of responsibility.

In both episodes the Union acted unexpectedly to bring the situation under control. The old rule-making factory's failure and overestimation of itself, in evidence even in these emergency situations, had to be offset by the means and authority of events-politics. This was accompanied by arguments, by doubts and ineptitude, but also by two remarkable breakthroughs. Just as in the euro crisis the monetary orthodoxy of the rules had to make way for the higher good of financial stability, the survival of the common currency and ultimately of the Union itself, so in events at the border a discourse about an inviolable value twice yielded to the higher interests of peace and security (which are also values, of course).

First, to help to end the war between Ukraine and Russia, in February 2015 Chancellor Merkel and President Hollande brokered a compromise between Ukrainian President Petro Poroshenko and his Russian colleague Vladimir Putin, giving priority to the chances of peace and the sparing of human lives over the value of strict adherence to international law. Then, to dam the torrent of refugees pouring from Syria to Greece, in March 2016 European leaders made a dubious deal with President Erdogan's Turkey, in the name of higher political interests. Two fascinating decisions of events-politics, which raised the tension between the Union as a moral beacon and as a player of power-politics: this was at one and the same time self-denial and a new maturity. In those turbulent years, Europe lost its geopolitical innocence.

This was not entirely without precedent. On 8 August 2008 war broke out between Georgia and Russia at a time when the six-month presidency of the European Council had fallen to Nicolas Sarkozy. In line with the French vision of the Union as a lever for diplomatic power, and in his role as one of its top political leaders, Sarkozy used his position as a springboard for European action. Within four days the French president had flown to Moscow and Tbilisi with his foreign minister to arrange a ceasefire. The initiative was far from irreproachable, but at least it averted the occupation of the Georgian capital by the Russian army, which some believed was imminent. As seldom before, the Union acted in a matter of war and peace, and without splitting apart or being overtaken by events. Furthermore, its mediation took place without, in fact in opposition to, the Americans. The Georgians had received funding and military advice, and incitement, from Washington, which – in the final days of Bush Jr – was eager to steer them towards NATO membership.

It could be argued that Sarkozy was taken seriously by the Kremlin as a Frenchman, not as a European. France does indeed have a substantial army and is a permanent member of the UN Security Council. The Slovenian premier, president of the European Council for the previous six-month term, could not have got Moscow to agree to a ceasefire. But, conversely, Sarkozy would have been on less firm ground as merely a Frenchman than he was now that he could speak "in Europe's name".

So how did mobilization "in Europe's name" come about? Beforehand, on 11 August, Sarkozy talked by phone with Angela Merkel in Berlin and Silvio Berlusconi in Rome, and through staff he was in contact with fellow leaders in London, Madrid and Warsaw.[11] Afterwards a meeting of the 27 foreign ministers took place, followed in early September by a summit of government leaders, partly to put pressure on the procrastinating Russians. In a follow-up visit to Moscow and Tbilisi, the tireless Council president was accompanied by EU foreign policy chief Javier Solana and Commission president José Manuel Barroso. Sarkozy's initiative was now clad in the authority of all the governments at the highest level and could if necessary be pursued by other players. To round everything off, the Union reached into its diplomatic toolkit and sent a mission to observe the ceasefire.

Just as his predecessors liked to say *"la France"* when they meant "I", so Nicolas Sarkozy availed himself of the superlative after his Moscow trip. "Europe has acted, Europe has spoken", he repeated jubilantly at press conferences and in speeches.[12] He declared that Europe had behaved as a body politic. With his bold performance, Sarkozy unveiled, for the first time, the political infrastructure for events-politics in the Union; with improvisation, willpower and bluff, he revealed the presence of a supreme authority and a joint capacity for action. The public applauded.

Four episodes

A confrontation with its most significant opponent on the continent was an excellent test case for Europe's foreign policy in action. After the Kremlin made clear in August 2008, in response to a Georgian provocation, that it would not eschew violence, everyone could see the next trial of strength coming. As early as 2009 it was possible to write critically of Europe's then foreign policy that it was "a good deal less ambitious than – imagine! – trying to keep the Ukrainian Crimea out of the clutches of Russia by dispatching European troops or gunboats".[13]

The following four episodes, four key moments from the Ukraine crisis, show how the Union works as a magnet ("In Vilnius"), how it assists a neighbouring country in democratic transition ("On and around Maidan"), how it reacts to territorial expansionism ("After Crimea") and finally, hardest of all, how it holds an armed conflict in check through negotiation ("Merkel in Munich and Minsk"). Four snapshots of emerging events-politics, with the underlying question of whether Europe is developing an awareness of its independent interests or remains trapped between America and Russia.

IN VILNIUS: DIVISIVE POWER OF ATTRACTION, 28–29 NOVEMBER 2013

The anticipated diplomatic festivities ended in failure. On 28 November 2013 there was a gathering in Vilnius for the Union's 28 government leaders and the leaders of its six eastern neighbours. Three of the six – Ukraine, Belarus and Moldova – have borders with one or more member states. The other three – Georgia, Armenia and Azerbaijan – are at the periphery of the continent between Russia and Turkey. Of the six, Ukraine, larger than France and with 45 million inhabitants, was by far the most important.

The six former soviet republics found themselves tugged towards opposite poles. Since 1991 they had been seeking their place between Russia and the European–Atlantic structures. At the Western pole, Washington showed itself willing in the spring of 2008 to admit Georgia and Ukraine to NATO, but Paris and Berlin resisted – mainly so that Russia would not feel encircled. A short while later the European Union, on the initiative of the Polish and Swedish foreign ministers, invited the six neighbours to join an "Eastern Partnership", a framework for political cooperation and economic integration that might lead to an "Association Agreement".

The partnership was emphatically not an antechamber to accession. Western European public opinion was expressing itself tired of enlargement, so the Union kept its biggest magnet, the prospect of membership, in its pocket. This was not what leaders in Chișinău, Kiev and Tbilisi wanted to hear; for some, Union membership was the top priority. A dilemma for Europe's diplomats: they wanted to support pro-European forces in the neighbouring countries but could not make promises that went against the wishes of their own voters. The result was semantic ambivalence. In 2008 the European Council recognized Ukraine as a "European country", still one step away from the coveted status of "European state" that would mean it could formally lay claim to membership. The subtle distinction was unsustainable. Knowing that these countries wanted to enter yet without promising to hold the door open, in its official declarations the Union repeated the Jesuitical formula "We recognize your European aspirations". In other words: no harm in trying. Downplaying the difference between inside and out, the European commissioner responsible, in a speech in October 2010, described the future relationship with the eastern neighbours as "EU Accession minus 1%".[14] The temptation to deploy the magnet had trumped the need to draw a boundary.

Moscow developed an alternative project in parallel. In 2007 President Putin had launched the idea of a continental economic space "from Lisbon to Vladivostok" – a successor to Gorbachev's "European House" and a distant cousin to De Gaulle's "From the Atlantic to the Urals" – but there was no response to this opening. In 2010 Russia established the Eurasian Customs Union with Belarus and Kazakhstan, which the Kremlin would have liked Ukraine to join, an integration project based on the Brussels model. The European magnet now had a rival.

This development laid a trap for Ukrainian President Viktor Yanukovych. Initially he played the market trader looking to see from which bidder he could extract the highest price. The Brussels negotiators, determined not to be suckered by such horse-trading, underestimated the existential difficulty behind Yanukovych's opportunism. Ukraine, which literally means "Borderland", truly cannot decide. Choosing between "Brussels" and "Moscow" is deeply divisive. The population is split between wanting to be part of European modernity and wanting to preserve old ties with Russia. The dividing line is a cultural rift that coincides to some extent with the distinction between Ukrainian speakers and Russian speakers. The choice between the two is therefore supremely political for Ukraine. The Kremlin, with strategic interests at stake, understands this better than Brussels.

From the summer of 2013 onwards, the tension increased. Yanukovych, along with a small majority of the population, was inclined to opt for Europe; in August he said he was minded to sign the Association Agreement at the forthcoming Vilnius summit in November, and he repeated this in September in New York to both the EU presidents, Van Rompuy and Barroso. Moscow realized over the summer that it could well "lose" Ukraine and it started a trade war against the country; Putin's economic adviser warned against the "suicidal step" of signing.[15] Things grew serious. Brussels, however, was busy in the wings: Kiev was being slow to meet the final preconditions in the fields of human rights and the judiciary. In practice it was possible to skirt around many of the bureaucratic benchmarks, but not so the law under which Yulia Tymoshenko, the jailed opposition leader, should have been allowed to travel abroad for medical treatment. As long as the face of the Orange Revolution of 2004 was behind bars, it was hard for Western European governments to sell a warm welcome to Ukraine at home. Meanwhile, in early September, Armenia, militarily dependent on Russia, opted for Putin's customs union and relinquished its European aspirations. Moscow had been exerting pressure on Yerevan. A week before "Vilnius", Ukrainian premier Mykola Azaov – after a meeting with his Russian counterpart Medvedev – announced that his government was putting the Association Agreement on hold. Protests broke out immediately on the central square in Kiev, Maidan. The demonstrators demanded a choice for Europe.

On Thursday 28 November 2013, on arrival in Vilnius, President Yanukovych said he would sign after all. Behind closed doors it transpired that he could see two ways out. One was for Europe to pay millions to compensate for the expected loss of exports due to punitive measures by Russia. The gathering had little enthusiasm for that. The other way out was dual membership, allowing Ukraine to be a member of both clubs, the European Union and the Eurasian customs union. The Brussels side was not willing to grant Yanukovych this wish. One notable detail: the argument was settled by recourse to World Trade Organization rules; the rigidity of the politics of rules had taken the place of strategic interests.[16] The politically precarious situation required more than bureaucratic implementation, and the gathered heads of government had the authority to make an exception, or at least to investigate one. But they stuck to the charted course. The Union did not take up Yanukovych's proposal and Yanukovych could not choose the anti-Moscow option. The next day the Ukrainian stepped outside, sombre, his smile empty. He knew something had snapped. The deeply disappointed Brussels presidents made clear that their offer remained on the table. "We must not miss this rendezvous with history", said Van Rompuy. His colleague Barroso explained why he had rejected the idea of talks between Europe, Ukraine and Russia: "For a bilateral agreement between EU and Ukraine, there should be no trilateral format. The times of limited sovereignty are over in Europe."[17] Technocratic overreach.

The summit in Vilnius proved a turning point and set in train a fresh series of events. But even aside from the consequences, it was a significant moment. Close to the finishing line, with all the leaders together, the European magnet could not (or, people comforted themselves, could not yet) pull Ukraine into its sphere. The counterforce exerted by Moscow was too strong, and the Brussels side did not have the words with which to parry or eliminate that counterforce. In a strict sense it could not understand what was happening. Ukraine, as well as being between two opposing forces, was stuck between two incompatible discourses, two irreconcilable narratives.

The Kremlin was playing a geopolitical power game about the place of Ukraine in the continental order and it saw a Union with an urge to expand. It therefore read in the Association Agreement not just the 300 pages of trade regulations but the 12 pages of political cooperation, including an obscure paragraph on defence of which no one in Brussels realized, or was willing to acknowledge, the geopolitical impact. The European Union refused to think in terms of spheres of influence; that, as President Obama would say later, was a nineteenth-century concept, unworthy of the twenty-first century. Against political antagonism it set a story of economic interlinkage. The trade agreement was presented as advantageous to all parties. It would immediately save Ukraine €500 million in import duties and in the longer term it would create 6 per cent annual growth, according to Barroso after the summit ended. This was not a zero-sum game, economist Van Rompuy agreed; prosperity in Ukraine would confer benefits on its neighbour Russia. According to Brussels logic this win-win principle of trade was beyond dispute. It is the Union's *raison d'être*. Anyone who thinks or acts differently is beyond the pale. This conceptual rigidity revealed itself gloriously when Commission president Barroso firmly announced (without mentioning the man in the Kremlin by name), "This is a process not against someone. This is a process for something. It is for democracy, for stability and for prosperity. It is not against someone, because I don't believe someone should be against democracy, against stability or against prosperity."[*18] This was the ideology of the Brussels magnet in its most depoliticized, moralistic form. It sounded shrill. Impotent swagger.

Germany alone sounded a different note. Chancellor Merkel, who had spoken several times in private with Yanukovych in Vilnius, said, when the summit was over, that member states must "get away from the either/or of either a bond with Russia or a bond with the European Union".[19] A compromise was needed. Yet the outcome of the preceding 24 hours belied this intention.

ON AND AROUND MAIDAN: "FUCK THE EU", FEBRUARY 2014

Over the winter the demonstrations in Kiev, which had begun as "Euromaidan", turned into a Ukrainian revolution. In January 2014 there were fatalities during scuffles between demonstrators and riot police. By February the country was on the verge of civil war.

European politicians, unaccustomed to such enthusiasm after years of euro crisis at home, watched in fascination as ordinary citizens in Kiev waved the European flag. The German, Swedish and Dutch foreign ministers, and several Euro-parliamentarians, gave speeches on Maidan Square about values, freedom and democracy. CNN was there too. This was "History in the Making", another milestone on the universal march to freedom.

---

* The published communiqué reads "is", but in the video recording Barroso clearly says "should be", a choice of words that accurately reflects the difference in perspective between the Union and Russia.

Behind the scenes the Americans endeavoured to form a transitional government, as the world discovered when, on 6 February, Moscow revealed a tapped telephone conversation between President Obama's envoy, Victoria Nuland, and the US ambassador in Kiev. In the recording, prospective members of a new government in Kiev are assessed one after another, and there too was the United Nations, in the role of "midwife" to the process. Nuland preferred to keep the Europeans out of it, as attested by her heartfelt cry of "Fuck the EU".

In Brussels, in the glow of the Ukrainian revolution, the 28 foreign ministers, led by Poland, went further than ever on 10 February in holding out to the country its European prospects. To encourage the demonstrators they waved their ultimate trump card, a promise of membership. They declared that "the Agreement does not constitute the final goal in EU-Ukraine cooperation", thereby stretching the semantic ambivalence to the utmost. It was improvisation on the spot, but careless: the politically highly charged text was not backed by their bosses.[20]

The situation in Kiev escalated. On 19 February snipers killed dozens of demonstrators. To prevent further bloodshed, the Europeans put themselves forward as mediators. In consultation with their colleagues meeting in Brussels, the German, French and Polish foreign ministers left for Maidan on 20 February. After fourteen hours of negotiations they acted as midwives to an accord between President Yanukovych and the opposition. In a sign of how tensions were rising, the Pole, Radosław Sikorski, said to an opposition leader, "If you don't support this [deal] you'll have martial law, you'll have the army. You will all be dead."[21] A Russian envoy was present too. The Americans stayed away.

In Brussels there were complaints that "the EU" should have been present in Kiev (meaning its high representative Catherine Ashton) rather than three "national" ministers. This was to misconceive the nature of the Union, which is not merely "Brussels" but the member states jointly. For the Ukrainians, the Russians and the rest of the world, the Steinmeier-Fabius-Sikorski trio was evidently speaking "in Europe's name". The protocol was reassuring: they were assisted not by three national ambassadors but by the one EU ambassador in Kiev, and they signed the accord, in the early hours of the Friday morning, as witnesses "for the European Union" on an equal footing with those "for the Russian Federation".[22] This was successful European improvisation, at least as regards form.

As to substance, the accord was inherently brittle, however. Too brittle, as became clear in the hours that followed. The demonstrators – some had been camping out in the cold for three months – demanded the immediate departure of Yanukovych. The Ukrainian parliament voted for the release of his arch rival Tymoshenko, a humiliation. The street kept up the pressure. Towards evening the president fled the country. Minister Fabius had by then left for China on other business; his colleagues Steinmeier and Sikorsky were unable or unwilling to stop the revolt. The Kremlin drew its own conclusions and saw its suspicions of hypocritical European expansionism confirmed.

AFTER CRIMEA: SANCTIONS, FEBRUARY–JULY 2014

On 27 February 2014 Russian soldiers invaded Crimea, where unrest had prevailed since the Maidan events. This invasion marked the start of the most serious crisis in the European order of states since the Cold War. The violation of the border necessitated a response from the European side. But what?

War and peace on the continent are a *Chefsache*, a matter to be dealt with at the very highest level. Van Rompuy called the European Council together on 6 March. At the start of the session, the new Ukrainian premier Arseniy Yatsenyuk – according to the Nuland tapes a favourite of the Americans – impressed his 28 EU counterparts with the emotionally restrained speech of a leader in wartime: helping Ukraine economically and politically should be one half of the strategic response, punishing Russia the other. During that session, the message arrived on several Blackberries that Putin intended to organize a referendum on making Crimea part of the Russian Federation. The news hardened attitudes; the meeting was stormy.

Some countries – Poland, the Baltic states, Britain and Sweden – wanted to hit the aggressor hard. Others were keen to avoid confrontation, to protect trading interests and the green shoots of economic recovery at home: roughly Southern, Central and Eastern Europe, plus Benelux. In between were Germany and France. Yet all recognized the importance of unity. The unanimously accepted compromise was a sanctions regime in three stages.

Stage one: diplomatic sanctions, starting immediately; summit meetings with Russia were cancelled. Stage two: targeted blacklists, to be introduced if Russia did not change tack "within a few days"; this involved a travel ban for people connected with Russia's military operations and the freezing of their financial assets. (The first blacklist was published ten days later.) Stage three: economic sanctions, to be implemented if Russia further "destabilized" Ukraine. These are the heavy guns. A decision of the latter kind is the hardest because anyone hitting someone else with trade sanctions suffers pain too. That "rebound" pain needed to be shared evenly – some countries export weapons (France's sale of two aircraft carriers to Russia was a focus of attention), some financial services, others cars, or fruit and vegetables. The leaders therefore preferred not to name specific sectors yet but asked the Commission for a balanced proposal.

While Russia formally annexed Crimea on 21 March and pro-Russian rebels in eastern Ukraine proclaimed two mini-republics and seized terrain, the European debate over economic sanctions dragged on. For months. Between and within member states. In Germany it ignited a fierce public argument between Putin-sympathizers and hardliners.

This ended on 17 July 2014. When the civilian airliner MH17, on its way from Amsterdam to Kuala Lumpur, was shot down over eastern Ukraine with 298 people on board, the debate was over in a flash. Even the German business world and the Dutch gas lobby realized that geopolitical stability is a precondition of trade. No special summit this time – it was the holiday season and there was little enthusiasm – but the matter was clarified in telephone calls between leaders and at ambassadorial level in Brussels. On 29 July both the EU presidents, Van Rompuy and Barroso, reported that unprecedented economic sanctions were to take effect. The intended signal to the leaders of Russia: "Destabilising Ukraine, or any other Eastern European neighbouring State, will bring heavy costs to its economy".[23]

When the heat is on, when the unity of the members of the Union as a club is at stake, its political *raison d'être* trumps purely economic interests. That was clear in the summer of 2012 during the euro crisis and it became clear again in this business of war and peace. The tough sanctions against Russia were extended by unanimous agreement several times after 2014, most recently until the end of July 2019. Despite considerable differences

– between the Italians and the British, between the Portuguese and the Lithuanians, between Bulgarians and Poles – the 28 leaders were unanimous on the fundamental nature of the threat and the strategic importance of a united front.

There was, however, an inherent limit to this show of strength. Introducing sanctions means closing your market to products and your border to individuals, in other words: reversing the force of the magnet. Causing pain by pushing away. It takes great resolve and has a potentially powerful effect, but it is not action. As a political tool, sanctions are therefore limited. Europe's new politics demands a more ample toolkit: not just attraction (magnet) or rejection (sanctions) but rhetoric and action.

MERKEL IN MUNICH AND MINSK:
ARMS OR DIPLOMACY, FEBRUARY 2015

After the invasion of Crimea, leaders in Washington, London, Paris, Brussels and Berlin engaged in countless telephone conversations with the Kremlin. No one, however, got on a plane, as Sarkozy had done in 2008. The European Union did not immediately take upon itself the role of mediator between Kiev and Moscow. That was difficult anyhow, because unlike the 2008 episode, which concerned NATO, the EU was in a sense a party to the conflict.

Yet three weeks after the Crimea invasion, a plane stood ready at the military airfield outside Brussels to take Sarkozy's successor as president of the European Council, Herman Van Rompuy, to Moscow for talks with Putin. It was 18 March 2014, two days before the scheduled March summit, a good moment to look into the lion's mouth and then report back to all the government leaders. Van Rompuy had wanted to keep the mission a secret, but that failed as a result of clumsiness on the Russian side.[24] Diplomatic channels got wind of it, the Poles immediately grew nervous – ever fearful of concessions to the Russians behind their backs – and to be on the safe side the president cancelled the mission. The Belgian did not possess the French ability to bluff that had been Sarkozy's strength.

The ball landed in the court of the leaders of France and Germany. That spring tensions rose between Moscow and Washington, partly because of intimidating military movements on land, at sea and in the air by both the

Russians and NATO. On 4 June the annual G8 Summit was to take place in Sochi, Russia, with Putin as host. It was boycotted by Obama and the other guests. The absentees met as the G7 in the Justus Lipsius building in Brussels; there was an old-fashioned feeling of "the West" against Moscow. Then the French president cut through the Cold War dynamic. History lent a helping hand; on 6 June the Allied landings in Normandy were to be commemorated and the French president, feeling it would be inappropriate to take the Russian leader off the guest list, spotted an opportunity. On the beach the host arranged a meeting between Putin and new man Petro Poroshenko, elected president of Ukraine ten days earlier. Merkel helped break the ice and made her weight felt. Obama and Putin also met for the first time since the crisis began. They all expressed a desire for a quick end to the bloodshed in eastern Ukraine. A ceasefire was not in fact reached until three months later, after the shooting down of MH17.

In January 2015 the conflict flared up again. Pro-Russian rebels seized the airport at Donetsk and began an offensive towards the strategically important town of Debaltseve. Fear of all-out war intensified. In Washington, both in the White House and in Congress, there were increasing calls for military support for Ukraine. Influential Republicans and Democrats wanted to send weapons: the peace-loving Ukrainians must surely be helped to defend themselves against Mr Putin. This betokened a dramatic escalation. Kiev requested high-tech weaponry that required the sending of military advisers to operate it. In no time at all, America and Russia, the world's biggest nuclear powers, would be at war through intermediaries. A war by proxy on European soil. A nightmare. Angela Merkel seized the initiative along with François Hollande. A tireless February week saw her in Moscow, Kiev, Munich, Washington, Minsk and Brussels.

Particularly memorable was her appearance at the Munich security conference on Saturday 7 February. Just back from Moscow and Kiev, she spoke to a critical audience. American Vice-President Joe Biden, Ukrainian President Petro Poroshenko and Senator John McCain, always up for a fight, were sitting in the front row. The reproach of "appeasement" hung in the air, of cowardly deals with dangerous opponents, like Chamberlain's 1938 deal with Hitler. Victoria "Fuck the EU" Nuland, Obama's Europe adviser in the White House, drove the point home to 20 American diplomats and senators in a hotel room;

the German defence minister was referred to as the "defeatism minister" and there was talk of "Moscow bullshit" being uttered by Europeans.[25]

In the plenary chamber Angela Merkel's speech was good, in the question-and-answer session she was outstanding. Why deny ourselves the kind of weapons Putin is using? was the indignant question from the audience. Merkel's response: "I cannot envisage any situation in which an improved equipment of the Ukrainian army will lead to a situation in which Putin is so impressed that he will lose militarily. [...] I think one has to look reality in the eye." This was enough to undermine the sense of good and evil. Merkel then drew on deeply personal experience:

> You know, I grew up in the GDR. As a seven-year-old child I saw the Wall being erected. No one, although it was a stark violation of international law, believed at the time that one ought to intervene militarily in order to protect the citizens of the GDR and the whole Eastern bloc from the consequences of that, namely to live in lack of freedom for many many years. And I don't actually mind, because it was, I understand this, it was a realistic assessment [...] but I also had the experience that you standing up for the unity of Germany led to my sitting here today. [...] I'm a hundred per cent convinced that our principles will in the end prevail. [...] No one knew when the Cold War would end at the time, but it did end.[26]

A strong narrative countermove, setting "the Wall 1961" against "Munich 1938"; counterbalancing moral conviction with patience and a steady moral compass through time.

Two days later, on the Monday, the chancellor was in the White House. Obama let it be known that he was under considerable pressure. He alone still stood between the cries of the hawks and weapons deliveries to Kiev. If the Europeans wanted to solve the conflict through diplomacy, it would have to happen the day after tomorrow in Minsk. For her part, Merkel impressed upon him that he should pay more attention to Putin.

On Wednesday 11 February 2015 all these efforts came together in Minsk. Belarus' President Aleksandr Lukashenko, nicknamed "Europe's last dictator", had put his Independence Palace at the four leaders' disposal. In the vast ornate room, Merkel, Hollande, Putin and Poroshenko talked all night about

terms for a ceasefire. A short distance away, pro-Russian rebel leaders negotiated with a Swiss envoy of the Organization for Security and Co-operation
in Europe (brought in at the request of Kiev, having both Ukraine and Russia
as members). At 8.00am, after 14 hours of talks, the envoy emerged with bad
news: they did not want to sign. It had all been for nothing. Confrontation
threatened. The four leaders now consulted in private. More endless talking.
Then Putin withdrew to an office set up for him. He phoned both the rebel
leaders. The others did not know what was being said. Two hours later both
signed. At 11.00am local time, without a press conference ("We have hope"
was how they summed up the shaky result), Merkel and Hollande flew from
Minsk to Brussels, where at 1.00pm they joined the plenary European Council meeting.[27] Like the German-French-Polish ministerial trio a year earlier in
Kiev, this German–French duo gave a European setting to its performance.
Just to make sure, the new European Council president, Poland's Donald
Tusk, also had Ukrainian President Poroshenko report to his European colleagues on the "Minsk Night". The war was not over, but escalation had been
curtailed and the chances of peace preserved.

Merkel's statesmanship in Minsk rested on her personal authority, on
German and European political and economic power (concentrated in unanimous sanctions), on a cool assessment of relations and on strategic patience.
She was little moved by the Western hawkish discourse about the dastardly
Putin, or indeed by the mirrored version of it in Moscow propaganda, but read
the situation in terms of power and powerlessness. The chancellor saw that
in this Ukrainian civil war the West did not have the will to win and Russia
was not willing to lose. Peace demanded a compromise: not just a ceasefire between the warring parties but a long-term underlying compromise,
between Europe and America on one side and Russia on the other, about a
security architecture for the continent.

For the attentive reader the beginnings of such a compromise could be
found in the Minsk accord. The visible elements were constitutional decen-
tralization of Ukraine and monitored local elections in separatist areas.[28]
These, however, pointed to invisible and more fundamental elements, of
which all parties were fully aware but that, if spoken about, would come up
against resistance from hardliners on both sides: in Kiev and Washington,
and in Donbass and Moscow. For Russia the crux was that Ukraine must not

become a NATO member; in return Kiev would regain territorial sovereignty over the Donbass and rebel regions in eastern Ukraine (though not Crimea), as long as a constitutional change gave those regions some kind of veto on NATO membership. Up to the present the mutual trust and political determination to put the deal into operation have been lacking. As long as the weapons are at the ready, there will be no majority in the Verkhovna Rada in Kiev for a new constitution; and as long as the Rada in Kiev does not adopt a new constitution, Moscow will not withdraw its weapons. The boundary has been drawn, the magnet played out: what now?

Between America and Russia

The battle over the borderlands breathed new life into old enemy stereotypes in Washington and Moscow. Cold War rhetoric unleashed fighting forces. Thus the conflict in Ukraine became a dangerous and existential moment. For the European Union it was also a moment of geopolitical awakening, and of cautious first steps on the way to its political independence between the United States and the Russian Federation.

Just as after 1989, no longer split by an Iron Curtain, Europe was able to manifest itself as a player on the world stage, so conversely a new Cold War threatened to place undesirable or unwanted constraints on its freedom of action. If it was to avoid being trapped between America and Russia, between protector and neighbour, it would have to develop a capacity to discern and defend its own interests and its own values.

Friction with America does not occur, or only to a limited extent, in the field of values. "Shared values" is the mantra of the transatlantic alliance. Freedom and democracy, three times tested in the twentieth century and victorious on all three occasions, in 1918, 1945 and 1989, made America and Europe into "the West". Although the two continents are slowly drifting apart and although since the Trump election "the end of the West" has been predicted more loudly than ever,[29] that inheritance will not vanish overnight. In this context the United States is the undisputed leader, because of its military strength, as was subtly but firmly made visible by Washington when on 26 March 2014 President Obama gave a speech in Brussels (seat of both the

European Union and NATO). A week before, in the Duma in Moscow, President Putin had given a rousing speech in defence of the annexation of Crimea. In the Centre for Fine Arts in Brussels, Obama replied with a well-told but standard story about the march of freedom and democracy, the battle of right against might. The decor, though, was striking. The American president spoke on a stage with almost forty flags around him. It was a while before I – one of an audience of 2,000 – managed to tease out the logic: they were the flags of all the NATO countries, as would be expected, plus those of all the member states of the European Union. You do not normally lump the two together: the US, Canada, Norway and Turkey are with good reason members only of one club; Sweden, Ireland and Cyprus with equally good reason only of the other. But in the tensions of the Ukraine crisis the Americans pushed such niceties aside in favour of a powerful *mise-en-scène*. The proud display of flags underlined American's leadership of "the free world". The American commander-in-chief had casually performed a masterly symbolic political embrace of the European Union. But who would feel any need to object; surely both sides share the same values?

Consequently the key question in determining and assessing Europe's policies on Ukraine and Russia is: aside from values, do Europe's political interests coincide with America's? If they do, then subordination to Washington is not a problem; it has traditionally been the outlook of the British, the Danes, the Poles and the Baltic peoples. Or is there an essential difference between Europe's dealings with a difficult neighbour and America's dealings with a superpower overseas, formerly its greatest enemy? If that is the case, then a degree of strategic autonomy is needed, as the French and many Germans feel it is. With Trump in the White House these issues only become more urgent, by reason of his unpredictability, but also his disdain for the language of values and his crude interest calculus, turning the Europeans from sacred allies into mere vassals.

Essentially, in the skirmishes on the eastern border – in Donbass in 2014–15, as in Georgia in 2008 – nothing less than Europe's geopolitical emancipation from America was at stake. After the invasion of Crimea, the EU and the US acted more or less in concert for a year; the sanctions against Russia were continually coordinated. Only the issue of weapons for Kiev drove a wedge. German–French opposition caused frustration in

Washington, and among hawks in Warsaw and London. Here and there Robert Kagan's sneer from the days of the Iraq war could be heard: "Americans are from Mars, Europeans from Venus" (Bush Jr's former ideologue could whisper it in the ear of Obama's Ukraine envoy in the bedroom; Kagan is married to Victoria Nuland). From the European side Merkel produced the most convincing counter-narrative, with words in Munich and with deeds in Minsk. Europe's reluctance to supply arms to Kiev was not simply a matter of weak knees, moral impotence or economic opportunism – although such frailties exist and the Kremlin makes grateful use of them. Rather it was rooted in the experience of what is politically possible. Whereas the postwar mainstream in American foreign policy sees demons everywhere and is eager to eradicate them right away, Europeans are scarred by the indelible tragedy of history. Curbing evil is an achievement in itself, in anticipation of better times. You will be branded a coward or a traitor, so this requires courage and determination.

Of course the United States too has a school of realist foreign policy, exemplified by Kissinger/Nixon, by Bush Sr and by Obama. The latter, in contrast to his predecessor Bush Jr, did not believe in the exportability of Western values, and in the Ukraine crisis, as a "realist and internationalist",[30] he kept the interventionist forces in Washington in check. With the election of Donald Trump the pendulum is swinging towards (at best pragmatic) isolationism. The gap between American and European interests is widening rapidly under the new president, even if domestic counterforces limit his room for manoeuvre. Trump defines America's interests more narrowly and egotistically than any of his predecessors since 1945 and is proud of the fact; it was his promise to his voters. For European countries over the coming years there will be an even more urgent need to be able to defend their own interests, and to build up their capacity to act, starting in their own wider region.

With Moscow the Union comes up against a different way of dealing with history. The Russians are masters at opportunistic events-politics and they have a system to match. Vladimir Putin did not invent it, but he does embody it. After his actions in Ukraine and also in Syria, where in August 2015 he suddenly became involved in the war and a year and a half later just as unexpectedly withdrew, both his friends and his enemies acknowledged that the man in the Kremlin had been a step ahead of everyone. Unsettled by such agility, Western commentators tend to write pedantically that Putin shows himself to be more an opportunistic "tactician" than a visionary "strategist", or that he has "unclear intentions". But the Russian president probably has no master plan for either Ukraine or Syria. Not because he is incapable of thinking of one, but because he regards it as a wasted effort: events always turn out differently.

This Russian attitude existed long before Putin and will not disappear with him. So some degree of diplomatic recall is indispensable for anyone wanting to face Russia well prepared in the future. In the midst of the Cold War, when much was at stake for those trying to understand Russian intentions, America's best ever diplomat in Moscow, George F. Kennan, observed the same phenomenon. In a memo written in 1952 he told his bosses in Washington that Russian agility is more than caprice. It arises from their own view of history and politics:

> I believe they [the Russians] are much more conscious than we are of the interplay of action and reaction in international affairs, of the way in which events mesh into each other and reflect each other, of the number of variables that can enter into the determination of a situation some years removed; and that they would be less inclined, for this reason, to feel themselves under the obligation to arrive at any firm or final judgement at the present time about the likelihood of war in a more distant future.[31]

This way of engaging in politics demands strong central leadership without any lasting accountability, precisely the kind for which the Kremlin is so well equipped.

In a democracy, improvisation is harder. Every move has to be elucidated, counterforces defeated – partly with words, partly through wrangling behind the scenes – and the public persuaded. All this costs time. Moreover, the arguments deployed go on to lead a life of their own. They take root. If you are forced to do something else three months later – new circumstances, new plan – you soon start arguing against your former self and are labelled a flip-flopper. A Kremlin leader is less troubled by that. In Russian dealings with chance, the leader has no need to feign sincerity and little to take account of, as long as the defence of national interests reaps results at the crucial moment and earns respect. We, by contrast, are troubled by the blind chance that reality serves up and demand, as a public, stories to tame it, preferably cast in moral categories that our own politicians must also believe in: the root melodies that are played.

Yet good improvisation-politics need not be mere opportunism. European leaders acting in the moment can still remain true to their own convictions; they too can steer by compass. This requires a clear definition of strategic aims, which change and evolve over time and are continually the subject of debate, along with an honest acknowledgement of the plurality of our values, which may, indeed will, collide. They define our power and individuality. If the classic American history is at its heart a morality play of right against might and Russian history a cynical chronicle of might against might, then European history has given us a tragic awareness that politics is very often right against right – peace against justice, equality against freedom, security against democracy. We Europeans do not play to win but to minimize losses.

It was in a different geopolitical crisis, not on Europe's eastern border but on the southern and south-eastern borders, not with shadowy little green men in Crimea but with those all too tangible orange life jackets on Greek beaches, that one such tragic dilemma arose, in full view of the European public.

3

Setting boundaries:
the refugee crisis

Besides, there are – because some have indeed said: you were tricked, overwhelmed, surprised or whatever – situations when it is necessary to make decisions. I could not have waited for twelve hours and contemplated the issues. Those people converged on the borders, and so we took this decision.

Angela Merkel[1]

What is the border for in the end? To unite us.

Régis Debray[2]

Conviction and responsibility

One and a quarter million refugees applied for asylum in the Union in 2015, twice as many as the year before.[3] The images were dramatic: small boats on the Mediterranean, handcarts on Balkan roads, full trains stranded on the way to the rich North. The influx of people looked to many like a mass migration, almost an invasion; and the public, in fearful bewilderment, had the impression the authorities had lost control. Could Europe act? Was Europe authorized to act?

The demand for action had a different character from that which accompanied previous crises. The Ukraine crisis of 2014–15 was a matter of war and peace; the Union itself had hardly any resources or powers to bring the conflict under control, so active intervention by the member states jointly was an obvious necessity. Moreover, application of the magnetic forces provided by the Brussels diplomatic toolkit, the showpiece being the association agreement with Kiev, had worked out badly. No one at that point, therefore, disputed the primacy of events-politics. In the fields of asylum and migration, by contrast, the Union had quite a few competences and regulations. The situation became unmanageable because the regulatory framework collapsed under divergent strategic interests and because of the disruptive impact of the situation on public opinion. For a long time Brussels was blind to the gap between what was administratively possible and what, in this exceptional situation, was politically required. Engagement by the highest political authority needed for events-politics was even actively hindered by some institutions, reinforcing the impression of a loss of control, of powerlessness.

The contrast with the euro crisis of 2010–12 is illustrative as well. To steer their poorly equipped currency through the storm, the leaders, at gunpoint, had both to design new tools and to deploy them immediately. They were therefore engaged in events-politics on two levels, firstly at the constitutional level, setting up institutions that had the power to act (the protective umbrellas, anchored in treaties) and establishing regulatory frameworks (fiscal treaty; bank supervision), and secondly at the level of action, using the new tools as soon as member states got into trouble (aid packages for Greece, Ireland and Portugal). The European Council served as both designer and enforcer. This connection between evenly recalibrated frameworks and adequate performance saved the currency and repaired the fracture between North and South. In the refugee crisis, by contrast, after a phase of technocratic overreach, events-politics vested with political authority emerged (the Turkey deal of March 2016), and institutions with the capacity to act were set up or strengthened (the agencies for border control and asylum), but the constitutional frameworks for asylum and migration were not recalibrated at the highest level, with the support of the public, to ensure they were ready for a future crisis. As a result, irritation and distrust proliferate to this day, in this case between North, South and East.

Three episodes from the refugee crisis are central, each characterized by one kind of political performance. We see how the Union decided to save lives ("At sea"), how it attempted to share out asylum seekers across member states ("Quota") and how the Union and its member states made the stream of refugees manageable ("Balkan dam and Turkey deal"). Feeling their way, the Europeans discovered what it means to share external borders.

Running through all three episodes is the tension between moral principles and practical responsibilities, between an "ethic of conviction" and an "ethic of responsibility". With this famous distinction from *Politics as a Vocation* (1919), Max Weber did not intend to assert that the former is equivalent to irresponsibility and the latter to a lack of conviction. "However," he claimed, "there is an abysmal contrast between conduct that follows the maxim of an ethic of ultimate ends – that is, in religious terms, 'The Christian does rightly and leaves the results with the Lord' – and conduct that follows the maxim of an ethic of responsibility, in which case one has to give an account of the foreseeable results of one's action".[4] According to Weber the two cannot be reconciled; you need to keep both viewpoints in mind and the outcome is never ideal.

In the refugee crisis, Pope Francis embodied like no one else an unconditional ethic of conviction, that of the gospel. His chosen name is already a programme. True to the saint from Assisi he makes a moral appeal with words and gestures of humility. In an Easter ritual in 2016 he washed and kissed the feet of twelve refugees, including three Muslim men. In a Mass on Lampedusa in 2013, not long after a horrific shipwreck, he used a cross and a chalice made of driftwood, having cast a wreath onto the water. In his sermon he was scathing about politicians: "Father, we beg your forgiveness for those who by their decisions on the global level have created situations that lead to these tragedies".[5]

It was and is the task of Europe's politicians to set acts of ethical responsibility alongside this.

Three episodes

AT SEA: SAVING LIVES AND CATCHING SMUGGLERS, 23 APRIL 2015

On the evening of Sunday 19 April 2015, just outside Libyan waters, a ship capsized with more than 800 refugees on board. Barely 30 were saved. It was the greatest tragedy in the Mediterranean since the Second World War. The press spoke of a "dark day" for Europe.[6]

For a long time the Italian government had relied on Libyan strongman Muammar Gaddafi to stop people smugglers; after his fall in 2011 there was a vacuum. At the request of Rome, the Union stepped in by mounting two modest coastguard operations. Some 20 member states contributed. It was a matter of "border management". The EU's border agency Frontex had no mandate for rescues at sea. Its ships stayed within Italian waters and did not have military assets. The Italians, frustrated at this lack of preparedness, set up their own mission, called Mare Nostrum, after yet another disaster off Lampedusa in late 2013. It had its own naval vessels, patrolled closer to the Libyan coast and picked up tens of thousands of shipwreck survivors. Rome felt it was acting on behalf of Europe as a whole and requested support from its partners, funding at the very least. Pressure on the Union to take over Mare Nostrum grew, but the border agency was not equipped for it, as those responsible acknowledged.[7]

A moral dilemma contributed to this reticence. The Italian rescue operation worked as a magnet, a "pull factor". People traffickers shamelessly made allowance for the European crisis of conscience in their business model. They took their clients out to sea and the coastguards took them to their final destination, asylum centres in the North. Mare Nostrum caused a dramatic increase in the number of attempted crossings, according to the director of Frontex: "I am afraid of saying it is a pull factor, but the smugglers have abused the proximity of this operation near to the Libyan coast to put more people in the sea with the assumption that they would be rescued very soon. This made it cheaper for them, they put less fuel, less food and less water on the boats which at the same time increases the risks of the migrants".[8] The paradox: saving lives could cost lives. It was another reason why northern European member states were opposed to a European Mare Nostrum. Their political appraisal ("pull factor") could, however, be concealed in legal language (no mandate). Only British Home Office minister Theresa May was prepared to embrace the deterrence argument, which the opposition at home saw as "immoral".[9] The agreement between the 28 ministers was half-hearted and when the Italians terminated Mare Nostrum nothing adequate replaced it. The EU mission, called Triton, which took over in November

2014, was not a rescue operation and did not sail so far south. It could do little about tragedies in Libyan waters.

After the catastrophe of Sunday 19 April 2015, all interior and foreign ministers came together within a day, at the invitation of High Representative Federica Mogherini, six months earlier her country's foreign minister. At the urging of Italian Prime Minister Matteo Renzi, Donald Tusk convened a summit of government leaders for 23 April. Both Italians seized the chance to finally make a national problem into a European problem.

The leaders endorsed their ministers' decisions, only in stronger language.[10] Saving lives and catching criminals were the main aims. Operation Triton saw its financing tripled, was allocated more ships and more staff, and was given the authority to carry out rescue missions in international waters with "no limits, geographic or legal".[11] It was barely lawful, but it made the European mission into a proper replacement for Italy's Mare Nostrum. This constituted a political turnaround for the northern-European member states, most conspicuously for Britain. The cold argument about the "pull factor" was simply unconvincing amid images of human suffering; the ethic of conviction swept aside the ethic of responsibility.

The leaders asked Mogherini to prepare a military operation that would "undertake systematic efforts to identify, capture and destroy vessels before they are used by traffickers".[12] This was bellicose language. It was to be done "in accordance with international law", but the feasibility of that was doubtful. The Libyan government let it be known right away that it would "'confront' any unilateral EU moves to attack sites used by people smugglers".[13]

Saving people and hunting smugglers were new forms of concerted action, in response to an unprecedented disaster. Events-politics. Yet the decisions of those April days did not give the impression of balance. This was a contradictory mix of compassion-born-of-guilt and full-bodied harshness, such that it seemed as if the latter was intended to compensate for the anticipated consequences of the former. Europe's ambiguous message to the refugees: we're coming to save you but we don't want you to be saved. And the message to the European public, internally split between opening and shutting the doors: we will not be suckered.

QUOTA: SHARING OUT THOSE WHO ENTER,
22 SEPTEMBER 2015

Analytically there are three ways to control a disruptive stream of migrants. First you can tackle the causes at source. This requires an active foreign policy focused on combatting poverty, resolving conflicts far and wide, and so on. Secondly, you can throw up a dam to stem the approaching flood. This is defensive border politics and it necessitates the deployment of robust means. Thirdly, you can opt for irrigation, for the redirection of incoming currents, so that they do no harm and even perhaps become an asset. This is an ambitious domestic political operation, which because of its intricate nature demands a strong central organization (as the pharaohs discovered in dealing with the Nile). You can also combine all three.

It is striking that after the Mediterranean shipwrecks of April 2015, European action was focused mainly on the second and third methods: dam and irrigation. Political energy was devoted to them, thinking was focused on them, a battle raged between them. Active foreign policy to address the sources of migration lost out to them both. Of course improvements to the situation in the Sahel or in Afghanistan cannot be achieved overnight and success depends on other players too. There is no solution here to an acute migration crisis. Still, Europe's minor role in the diplomatic efforts to put an end to the biggest source of refugees by far, the civil war in Syria, was disappointing. The names of those who led the peace talks in Vienna (2015) and Geneva (2016) are telling: John Kerry and Sergei Lavrov, foreign ministers of America and Russia.

In the summer of 2015 the main current of refugees switched from the Libya-Italy route to the Aegean Sea between Turkey and Greece. This changed the dynamic. Greece was now the number-one frontline state, and between January and September it received 213,000 requests for asylum. Strikingly, number two was not Italy but landlocked Hungary, with 143,000. This pointed to an out-of-control and collapsing asylum system, but also to administrative defeatism and lawlessness. Thousands of people had clearly travelled unchecked from the Greek islands northwards through Macedonia and Serbia, two non-member states, and were not registered on Union soil until they reached the Hungarian border. This phenomenon was not new. Stories had been doing the rounds for years about the Greek authorities sending migrants off into the night without a stamp, and the Italian police turning a blind eye if refugees took a bus or a train to Austria. There had been dozens before, perhaps hundreds, but now there were thousands, tens of thousands and more.

Such buck-passing was a consequence of the agreement that the member state of first entry had to grant asylum. This "Dublin" regulation placed an unfair burden on the southern and south-eastern member states with fragile external borders, which is why richer northern and western member states tolerated the resulting misconduct; they were glad not to be in the front line themselves. But an asylum system that has to maintain its political equilibrium by hypocrisy and evasion of the law cannot survive a shock. Now the shock had come. And the first victim of that shock would be European integration itself, or at least a symbolic and economic crown jewel: the open internal borders. If thousands of migrants were wandering around Europe, national governments would soon want to close their borders on public-order grounds, with all the inevitable consequences.*

From the perspective of Brussels the answer to the emergency situation was self-evident: the influx must be intercepted internally and equitably shared: irrigation. The crisis demanded solidarity – internationally with the refugees, and between Europeans. The salving of consciences and the logic of integration pointed in the same direction. In his annual major speech to the parliament in Strasbourg on 9 September 2015, Jean-Claude Juncker expressed this identification of Europe with solidarity in almost Franciscan tones: "Europe is the baker in Kos who gives away his bread to hungry and weary souls. Europe is the students in Munich and in Passau who bring clothes for the new arrivals at the train station."[14] The Commission president knew that this creed would go down well in the Europhile Parliament.

For the governments the matter was less simple. They had to weigh arguments from solidarity against other principles and interests. Borders and migration touch upon national sovereignty and identity, while the transfer

---

* A far from elevating foretaste was a Franco-Italian conflict over 26,000 Tunisians who ended up in Italy after the fall of dictator Ben Ali in 2011. The Italians gave the group temporary permits with quasi-encouragement to travel on to other Schengen countries. At that point the French stopped and checked several trains at the French-Italian border crossing, close to Ventimiglia, which led to a fierce diplomatic quarrel and newspaper articles about "the end of Schengen". The affair fizzled out.

of powers, or interference by Brussels, were not popular themes. In a time of fear of terrorism, a local incident with an asylum seeker could lose you a general election. Taking in extra refugees and distributing them is a drastic measure, way beyond day-to-day Brussels market decisions. The idea and its implementation require solid support. Yet the Commission rather insouciantly deployed a discourse of the ethic of conviction. It has less need to weigh solidarity against other interests than governments do (at root this is a consequence of its tenuous link with the public). Governments, by contrast, cannot engage in the ethic of conviction alone; their voters want an ethic of responsibility too.

As a result of such political and constitutional sensitivities, the heads of state and government said in April – at their emergency summit after the Mediterranean shipwrecks – that they did not want "compulsory" asylum quotas; in June they repeated that, to the fury of Juncker, whose Commission had proposed, in May, the centralized redistribution of 40,000 asylum seekers to relieve the frontline states. The fiercest resistance to this emergency measure came from Central and Eastern Europe, but elsewhere too there was a lack of applause. Reactions were attributable in part to the way the balance tipped. Whereas arrival countries such as Italy and destination countries like Sweden and Germany would benefit from redistribution (for them, solidarity and self-interest coincided), most other member states, including transition countries, stood to lose. It would therefore take time to get everyone on board.

But after the tragic summer of 2015 – with its images of life jackets on beaches and children pressed against border fences – Jean-Claude Juncker decided there was no more time. Europe must act now. Another emergency mechanism was needed, this time to relocate 120,000 people, and in due course an asylum system based on greater solidarity, he said in the Parliament. Radical ideas, but the president declared that "the mood is turning".[15] He was probably thinking of evidence of the hospitality of the European public. He was probably thinking of the millions moved by the photograph of the drowned three-year-old Syrian boy Alan Kurdi on a Turkish beach a week earlier. He was certainly thinking of the German chancellor.

Because it was also the summer of Angela Merkel. On 25 August an office of the Federal government let it be known on Twitter that Syrian refugees were no longer being sent back to their first country of arrival based on the

"Dublin" rules. The cry went out, resonating as far as refugee camps in Turkey and Jordan. At her summer press conference on 31 August Merkel said "*Wir schaffen das*" ("we can manage this"); the next day Syrians, Albanians and Iraqis at Budapest station chanted "Deutschland, Deutschland" and "Merkel, Merkel". When the trains ground to a halt, they set off on foot, towards Germany, towards Merkel, who in the night of 4–5 September decided to send trains to fetch them, because Germany has a human face. The chancellor, knowing that the mood can always change, wanted to bind the rest of Europe to these abrupt, historic decisions. Just as in the Federal Republic asylum seekers were spread out across the German states from Berlin, so the European Union must share them out among member states from Brussels. In June Merkel had still been urging the Commission to have patience, in September she could no longer wait. The German public deserved to know that it was not alone.

But how to overcome the resistance to quotas among those opposed? The Central and Eastern European blockade held, as became clear in the Council of Ministers on 14 September. In frustration the German minister, supported by his French counterpart, threatened to cut subsidies to the Eastern Europeans. This cantankerous power play indicated that the political means to persuade the obstructionists were lacking (in contrast to the euro crisis, when the dual pressure of the markets and the German purse pulled all the leaders across the line every time). Merkel, inconvenienced by this impasse, increased the institutional pressure. She rang Luxembourg premier Xavier Bettel, whose country held the rotating presidency of the Council of Ministers, to ask whether his justice minister could quickly organize yet another Council meeting on migration.[16] The chancellor was keen to have the quota debate out of the way before an extra summit, also pushed through by her, on 23 September.

What was impossible for the leaders was possible at a ministerial level in the case of this emergency decision about redistribution: a vote. It would certainly be highly unusual on such a thorny subject. Generally the sword of the majority serves to make the minority sufficiently accommodating, at the price of an exemption or a transition term, thereby achieving a unanimous accord. But Luxembourg minister Jean Asselborn, chairing the Council, believed that the "Community institutions" must be able to take difficult decisions even without government leaders; he was completely in agreement with the Brussels line of Commission president Juncker, his fellow countryman. When in the extra Council of Ministers of 22 September it turned out that Poland would abandon its Eastern European allies and join those in favour, the way was clear. Suddenly Asselborn proceeded to a vote. A large majority voted in favour, the Czech Republic, Slovakia, Hungary and Romania against, while Finland abstained. Afterwards relief and bitterness prevailed. "Europe has assumed its responsibility" said François Hollande on behalf of many.[17] But the outvoted spoke of a "terrible" atmosphere. Prime Minister Fico said that no compulsory quota would be implemented on Slovak territory as long as he was in power. Above all, being told to put their societies on a path towards multiculturalism by order of Brussels rankled.

On 9 October the first 19 Eritreans left Rome for Sweden. At Ciampino airport they were given a festive send-off by European commissioner for migration Dimitris Avramopoulos, Luxembourg Council chair Jean Asselborn and Italian minister of foreign affairs Angelino Alfano. The Commission announced that "it was an important symbolic moment which marked the start of a new, European approach to the way we treat asylum applications".[18]

The revolutionary decision on compulsory asylum quotas proved a fiasco. Of the 160,000 asylum seekers to be redistributed, after three months only a few hundred had moved, after more than a year a mere 5 per cent, and after eighteen months a little over 10 per cent.[19] This was clearly not purely the fault of recalcitrant Slovaks and Romanians. The formal decision of 22 September 2015 had no material consequences, or at best its workings were agonizingly slow. Attempting to demonstrate a capacity to act, Europe looked ridiculous.

What went wrong? In essence this: the Brussels machinery, encouraged by Berlin and facilitated by Luxembourg, tried to control an unprecedentedly dramatic event using the old prescriptions of the politics of rules. It had overreached itself. But the Commission and its allies could not see their mistake. Instead the failure was indignantly blamed on deficient implementation by "the member states". If only they would simply do as agreed. The law is the law.[20] Such reactions are facile. Reality cannot always be contained. In this case internal rules-politics fell prey to hubris – to triple hubris.

First of all there was technocratic overreach. The Commission, as was its habit, relied on its panacea of depoliticization but came up against political emotions that ascended to unparalleled heights, touching on citizenship, identity, sovereignty and even religion ("We don't have any mosques", the Slovak government defended itself). Yet Brussels shared out the burden of the asylum seekers as if dealing with fishing quotas or CO_2 emissions. If you had, say, 135 asylum seekers from Somalia, then you looked at the population of each member state, its wealth, unemployment rate and recent asylum efforts, and arrived at, say, a figure of 2.4 Somalis for Portugal. The result appeared neutral and objective. There was a failure to appreciate that the most virulent protests were not about "unfair" numbers but about the principle of central-ized redistribution, not poor implementation but the lack of a political basis.[*]

Then there was practical overreach. Sharing out asylum seekers is one thing, but how do you get them to their destinations? Even the relocation of the 19 Eritreans had required "intensive preparatory work on the ground by the Italian and Swedish authorities, by Frontex and other EU agencies, by local NGOs, and by the special envoys which the European Commission has deployed", according to a Brussels press release, not forgetting "outreach to the Eritrean community" to build trust. There were still 159,981 refugees to go. The fact that most frontline states had never set up the necessary reception centres and registration procedures became obvious. In Greece everything had to be built more or less from scratch. Chaos on the border; lack of basic amenities for new arrivals, staff, buildings, procedures for evalu-ation and selection: the scale of the practical problems was extraordinary and unprecedented.

Lastly there was institutional overreach. In the migrant crisis the Juncker Commission engaged in a battle with the European Council for prestige and power. To demonstrate its own political calibre it tried to exclude the cus-tomary crisis tamer, the forum of government leaders. It was "Community method" against "Union method". The Commission hereby deprived both

---

[*] Typically, Commission officials simply assumed that Hungary would collaborate with the emergency mechanism that was to provide 120,000 asylum places, given that 54,000 of them would serve to take asylum seekers from Hungary to other member states (the remainder were for those from Italy and Greece). During the Council of Ministers meeting of 14 September 2015 it was discovered that Budapest had no appetite for the initiative, pre-ferring to stick to the principles of the existing Dublin system and accept whatever troubles went with it. No one had asked the Hungarians beforehand; this objection on principle had been, it seems, unthinkable.

itself and the Union of the means to compensate for its other weaknesses, technocratic narrow-mindedness and practical ineptitude. Because what more effective means could there be of overcoming fierce public resistance in several member states than a summit, at which all governments commit themselves at the highest level and in full view? What better means of mobilizing the necessary capacity for action than to have the gathered leaders take the reins?

The vehicle of events-politics was blatantly passed over and ignored. The authority of the European Council was cast aside. Commission president Juncker wrote in late August 2015, "We have had many summits of government leaders [...] but what we need is for all EU member states to accept the European measures now and implement them".[21] For his part, Jean Asselborn reacted as if stung to the news that Merkel and her Austrian counterpart were requesting an extra European summit: "We're not in the African Union".[22] The Luxembourger wanted the relevant ministers to do their work according to the script of the Community method, in place of the government leaders, whose less formal gatherings require unanimity. The vote forced through by Asselborn on 22 September can be seen as an institutional victory for the old Brussels politics, but the price was high. The quota decision by ministerial majority lacked the political cohesion that even a weakened version at leader level could have achieved. The Luxembourg grouping had overplayed its hand.

The refugee theme might be new, but the risk of an administratively valid yet politically powerless decision was not. In an earlier situation Nicolas Sarkozy had drawn a line, making clear how, essentially, it should work. In 2008 the Union was negotiating reduced emissions of greenhouse gases and then too, opposition was greatest in Eastern Europe, as the agreements would have a major economic impact on regions dependent on brown coal. Then too, the Commission, Parliament and several of the more ambitious (in this case "greener") member states wanted to break the resistance by voting down the obstructionists. But the presidency of the Council, then still rotating at both ministerial and heads of government level and in French hands, thought a majority vote would be unwise and reached an accord by consensus at the summit of December 2008 after all. A week later Sarkozy countered criticism from the Parliament by saying:

I have accepted the principle of unanimity for a simple reason: the environmental choice Europe makes must not be a choice we endure but a choice for which we take responsibility. Imagine the weakness of a majority agreement whereby some of the countries did not endorse the pact. How lacking in credibility would an energy and climate package approved by majority be, when everyone realizes that unanimity provides the guarantee that we will meet our political obligations?[23]

Seven years after Sarkozy's speech, the import of his warning became clear. After the asylum quota vote of 22 September 2015, two outvoted member states immediately went to the Court; the Polish government that took office in October subsequently joined them. In October 2016 Hungarian premier Viktor Orbán reached for the weapon of a referendum so that his population could challenge the decision, which he could not so easily have done had he been made partly responsible for it himself.

BALKAN DAM AND TURKEY DEAL: STEMMING THE FLOW, 23 SEPTEMBER 2015–18 MARCH 2016

After the quota decision, designed to produce "irrigation", attention turned to the "dam". Redistribution could not be the only answer to the ever-growing torrent; some member states had been arguing for some time that a more solid dam would make irrigation superfluous. Several government leaders believed that Merkel had acted irresponsibly, underestimating the inviting impact of her words and shifting the consequences onto others. Hungary's Orbán was the only one to say this publicly, but he was *persona non grata*, with his razor-wire barrier going up at home.

At the summit of 23 September 2015 Donald Tusk reminded his colleagues of a few facts. Eight million Syrians had been internally displaced and another four million had fled to neighbouring countries, so potentially there were millions of refugees from Syria alone, "to say nothing of Afghanistan, Eritrea and other places", many of them determined to travel to Europe. Conclusion: "The greatest tide of refugees and migrants is yet to come. Therefore we need to correct the policy of open doors and windows. Now the focus should be on the proper protection of our external borders and on external assistance to refugees and the countries in our neighbourhood."[24] This message marked a new phase in the crisis. Control of the external borders became the watchword, but how?

The weak point, once again, was Greece. In October 2015, 200,000 migrants crossed the Aegean from the Turkish coast, an absolute record. It caused chaos, on the Greek islands, in the port of Piraeus and on the roads north. Turkish help was indispensable if the flow was to be dammed.

Such contracting out of border controls can work. Just as the Italian authorities worked with the Libyan leader Gaddafi for years to stop people smugglers, so from 2006 onwards the Spanish authorities developed a good working relationship with Morocco, Senegal and Mauritania, and with their local police and customs services. From then on considerably fewer migrants hazarded the crossing to the Canary Islands or southern Spain, and the deportation of irregular migrants who had reached Spain became far smoother. Why did those countries cooperate? It is a matter of service and fee, give and take, threat and promise. Nothing will come of nothing; quid pro quo. Trading contracts or visa commitments are obvious benefits that can be offered by the Union, but there are also matters that do not bear examination. It is an open secret that the Spanish state got its hands dirty with bribes for customs officials in Morocco, collaboration between secret services, even backdoor arms deliveries. The Brussels institutions and other member states chastely kept their distance, on the principle that "if you solve it, we don't need to know how".

Hence the difficulty of a deal with Turkey and why it led to the loss of Europe's geopolitical innocence. Who could negotiate and what could they put on the table? Who could get their hands dirty and who felt responsible? A bilateral deal between Greece and Turkey after the model of Italy and Libya or Spain and Morocco was pointless in the situation as it stood (quite apart from their conflict over Cyprus). Athens was politically and financially weak. Moreover, the refugees did not want to go to Greece but to other European countries, especially Germany. Then again, German–Turkish negotiations over control of the Greek–Turkish border, even if Europe chose to see it as the "Schengen"–Turkish border, would be strange. That seemed to be the outcome all the same; between October 2015 and May 2016 Chancellor Merkel travelled no fewer than five times to see President Erdogan in Ankara, who impressed upon her the power he held. But Germany could not speak on behalf of Europe; any agreement had to be embedded in the European Union. In this quid pro quo, not just the quo of border control but the quid of reciprocal action was a common concern. As well as financial support (which if necessary Berlin could have paid single-handed), Ankara was seeking faster visa liberalization for Turkish tourists and businesspeople, and the reopening of stalled accession talks. So the Commission negotiated an EU–Turkey action plan – Juncker's right-hand-man Frans Timmermans received his instructions informally from Berlin – and it was finalized on 29 November 2015 by the complete European Council in the presence of Turkish premier Ahmed Davutoglu. Through Berlin and Brussels, Ankara had negotiated with the Union as a whole.

But the power disparity was obvious. The Union as a Union is not equipped to play hardball. It is not a state, it has no secret services with valuable information, no dark vaults out of which to pay backhanders. Authoritarian neighbours of the calibre of Putin love to poke fun at this weakness. President Erdogan too, in a conversation with Tusk and Juncker several weeks before the November deal, let rip when the offer disappointed him: "We can open the doors to Greece and Bulgaria any time and we can put the refugees on buses". Tusk replied, "It is difficult with twenty-eight member states, but we really do want a deal with you". To which Erdogan responded rhetorically, "If there is no deal, how will you stop the refugees? Will you kill them?" (according to the leaked minutes, Tusk said that Europe could make itself less attractive to refugees but that was not the solution the Union wanted).[25]

When the images of Syrian women and children in the Balkan snow became tragic, when Turkey apparently could not or would not abide by the November agreements and in the cold of December another 100,000 people crossed the Aegean, when after one million refugees in 2015 the estimate for the new year rose to two million, panic broke out. On 4 January 2016 even refugee-friendly Sweden introduced border controls on its famous bridge to Denmark, supported by the local population. The euro, the internal market, Schengen: everything would be destroyed if the refugee crisis was not brought under control, Juncker said in his New Year speech.[26]

The key question that winter became: do we save Schengen with or without Greece? Plan A, with an A for Angela, was to keep Greece in by carrying on along the chosen path with Turkey, but more effectively. All smugglers on the Turkey–Greece border must be stopped and that service was worth a higher fee. More charitably too: we can dissuade the Syrians from risking their lives on the sea without disavowing our hospitality if we send back new arrivals in Greece while taking asylum seekers direct from Turkish camps. Only then does Europe remain true to itself. (Behind closed doors, Angela Merkel said, "I haven't kept the Greeks in the eurozone only to throw them out of Schengen now".) Plan B, with a B for Balkan dam, roughly took the following line: no, we don't need to keep a country with porous borders in Schengen at any price, we refuse to be blackmailed by border guard Erdogan, and we can restore control by closing the western Balkan route via Macedonia, Serbia, Hungary or Slovenia and Austria; in other words by sealing off Greece on the northern side, at the Macedonian border.

In the chaotic winter months of 2016, both these approaches worked side by side, sometimes head to head, until they reinforced each other. Plan B had its point of departure in a remarkable letter that Jean-Claude Juncker sent to Slovenian premier Miro Cerar on 25 January. The Commission president, raging against border controls only shortly before, drily let it be known that member states and non-member states (such as Macedonia) must shut their borders to migrants who simply wanted to travel through (to Germany), or who as economic migrants had no chance of being granted a residence permit.[27] In other words, closing off Greece was legally permitted. The letter went a step further. Looking at the southern end of the Balkan dam, Juncker wrote that although the Union could not help non-member Macedonia with border controls – so Frontex was held back – individual member states could. In other words, closing off Greece might be a matter to be tackled by Europe, de facto outside the Treaty, but nevertheless by the member states together. Four Central and Eastern European countries seized on the letter as an opening: "If Greece and Turkey fail to protect the outer border and we are unable to cope with strong migrant pressure, we will have to discuss a plan B".[28] Operationally the sealing off would progress from north to south; diplomats spoke of "cascading back" as the way to address waves of refugees. The Commission supported the operation, not with border guards but with emergency aid. The Union could not countenance the apocalyptic prospect of a humanitarian catastrophe in the Balkans when a great mass of people reached a closed border. Athens too was given extra support, to the tune of €300 million. In the camp at Idomeni on the Greek–Macedonian border conditions were dire. For the first time, resources intended for external emergency aid were deployed within the territory of the Union. This approach, despite resistance from Merkel who spoke of defeatism, was given the blessing of the European Council at its meeting on 18–19 February. Less than three weeks later, again to her displeasure but with the support of François Hollande and the others, the 28 government leaders declared "Irregular flows of migrants along the Western Balkans route have now come to an end".[29] One dam was up.

Meanwhile Merkel and her government were working imperturbably on Plan A, which would turn Turkey into Europe's border guard, keep Greece in Schengen and avoid the introduction of a ceiling to the number of asylum seekers accepted by Germany per year. She realized that only with a politics of responsibility on the external borders could she sustain her "ethic of conviction" narrative of a culture of welcome. In February, at the suggestion of German defence minister Ursula von der Leyen, NATO began to patrol the Aegean. Most of Merkel's European colleagues had no faith in her solo effort. She was supported by Alexis Tsipras, however, who found an unexpected ally in his opponent from the Greek midsummer euro saga of the year before, and by Dutch premier Mark Rutte, whose country had taken over the six-month presidency of the Council of Ministers from Luxembourg. A team of diplomats and civil servants from Berlin, The Hague and the Commission negotiated for weeks with Ankara over a new deal.

On 6 March came the breakthrough. In a conversation with Merkel and Rutte in the Turkish embassy in Brussels, on the eve of an EU–Turkey summit, Prime Minister Davutoglu made a surprising offer. Turkey was prepared to take back all asylum seekers who reached Greece if, in exchange, the Union would relocate Syrian refugees from the camps in Turkey, one for one. The German and the Dutchman did not believe it straight away, they posed critical questions, but the offer was real. Both leaders updated Tusk the next morning, who adjusted his battle plan. Refusal to respond to the proposal was not an option, but immediate assent was impossible because of all the Turkish demands. The leaders mandated Tusk to hold final negotiations with Ankara. On 17–18 March, in another dual European Council and EU–Turkey summit – after ten years of frustration over stalled accession talks, the Turks featured in the coveted "family photo" three times inside a few months – the deal was done.

The number of refugees arriving fell markedly in the weeks that followed, from 73,000 in January and 61,000 in February to 36,000 in March and 13,000 in April.[30] Relief all round: finally the capacity to act had been demonstrated; finally there was something that worked and could perhaps be repeated elsewhere. Yet in the media a battle of political narratives broke out. Was the success attributable to Plan B or Plan A? The truth was that it was down to both. The weekly figures show two downward kinks in the graph, the first when the Balkan dam was erected (around 19 February) and the second following the Turkey deal (shortly after 18 March). Perhaps the first dam was a precondition for the second. Only after Europe showed a willingness to stop the influx with a firm hand, countering Erdogan's disdain, did Ankara make the decisive offer. Of necessity. Cynically put, if Turkey's dirty hands became superfluous, the country would lose its leverage and opportunity to profit. Without quo, no quid. An alert *Financial Times* journalist correctly wrote, "In purely diplomatic terms, the Turkey deal was one of the first real examples of the EU playing *realpolitik*."[31]

But for that very reason a row promptly erupted after the deal. Were the refugee-return agreements valid under international law? Was Europe betraying its ideals in a dirty deal with autocrat Erdogan? Was Ankara secretly sending refugees back to Syria? Was Europe forcing them to take the more dangerous route via Libya and Italy, with more deaths at sea as a consequence? Painful questions. Human rights organizations and the UN refugee agency – accustomed to being in alignment with Brussels – were disconcerted.

It fell to Donald Tusk to point out to the public the tragic political choices Europe faced. Reporting on the two deals in the European Parliament, the traditional sounding board for moral indignation, the Pole said:

> The deal with Turkey and closing the Western Balkans route raise doubts
> of an ethical nature, and also legal, as in the case of Turkey. [...] While
> taking into account all the above-mentioned doubts, and even sharing
> some of them, I would like to recall that the main goal we decided on was
> to stem irregular migration to Europe. As I have frequently said, with-
> out this, and without restoring control over European migration policy,

we would be unable to prevent political catastrophes. Here I mean the collapse of Schengen; loss of control over our external borders with all its implications for our security; political chaos in the EU, a wide-spread feeling of insecurity; and ultimately, the triumph of populism and extremism.[32]

External borders and internal borders

After months of chaos, the Union managed to get the unprecedented influx of refugees of 2015–16 more or less under control by improvising. There will be no immediate repeat on a comparable scale by comparable means. Yet all parties realize that Europe needs to be prepared for new migration crises, whether prompted by war in the Middle East, poverty and population growth in Africa, or tensions between Russia and its westerly neighbours. Will joint action be mounted more convincingly in a future emergency? It remains to be seen whether the Union's turn towards *realpolitik* will prove lasting.

Under the pressure of events, politicians and policymakers rapidly supplemented the toolkit with new instruments for border control and asylum. So next time the tools will be available. The public has discovered that Europe's external border is in part a shared border, for example that the border of the Netherlands, Belgium or Germany is formed in the south by the Mediterranean Sea. But these experiences have yet to settle into the stable political and legal equilibriums that would allow us to meet a new test with calm confidence.

Each of the three ways of controlling a disorganized flow of migrants that the Union deployed – at the source, with a dam at the border and by "irrigating" the territory – entails its own tensions and uncertainties.

As far as work at the source is concerned, efforts undeniably increased. Ever since a migration summit between African and European leaders in late 2015 in Malta, the Union has been working on comprehensive migration agreements with source countries in Africa. They include help to improve employment prospects, aid to security forces and action against smugglers, the quid pro quo being the more rapid return of rejected asylum seekers. The

EU diplomats who negotiate these agreements, mostly from the Brussels department for development aid who have grown up with magnet thinking and philanthropy, take time to get used to thinking in terms of trade-offs, and they have a certain facility to obstruct. They are accustomed to grateful responses from partners in their target countries and are not exposed to the mood of electorates at home. So government leaders keep up the pressure on them and do not leave Africa purely to their foreign ministers. It was Matteo Renzi who, until he resigned as Italian premier at the end of 2016, kept his former foreign minister, EU High Representative Federica Mogherini, focused on the task. Also striking was the three-day visit by Chancellor Merkel in October 2016 to source countries Mali, Niger and Ethiopia – a diplomatic novelty and a signal to the public at home that Africa's future affects Germany. But this is all part of a long process. Demographics, climate, Islamic extremism and corruption: there is plenty to indicate that migration pressure from Africa will continue for two or more generations yet.

The continuing lack of European involvement in efforts to secure peace in Syria, the largest source of refugees, is all the more stark in light of these efforts in Africa. Although France, the UK and a handful of other countries sent troops to combat ISIS, Europe has hardly any real influence in Syria or its neighbouring countries.

This makes work on the dam, the object of the turn towards *realpolitik* in the spring of 2016, all the more important. That the Turkish dam has been effective is beyond dispute. In the eight months before the deal with Ankara, some 850,000 irregular migrants arrived in Greece, in the eight months after it that number fell to 23,000.[33] The uncertainty relates to the durability of the agreement. Doubts about the desire of President Erdogan to fulfil the agreement grew after the failed coup in Turkey of summer 2016 and his power grab by referendum in the spring of 2017. European governments are troubled by the promise of visa liberalization and steps towards accession – an electoral goldmine for domestic populist challengers. Should the Turkish dam collapse, the Union will have to play border guard itself on that flank and there will be pressure on the Balkan dam. In anticipation of such a situation, in September 2016 other member states granted Bulgaria support in guarding its frontier. With unprecedented speed the unimpressive Frontex was dressed up as a European Border and Coastguard Agency able to help member states in tasks of border control, reception and return, with its own equipment plus a pool of 1,500 staff to call on. This decision too shows that preparedness to take responsibility for a shared external border is growing, defensively at least.

The southern flank is the other cause for concern. After the closure of the route via the Aegean, the central Mediterranean route – from Libya, Tunisia or Egypt to Italy – came fully back into the picture. The number of people who drowned on that route was higher in 2016 than in the disastrous 2015. Three quarters are West Africans in search of a better life, who have little chance of asylum.[34] This migrant influx was overshadowed for a time by the astonishing flow of Syrian refugees, but it remained and remains undiminished. The anti-smuggling mission in Libyan waters launched by the Union after the shipwrecks of April 2015 saved the lives of thousands of migrants. At the same time it came up against the same dilemma as Italy's Mare Nostrum before it: the presence of naval ships close to the African coast works as a magnet. Knowing that rescuers are waiting, unscrupulous smugglers send their clients out in increasingly unseaworthy vessels. Humanitarian organizations, for which every death is one too many, deploy ships of their own. So the rescue boats of morality and the rescue boats of public power crossed the Mediterranean[35] – an image of the unresolved tension between the ethic of conviction and the ethic of responsibility.

The balance is shifting, however. An Italian populist-led government, which was in power from mid-2018 until mid-2019, refused to accept any more NGO rescue boats, sending them on to France and Spain. Under pressure from Rome, other governments also hardened their line and started to push for the "disembarkation" of rescued migrants on the African side of the Mediterranean. This approach requires agreements with the countries concerned, along the lines of the Turkey deal of March 2016. But less is heard now of the subtle linkage between border control and hospitality – between responsibility and conviction – which that deal embodied. A firm dam at the Union's southern border has priority. To achieve it, quid pro quo agreements will have to be made with Tunisia and with Egypt, where strongman Al-Sisi is playing hard to get. Libya is a case apart because of the lack of a central authority. The political instability of these countries and the migratory drift due to despair in large parts of Africa are a political time-bomb.

While work on the source and the dam battles uncertain realities, "irrigation" initiatives, the third means of making a flow of refugees manageable, suffer from internal tensions. The conflict of September 2015 over compulsory quotas for asylum seekers was still unresolved in late 2019. The Poles, Hungarians, Slovaks and Czechs maintain their resistance. The four of them proposed seeing the migration issue as a single whole, such that every member state would take on part of the necessary work, according to its wishes and capacities. They could then compensate for a refusal of asylum by performing other tasks. In the autumn of 2016, when Slovakia held the rotating presidency, the four coined the term "flexible solidarity" for this concept, a semantic provocation that was later adjusted to "effective solidarity". The other member states did not reject the idea outright. But how could anyone's contribution be assessed as fair and proportionate? Could you equate the acceptance of a hundred asylum seekers to the provision of ten border guards? Could such a thing be expressed in hard cash, as the Commission was contemplating? In the end the discussion ran aground: such efforts could not be quantified.[36]

There is agreement on the essence. The asylum system currently in place ("Dublin") is not equipped for shocks and needs adjustment. As in the euro crisis, there was a search for balance in terms of responsibility and solidarity.[37] Responsibility remains the watchword in the case of low or normal flows, when everyone needs to take care of border controls and the accompanying registration and accommodation of asylum seekers. Solidarity comes into play when the influx suddenly and uncontrollably increases and collective action is needed. At that point other member states, bilaterally or through EU agencies, must help frontline states with border control, registration and reception. A crisis mechanism, in other words, along the lines of the Stability Mechanism for the euro. Yet it is hard to negotiate the parameters: what level of flow merits a collective response and who declares it reached? Can anyone be obligated to receive asylum seekers? Can a meaningful distinction be made between "normal" peaks, for which the existing rules apply, and exceptional circumstances that require the political authority of the European Council?

The Union will have to strengthen its capacity to improvise. As in the euro crisis, successful improvisation has three elements: unified action by all, well-chosen and visible acts that can shape the future, and a balanced appeal to a root melody that will find resonance with the European public. Or, put another way: successful improvisation avoids division, powerlessness and arbitrariness. Only when it is achieved will the public be able to evaluate such a political performance and relate to it. Up to now this has not worked well. Yet however difficult, it must be possible. Border politics is identity politics.

The refugee crisis made crystal clear to the European public at large that the Greek–Turkish border is a European–Turkish external border. Why then is it so difficult to translate this awareness of shared responsibility for the external border into political commitment and an adequate structure?

One major reason is that the burdens of having shared external borders are not coupled with the benefits of dismantling the internal borders. Attending to the external border is a chore, a thankless task, while the price of dodging that duty is very low. Hence the irresponsible behaviour, first of Greece and Italy in the South (who for years let countless people walk through), and simultaneously of Germany and others in the North (who knew perfectly well that the "Dublin" rules placed an unfair burden on the South), then later of the Hungarians and their allies in the East (who do not want to grant asylum to others). To address this problem, the three camps need to improve their act more or less simultaneously, and the cost of refusing to participate must rise too.

So the Union needs to work towards a system that links looking after the shared external border politically and legally with benefiting from open internal borders. Public opinion will understand the connection. Translated into policy it means creating a visible balance between "Dublin" and "Schengen". True, this is not simple in legal terms, given that the two regimes do not coincide in their membership, but politically and for the public it is an obvious pairing. Illustrative in this sense is a stipulation in the provision that set up the European Border and Coastguard Agency in September 2016. If a member state neglects its border and so endangers the security of the whole, can the Agency intervene on its territory even against the will of that member state? For the constitutional nature of the Union it is a decisive question. Who has power in an emergency? The Union as a whole or its constituent parts? (As Carl Schmitt famously put it: "Sovereign is he who decides on the exception".)[38] As might have been expected, the Commission and

Parliament advocated that "Brussels" should have the upper hand in emergencies, whereas for member states with a vulnerable external border this was unacceptable. The Poles did not want to see German customs men on the Polish–Russian border without their permission, nor the Spaniards the French (it seems that not just Hitler but Napoleon is a recent memory). The outcome was a balancing act: if the member state concerned does not cooperate within 30 days and there is a fully developed emergency plan in place backed by the Council, the Commission can start the process of expelling the country from Schengen.[39] So the Union cannot, for example, send border guards to the Greek border against the wishes of Athens, but if all else fails it can exclude the country from freedom of movement. This solution makes sense in terms of sequencing, proportionality and cost. The Union must be able to close a possible hole in the border.

It makes obvious sense to include a comparable emergency clause in agreements about asylum. The argument goes that you endanger Schengen not only by neglecting your external borders but by failing to have your asylum system in order, or by failing to cooperate with a joint effort to deal with a major influx of refugees. Just as the emergency measure regarding the coast-guard can force frontline states Greece and Italy to behave responsibly, so this same agreement – and possibly only this agreement – could force Hungary, Poland and Slovakia to make a clear choice. No open internal borders without shared concern for all aspects of the common external border: both security and hospitality.

Only then does the tension remain bearable between the demands of protection necessitated by Europe's geographical position and the magnetic power of attraction exerted by Europe's prosperity, freedom and tolerance. Or, as the liberal realist politician Donald Tusk said on 6 May 2016, at the ceremony where the Charlemagne Prize was awarded to Pope Francis, in a suitably elevated tone for the occasion: "Why should we be proud of Europe? Why is it worth our concern, and – if need be – our protection and defence? It is because the spirit of love and freedom is still present here."[40]

In short, in Europe there can be no ethic of conviction without an ethic of responsibility.

4

Uprising:
the Atlantic crisis

The republic was not timeless, because it did not reflect by simple cor-
respondence the eternal order of nature [...]. The one thing most clearly
known about republics was that they came to an end in time, whereas a
theocentric universe perpetually affirmed monarchy [...]. It was not even
certain that the republic was the consequence of a principle.

J. G. A. Pocock[1]

Sovereignty does not reside in abstract principles. The French people did
not emancipate themselves from absolute monarchy in 1789 with the
declaration that "the principle of any sovereignty lies primarily in the
nation". True emancipation arrived in 1792, when citizens across France
rose up to defend the revolution against foreign kings. It is when a people
makes its own choices that it becomes sovereign. It is time for Europeans
to become sovereign.

Emmanuel Macron[2]

"Till death do us part"

The introduction of the right to divorce was never an innocent act. In Eng-
land of all places this should come as no surprise. The country's tumultuous
first "exit" from a pan-European order, by means of the 1534 Act of Supremacy, was the result of a Tudor king's wish to divorce his queen. It was Brexit
avant la lettre. The political and legal order challenged by Henry VIII, the

Church, was called "Rome". Today's second exit, *Anno Domini* 2020, will be from another order founded in "Rome", the Rome of the Treaties.

In 1957, at that Roman founding moment, membership of the European Economic Community was entered into for an indefinite period. For eternity, in other words. The six founding states stepped into a new era. To celebrate the rite of passage, on 25 March all the bells of the Eternal City rang out. The perpetuity stipulation was exceptional. The coal and steel treaty signed by those same six states in Paris six years before was for a mere 50 years. This infinite duration was an invention of Belgian minister Paul-Henri Spaak, chair of the treaty negotiations. Lawyers protested, but Spaak stuck to his guns.[3] Ties with the Community had to be irreversible and indissoluble, as in a marriage.

Something of this same *esprit communautaire* could be felt in the consternation among true believers when almost half a century later there was talk of an exit clause. Eastern European countries, on the threshold of accession, clung to the symbolic assurance that this Union was no prison of the peoples like the Soviet Union. But representatives of the six founding states, in some despair, wondered: What about the political bond? Was the Union like a station concourse where you could come and go at will? And would they not be offering Eurosceptics an open goal? On the contrary, said its advocates. Such a provision would not be used lightly.[4] Eventually it ended up in the Lisbon Treaty of 2007. "Any Member State may decide to withdraw from the Union in accordance with its own constitutional requirements." So begins the now famous Article 50, introducing the withdrawal procedure.[5]

It is worth recalling that no one anticipated the political forces this provision would unleash, first of all now, in Britain. But even back then, the symbolic significance for the Union of this finitude clause should not have been underestimated. The introduction of the right to divorce represents an existential departure from Brussels perpetuity thinking. The Union had to establish its existence on a new basis. It could no longer simply rely on a "yes" at the altar but needed to earn the support of unpredictable populations, day in, day out. The option of divorce made the Union, at a stroke, both more perishable and more democratic.

Out of the experience of a democratic republic's own transience and mortality there may arise a political will to manifest itself as a sovereign player in

116

historical time. This is the thesis of J. G. A. Pocock in his brilliant *The Machi-avellian Moment* (1975). The author locates the creation of modern political thought – by Machiavelli and his contemporaries such as Guicciardini – in the recognition of the finite nature of the *polis*, which entails both political emancipation and theological liberation from a history of salvation. Pocock speaks of "the moment in conceptualized time in which the republic was seen as confronting its own temporal finitude, as attempting to remain morally and politically stable in a stream of irrational events conceived as essentially destructive of all systems of secular stability".[6] Those who know themselves to be mortal must regard and arm themselves as chance entities in the river of time: an existential experience.

Something of that nature seemed to be happening to the European club of member states after the uppercut of the British referendum result of June 2016. The divorce disturbed its long cherished self-image and for a moment it feared for its survival. This awareness became even clearer after a right hook that came five months later, delivered by American voters in the form of their new president, when out of the experience of its own vulnerability a new will to live came to the fore. A self-definition in time and therefore also in space.

In three sequences I will show how, after that double whammy, the Union got up and dusted itself off, rather groggy but freed from the illusion of eternal fidelity and constancy.

Three episodes

AFTER THE BREXIT SHOCK: "WE'RE STILL ALIVE", 24–29 JUNE 2016

The result of the British referendum caused a huge shock on the morning of Friday 24 June. Many a European government leader had gone to bed around midnight that Thursday with an expectation that the result would be favour-able. Not without reason. In London, when the polling stations closed and for hours afterwards, opinion pollsters predicted victory for Remain; Tory champagne was on ice for a relieved celebration. The astonishment at dawn was immense. An abstract possibility suddenly became a political fact.

While that morning events and vituperations in London held the world spellbound, the spotlight moved across the rest of the Union. For months European leaders, at the request of 10 Downing Street, had done little but wait, watch and burn candles. Now suddenly the future not just of Britain but of Europe was at stake. An awareness sank in that "Brexit" would bring uncertainty and danger to the continental side of the Channel too. The departure of Europe's second largest economy – a major military and diplomatic power, proponent of the internal market, 12 per cent of the EU population – meant that the internal balance of power in the union would shift and Germany would be even more obviously the largest. Populists felt emboldened, from France to the Netherlands and Austria; further departures might follow and cause the Union to fall apart. Then there was the mutilated vision of Europe. A British departure did not merely betoken a loss, it was an amputation, a farewell to a country that for many had been a political, historical and cultural beacon – from Shakespeare to Parliament to The Beatles – and belonged indivisibly to "Europe".

In early reactions from Brussels, the consternation and indignation were tangible. Towards 7.00am, president of the European Parliament Martin Schulz rang Commission president Juncker: "Jean-Claude, this isn't looking good."[7] Both wanted the "deserters"[8] (Juncker's word) to initiate divorce proceedings right away to preclude uncertainty. In The Hague, Prime Minister Mark Rutte, whose country held the rotating presidency of the Council of Ministers, was thrust into a car heading to Brussels for emergency talks. "No hysteria, please," said European Council president Donald Tusk to the press shortly after 9.00am. "There is no legal vacuum". Moreover, "That which doesn't kill us makes us stronger".[9] (He thought he was quoting his father, rather than Friedrich Nietzsche.) Tusk's saying goes to the heart of the matter: the Union's priority was to demonstrate a will to survive; the departure was not a deathblow.

Around midday the Tusk-Schulz-Rutte-Juncker quartet issued a business-like declaration on behalf of the institutions and coordinated with the capitals: the Union regrets but respects the decision of British voters; this is an unprecedented situation but we are united in our response. The four staked out a remarkable number of positions regarding the coming divorce: it is best to follow the procedure for departure laid out in Article 50; there will be no renegotiation of the special British settlement reached with Cameron in February; we hope that the United Kingdom will remain a close partner; any agreement made with the departing member as a "third country" must reflect the interests of both sides and be balanced in terms of rights and obligations.[10] Plus – at the request of Schulz and Juncker – please make a start as soon as possible. (That same evening on German television, Schulz described it as "scandalous" that Cameron wanted to wait until October, thereby "taking an entire continent hostage", while Juncker, on another German channel, let it be known, with injured vanity, that he would "have liked the letter immediately".[11])

It was Chancellor Angela Merkel in Berlin who tempered their haste. In her declaration, around midday on the Friday, she spoke of a "blow to Europe", a situation that demanded "calm and prudence" and "historical consciousness", and therefore no jumping to conclusions.[12] Behind her caution lay a lack of preparation. Until 23 June there had been a quasi-ban at the Federal chancellery on thinking about a British departure: it simply must not happen. In Paris, President François Hollande showed a desire for decisive action. "Today History is knocking at the door", he said, without fear of cliché, so the Union needed to make a "leap forwards". Hollande said he would soon be discussing concrete initiatives with Merkel.[13]

That same Friday, the 28 secretaries of state and ministers of European affairs had their monthly meeting. Unusually, because of the dramatic situation, the French, German and Italian foreign ministers, Ayrault, Steinmeier and Gentilone, were in attendance. Disillusionment prevailed. During a private lunch, Britain's David Lidington spoke of "a bitter blow", others of "a day of mourning". Here too, with one voice, London was called upon to provide clarity quickly. In their written resolutions, however, the ministers deferred to their bosses; the summit several days later must set out the line to be taken.[14] Despite this, the next day six ministers came together before the eyes of the world in a Berlin castle, at the invitation of Frank-Walter Steinmeier. The foreign ministers of the six founding states – Germany, France, Italy and the Benelux countries – felt a special responsibility for Europe at this historic moment.[15] Their consultation created ill-feeling among those excluded, especially Spain and Portugal. The German chancellor too was discomforted: no new fault lines now; the unity of the 27 takes priority.

It was too soon to adopt the kind of hard line that advocates of a punitive expedition were contemplating. In many capitals people still hoped – like many in Britain itself – that the British might step back from the brink, after a second referendum perhaps, or a general election. Perhaps a fudge could be found that would reverse the whole thing. And the instinct for harshness was not universal. Brexit did not hit all member states equally, either politically or economically. The Irish lamented the departure of their neighbour, the Dutch and Scandinavians of a liberal, Atlantic ally, the French of a counterweight against the Germans, whereas in some circles in Belgium and Brussels there was a sense of release from a permanent spoke in the wheel and in Berlin, too, far from everyone was plunged into mourning. Given such diverse strategic interests, the preservation of the unity of the 27 was a challenge and a necessity that should not be underestimated.

What the 27 feared most were British delaying tactics. Within a few hours of the result, David Cameron announced his resignation. After the referendum he lacked the authority to start divorce proceedings; only a new prime minister could bear responsibility for the uncertain political and economic consequences of Brexit. But it might take months to appoint a successor. To prevent the British from using the intervening period for exploratory talks that could undermine their united front, on Sunday 26 June, the 27 – at the level of the EU ambassadors and the "sherpas" of the government leaders – agreed a common stance: "No negotiation without notification". The slogan worked as a barrier, behind which they waited en bloc for their opponent. All were keenly aware that Article 50 stipulates that the departing state leaves after a maximum of two years of negotiations, with or without a deal (unless the term is extended by unanimous agreement);[16] as a consequence, once a divorce letter was sent, the clock would be ticking. This inevitably worked to the Union's advantage.

After the weekend, the baton passed to the heads of government. Everyone rang everyone else. Summit chair Tusk travelled to Paris on the Monday morning and then in the afternoon to Berlin. In the light of the cameras, Angela Merkel received François Hollande and Matteo Renzi that evening. At the European Council meeting of Tuesday 28 June, David Cameron informed his European colleagues. They had little more to discuss with him. The written conclusions – devoted to migration, economics and foreign policy – limit themselves to a laconic statement on the final page: "The UK Prime Minister informed the European Council about the outcome of the referendum in the UK".[17] Cameron was given a message for his successor: his compatriots should not expect to have the benefits of membership without its burdens.

It only remained to have a good diplomatic weep. Afterwards Cameron told the British press it was a shame that people at home had not been able to hear it: The prime minister of Estonia telling how the Royal Navy once helped to preserve the independence of his country. The prime minister of the Czech Republic on the many Czechs who made their homes in Britain after fleeing persecution in 1968. The French president on how he would join Cameron later in the week to commemorate the soldiers who died on the Somme for freedom and democracy. The Irish taoiseach on how the two neighbours, despite conflict dating back many centuries, are such good partners today.[18] Briefly the Brussels shutters opened, briefly fragments of European history could be seen – which the prime minister had never managed to place in the limelight during his utilitarian "Remain" campaign – and briefly the historical-political basis of the Union shone through. But it was far too late – emotion for politeness' sake.

The informal special summit the next day was crucial. The heads of government of what quickly became known as the EU27, plus EU presidents Tusk and Juncker, discussed their shock. Behind closed doors the mood, according to one of those present, was "halfway between panic and bravura". The public declaration was sober and considered. Everyone now realized that the British government controlled the timing of the divorce application; there was no point frustratedly demanding notification. The leaders confirmed their position concerning the procedure and the negotiating principles that had been staked out before the weekend by the quartet. They also reinforced an important point, stressed afterwards by Tusk: "Leaders made it crystal clear today that access to the single market requires acceptance of all four freedoms, including the freedom of movement. There will be no single market à la carte."[19] Patience with British cherry-picking had run out; if everyone signed up for the perks alone, the Union was finished. Looking to themselves, they decided on political reflection on their future at 27, beginning in the autumn. Within five days of the referendum panic, the European Union had recovered its composure. It would face the British in battle formation: the divorce principles, procedure and chains of command were clearly outlined. An unexpected success, proof of a survival instinct.

Danger unites. The European Union might fall apart. The atmosphere of threat and fear, tinged with resentment and anger towards its originator, explains how quickly all parties agreed to the principles according to which the divorce negotiations would be entered into and how firm they would be in their stance towards London. "We are determined to remain united and work in the framework of the EU" was the message after the meeting.[20]

A basis for the procedure was there in the Treaty. Article 50 provides a framework for the "orderly withdrawal" of a member state, as opposed to a disorderly break taking place outside Union law. It was the only way to prevent economic and legal chaos. The departure clause had never been used, however, and it left a great deal open, so every word was weighed.

Chains of command quickly became clear as well. In the first few hours after the referendum a typical Brussels battle broke out. Who would negotiate with the British on behalf of the EU27? The Commission – Juncker's chief-of-staff was already warming up for the role – or the European Council, which on Friday 24 June had with all speed formed a task force? Not just obvious rivalry between the institutions this, but a conspicuous clash of visions for the Union's future, such as can emerge precisely at moments of truth. Within a few days the European Council took charge. The assembly of heads of government, of which the Commission president is a member, set out the parameters and the other institutions played their roles within them. Brexit was a *Chefsache*.

The resolute front against the British contrasted with uncertainty about the European Union's own future. Survival, fine, but to do what? Because of that doubt, the 27 made a rudderless, feeble impression. Hesitation in thinking through the consequences of Brexit was understandable. A politician who recognizes a problem is expected to provide a solution. None was on offer. In the first few days there were merely declarations of intent, on loosely grouped topics such as border controls, defence and youth unemployment. Expansion of policy instead of new politics. It convinced no one.

The referendum result ran counter to the axiom of old European politics. Since the coal-and-steel days of Schuman and Adenauer, the interweaving of economic interests had been taken as a guarantee of peace and prosperity; economic interdependence would automatically produce grateful populations. British voters gave the lie to this axiom by 52 per cent to 48: rather control over immigration and our own laws (through exiting) than economic growth (through the internal market).[21] In founding logic this was unthinkable, and yet the simplicity of the Brexiteers' slogan "Take back control" trumped any such presupposition. It demanded an adjustment to the doctrine.

Another fundamental Brussels assumption perished too: the certainty that Europe's movement always goes in one direction, according to an irresistible logic of "spill-over" – more countries, more policy fields, an "ever closer union". This irreversibility proved an illusion. Suddenly the European Union became aware of its historical vulnerability. It did not thank the British for its rude awakening.

Yet this was an existential moment: a body politic experiencing its own mortality has to detach itself conceptually from its timeless foundations. It was Europe's Machiavellian moment, time for it – to translate Pocock's term into the words Angela Merkel would use a year later – to "take its destiny into its own hands".

THE LONG WAIT FOR A LETTER: 30 JUNE 2016–25 MARCH 2017

Having survived the first shock, the European club was faced with two tasks: organize the divorce and forestall copy-cat moves. The first was easier to achieve than the second – there is a stark contrast between the united front shown towards London and the fumbling declarations about the Union's own post-Brexit future.*

---

* A stern Henry Kissinger said in mid-July 2016, "Three weeks after Brexit, not one European statesman has articulated a vision for Europe's future. They are the continent that built the international world. And no one has stood up with the vision of Churchill. They're talking about tactical matters while they're in the process of giving up the essence of what they struggled for and what they've represented throughout history" ("World Chaos and World Order: Conversations with Henry Kissinger", online verbatim transcript of an interview by Jeffrey Goldberg, published in *The Atlantic*, December 2016).

By the end of June, the EU27 had resolutely lined up behind the barrier marked "No negotiation without notification". As long as no divorce letter came from London, there was no need to negotiate. To their own astonishment – every capital knew from experience the British art of fomenting discord – this front held, even when the wait proved far longer than expected. David Cameron's successor Theresa May, taking office in mid-July, asked to be given until her party congress in Birmingham in October. There the new prime minister announced that she would not send the letter until late March 2017, nine months after the referendum.

The Union did not allow the wait to go to waste. The procedure and principles of the divorce, the broad outlines of which were laid down immediately in June, were elaborated upon from the summer onwards. Article 50, although short and untested, gave the EU27 self-confidence. While in Britain public and politicians debated passionately for months over the first two sentences (Who sends the departure letter? Can the government send it without the permission of parliament?), the Union was preoccupied with the third. It runs, "In the light of the guidelines provided by the European Council, the Union shall negotiate and conclude an agreement with that State, setting out the arrangements for its withdrawal, *taking account of the framework for its future relationship with the Union*".[22] In this ambiguous clause Brussels lawyers read: first the divorce settlement, including the bill for outstanding obligations on the part of the leaver, then an agreement on the future relationship. In London the interpretation was different and there was a desire to see both conversations run in parallel. So a battle arose over the sequencing.

For the internal organization – Who decides? Who negotiates? Who makes an agreement? – little improvisation was needed. The Treaty provides for a subtle interplay between institutions and there was a desire to stick to that closely.* In late July 2016 president Juncker opted for Michel Barnier, former EU commissioner and former French foreign minister, as

---

* After the sentence cited above, which allows the European Council of heads of government to establish the "guidelines" for arrangements for leaving, Article 50 goes on: "That agreement shall be negotiated in accordance with Article 218(3) of the Treaty on the Functioning of the European Union. It shall be concluded on behalf of the Union by the Council, acting by a qualified majority, after obtaining the consent of the European Parliament." Article 218 points to the Commission as negotiator, mandated as such by the Council of Ministers.

negotiator-in-chief for the Union. Of course there was no escaping institutional tensions. When the Commission stole too much of the limelight for the member states' liking – the capitals watched like hawks the influence of Juncker's hardline chief-of-staff – government leaders pushed back. At the summit of December 2016 they declared that the European Council would remain "permanently seized of the matter" – something new for an institution that on paper comes together just four times a year – and amend the guidelines as necessary.[23] True, the degree of organizational detail suggests bureaucratic battles were going on under the radar,[24] but the gathered leaders claimed the political leadership. Their guidelines were ready as an answer from the Union side to Theresa May's divorce application, whenever it came.[25]

More problematic was the self-reflection that Brexit forced upon the 27. After the summer, the phase of denial was over. Anyone still regarding British Euroscepticism as a local phenomenon was making a "fatal error".[26] The Union had an existential problem. How could the confidence of its own citizens be restored? What should be the goal, now that its eternal foundations were challenged? Such questions were postponed until a series of summit meetings that ran from Bratislava in September to a festive summit in Rome on 25 March 2017, the sixtieth anniversary of the Union. At the same time there was a realization that effective initiatives had little chance of success before the French and German elections in 2017. Without a fresh mandate from their electorates, Berlin and Paris could not commit to real change, so a debate about the future risked remaining unsatisfactory for a while. Nevertheless, this phase revealed a great deal about the wounded Union's will to survive.

Three phenomena stand out. First, Germany visibly took the lead, while the balance of power on the continent shifted. Angela Merkel seized the initiative. Disintegration was a threat to Germany economically and politically. In one August week the chancellor met no fewer than fifteen fellow heads of government. She adopted a coordinating role, inventoried all their positions – not behind the scenes as she had done repeatedly during the euro crisis but in the full light of day. On Monday 22 August she went with François Hollande to visit Matteo Renzi on an island off the Italian coast. Countless front pages showed pictures of the aircraft carrier from which the trio came ashore.

Such photos threw the Italian host into ecstasies. After years of frustration at the Paris-London-Berlin power triangle, Brexit suddenly made Italy part of "the new Big Three". In Warsaw the chancellor met the prime ministers of Poland, Hungary, the Czech Republic and Slovakia – the Visegrád quartet. The Balkans came to Berlin a day later, with Bulgaria, Croatia, Slovenia and Austria, while the Netherlands was invited to dine with Denmark, Sweden and Finland (to the dismay of Belgium and Luxembourg, who saw their cherished Benelux split apart, Dutch Prime Minister Mark Rutte accepted). By coordinating all these groups, Germany placed itself where Merkel feels most at home politically: at the centre.

Secondly, from Brussels came the beginnings of a response. EU presidents Tusk and Juncker used the summer to formulate a substantive answer to the Brexit vote. They each presented it on their own stage in mid-September: the Bratislava summit (16 September) and the annual "State of the Union" in Strasbourg (two days earlier). Although the Brussels press corps detected rivalry, it is striking that both men announced the same change of course: Europe must learn to protect. In a firm letter of invitation to Bratislava, Tusk wrote to his colleagues, "People quite rightly expect their leaders to protect the space they live in and ensure their security. If the belief that we have abandoned this responsibility is further strengthened, they will start looking for alternatives. And they will find them." In other words, the revolt of British voters might occur elsewhere too. The European Council president concluded that it was crucial to restore the balance between freedom and security, and between openness and protection.[27] Given that the Union became great by opening borders, presenting opportunities and creating space, this was a sharp and substantial volte-face. In his Strasbourg speech the Commission president likewise used terms such as "protect", "defend", "make resilient" and "preserve our way of life".[28] He too concentrated on immigration, terrorism and globalization, on extra border guards and sharper controls on the external borders, without forgetting Europe's "social dimension", the counterweight to freedom of movement. And whereas a year before he had passionately spoken out about Europe's evangelical task in the refugee crisis, he was now humble and stuck to the script; this was no time for Brussels missionary zeal. Both presidents gave their institutions a crucial assignment for the new Union: translate a better balance between openness and protection into concrete decisions. (The immediate outcome of the Bratislava summit was disappointing: a mere 200 European border guards to assist the Bulgarians at the Turkish border.)[29]

The third remarkable phenomenon during those winter months of waiting for a British letter was that a call for "flexibility" put the unity of the club to the test. Yes, the 27 needed to maintain a united front, but also – so it was said in several West European capitals – they had to demonstrate mobility and vitality, and show citizens results. If not all countries wanted to take part in initiatives, an advance guard must be able to move "forward". This is a long-standing tendency, its terminology thrashed out over the years by academics and think tanks ("inner group", "two-speed Europe", "core Europe", "differentiated integration"), but a vital desire to break out of stagnation gave it a fresh boost. There was resistance too. Poland and other Central and Eastern European countries were nervous of ideas that entailed A- and B-membership, which explains why Berlin had always been reticent. But in early 2017 the chancellor released the handbrake, as did the Benelux countries.[30] At a meeting in Versailles shortly before the meeting in Rome, the leaders of France, Germany, Italy and Spain declared themselves in favour of "a multi-speed Europe". Countries that wished to move forward a little more quickly than others must be allowed to do so. The Commission also proposed such a scenario in a white paper on the future of Europe.[31] However, the question remains: might not this debate about "how", engaged in with such passion, in fact be compensation for disunity on the main question of "what"?

On Saturday 25 March 2017 the festive summit took place in Rome. Theresa May stayed at home, her letter still not sent. In the room where the Treaty of Rome was once signed, speeches were held, the occasional tear was shed and the leaders put their names to an insipid declaration.[32] Yet there was a great sense of satisfaction. At a difficult moment the 27 had demonstrated unity and the will to face the future together. Their club had survived a life-threatening attack. Acutely aware now of its perishability, leaders mustered a new readiness to defend and protect the Union, highlighting its capacity to change and to provide security for their citizens. They were made all the keener to do so by the fact that this festive moment was rather more difficult than anybody had imagined six months before.

AFTER TRUMP: MERKEL AND MACRON SPEAK OUT,
8 NOVEMBER 2016–28 MAY 2017

Two men in a gold-plated lift, one giving the thumbs-up, the other grinning. The photo was published in all the newspapers and it was a nightmare for many. 12 November 2016, New York. On the left, Donald J. Trump, three days earlier elected as American president. On the right, Nigel Farage, former UKIP leader and self-styled boss of the Brexit camp. The political year 2016, with its dual electoral assault on the postwar liberal order, captured in a single image. Analysts were not alone in pointing to the parallels; an enthusiastic Trump had himself held out to his supporters the prospect of his victory as a glorious "Brexit plus plus plus (you know what I mean)".[33] Even worse for politicians and diplomats in Berlin, Paris and London, Farage was the first politician from Europe to meet the president-elect. He apparently possessed that coveted thing: access to the new power. To make sure all knew it, he circulated the photo himself on Twitter.

With Trump, Brexit suddenly appeared in a more ominous light. Until then the rest of Europe had been able to regard the British as apostates, lamentable victims of a false doctrine; perhaps they would backtrack once they saw the error of their ways, once departure from the world's largest trading block started to cause economic pain – as was bound to happen. Trump disturbed that picture. The world-historical perspective threatened to shift. Now the Brexiteers had the most powerful man in the world as their best friend, an ally in the White House. Their grinning said: Who's on the winning side of history now? Who's so smart?

The hope that it would not be as bad as was feared, that the new man would speak a different language as president than he had during the campaign, proved groundless: it was still America First. In mid-January 2017, a few days before his inauguration, Trump gave a lengthy interview to *Bild Zeitung* and *The Times* in which he took aim at European unification, a strategic priority in Washington since Truman and Eisenhower. He called the British exit "smart", predicted it would be a great success and said, "So if you ask me, I believe others will leave".[34] A categorical undermining strategy. Aimed directly at Berlin. Trump called the Union at root "a vehicle for Germany", grumbled about the German trade surplus and called the German chancellor's open door policy a "catastrophic mistake".[35] Asked whom he trusted more, Merkel or Putin, he said, "I start off trusting Putin and Merkel – but let's see how long that lasts, it might not last long at all".[36] Not the slightest distinction between a democratic ally and an authoritarian former Cold War rival.

That same 16 January Angela Merkel reacted to the interview with two as yet little noticed sentences. "I believe we Europeans have our destiny in our own hands. I will continue pressing for intensive and most importantly forward-looking cooperation between the 27 member states."[37] In line with her words and deeds since the Brexit summer, European unity remained her strategic compass, but now, in the Trump winter, she linked that commitment to new words that sounded striking from the mouth of a German: our destiny as Europeans, in our own hands. The new president truly was prepared to let go of Europe. His uninhibitedly nationalistic inauguration speech of 20 January confirmed as much.

How did Europe respond? The first public blow was struck by the national-populist front. In Koblenz, the day after Trump's inauguration in Washington, Marine Le Pen, Frauke Petry, Geert Wilders and Matteo Salvini, standard bearers of the nationalist Internationale, stood together on stage for the first time, exuding self-confidence. In Brussels there was silence.

Earlier that week Commission president Juncker had tried to dissuade the White House from promoting Brexit: "We don't go around calling on Ohio to pull out of the United States".[38] A slightly misplaced remark, given that it assumes a relationship between equals – don't shoot at me and I won't shoot at you. That is, of course, the rub. The pairing is far from symmetrical. Europe depends on America for its security, on the US army and US nuclear weapons. Ironic threats are therefore no less feeble than appeasement by a vassal unless underpinned by power, by the capability to take one's destiny into one's own hands.

The classic term for the capacity of a state to act on its own behalf, theorized upon in the wake of Machiavelli since Bodin, Hobbes and Locke, is "sovereignty". On that basis the European states gave shape to their diplomatic relations after the Thirty Years War (1618–48) and by extension shaped the international world. And it was from that foundation that they turned away, after three centuries and two devastating world wars (1914–45), to build a new order based on treaties and universal values, a "post-sovereign"

Europe. They prefer to ignore the fact that this new order is determined and defended by American sovereignty. But now that, under Trump, America's protection can no longer automatically be relied upon, such willed blindness is not just hypocritical, it is becoming irresponsible.

Strikingly, the term "sovereignty" is making a comeback. It has of course been a battle cry of anti-integration forces since the Maastricht Treaty ratification debates, if not before, coming from bastions as diverse as the French Gaullist right, the German Constitutional Court and the British Parliament. The 2016 Brexit referendum forms the apotheosis of this discourse that sets national sovereignty and European integration in opposition to each other; the slogan "take back control" reignited a sovereigntist claim to be reconquering lost domains, leaving the Remain side speechless. But now the term was appropriated by the other side too. "European sovereignty" was the subject of a major speech by the young, unapologetically pro-European French presidential candidate Emmanuel Macron, on 10 January 2017 at the Humboldt University in Berlin. Why concentrate on "sovereignty"? "Because sovereignty means the capacity of acting in concrete terms to protect ourselves and defend our values. Because I cannot accept leaving the idea of 'sovereignty' to far-right or far-left populists and their lies."[39] Summit chair Donald Tusk chose the same vocabulary a few weeks later in a letter to the 27 heads of government. Unprecedented was the way the Polish liberal addressed in the same sentence the "worrying declarations" by the new American administration and threats from Russia, China and the Middle East. He wrote, "The disintegration of the European Union will not lead to the restoration of some mythical, full sovereignty of its member states, but to their real and factual dependence on the great superpowers: the United States, Russia and China. Only together can we be fully independent."[40]

Both men encouraged the Europeans to look their historical situation in the face. Under the American defence shield, the European states had built a Union of trade, laws and values, a thing of great worth, but to defend themselves and their Union in the era of Trump – which is also the era of Putin, Xi, Erdogan and Assad – they must also give themselves the capacity to act.

In the geopolitical jungle, economic power is a major trump card, as we learnt from the battle for the White House fought between Brexit-London and the Union. On 28 January 2017 British Prime Minister Theresa May became Trump's first foreign visitor after his inauguration. A diplomatic coup. Ten days earlier she had outlined in a major Brexit speech her vision of a "Global Britain" and, in passing, said to the public at home and to her European partners, "No deal [...] is better than a bad deal".[41] In other words, I can always walk away from the table. But then Britain would lose its largest export market and face possible economic chaos. Without an alternative the threat is not credible. She therefore needed just one thing from the White House: the promise of a quick US–UK trade agreement. Otherwise the ominous statement by Obama of April 2016 on the prospects for such a bilateral deal ("back of the queue") would remain hanging over the Brexit future like a curse. To propitiate Trump the dealmaker, Theresa May was prepared to roll out the reddest of all carpets; she offered the president, rather unpopular among the British, a state visit, including a round of golf on the royal course at Balmoral. The charm offensive worked. During a walk he grasped her hand flirtatiously within sight of the cameras. May beamed (to the dismay of many women in her home audience).

Two months later, on 17 March, Angela Merkel visited the White House. Again a memorable moment took place in public around a handshake, when the host, despite urgings from photographers, gruffly refused. (A lesser guest would have been humiliated, but with a sovereign smile at such small-mindedness the chancellor made allies of the press posse and through them the global audience.) This visit too was all about trade. Negotiations on the ambitious European–American trade deal TTIP were at a standstill because of resistance from the public on both sides. Several times Trump tried to tempt the chancellor into a bilateral accord between the United States and Germany. He failed. Afterwards the way that happened leaked. *The Times* quoted a highly placed German politician as saying, "Ten times Trump asked her if he could negotiate a trade deal with Germany. Every time she replied, 'You can't do a trade deal with Germany, only the EU'. On the eleventh refusal, Trump finally got the message, 'Oh, we'll do a deal with Europe then'."[42]

Meanwhile European voters were also responding to Brexit-&-Trump. The national-populist wave that rolled towards them over the Atlantic Ocean and the Channel broke against the mainland. In a first test in December 2016, the re-run final round of the Austrian presidential elections, the pro-European green candidate Van der Bellen defeated his right-wing-nationalist opponent Hofer, advocate of an "Öxit", by a larger margin than in the annulled pre-Trump duel. All of Europe then watched Geert Wilders' national-populist Partij Voor de Vrijheid fail to achieve a historic score in the Dutch national elections on 15 March, in which the centre right came out on top and the pro-European liberals and the greens significantly increased their share of the vote. But the contest that truly held the Union in its thrall was the French presidential election, with its final bout between pro-Europe centrist Emmanuel Macron and Front National leader Marine Le Pen. An antifascist left-right alliance, plus her confused plea for an exit from the euro, put paid to her chances; Macron won with two thirds of the votes. On 7 May French and European flags flew around his victory podium in Paris; the new man stepped up onto it to the sound of Beethoven's *Ode to Joy*, anthem of the Union, and after his speech came the *Marseillaise*. Message: France is staying; France is back in Europe. After France the sense of relief was nowhere greater than in Germany.

So ten months after the Brexit vote, partly thanks to the spectre of Trump, the acute danger of an Öxit, Nexit or Frexit had been averted. But the American president had not just poked the Brexit fire for a moment, he had revealed a deeper vulnerability. More threatening than the undermining of the European Union (bad enough in itself) was the detrimental impact Trump might have on the security of the European continent, as safeguarded by the North Atlantic Treaty Organization. During his election campaign he had called NATO "obsolete". For decades he had believed that the American taxpayer was being fleeced and allies in Europe (and Asia) should pay more. Was the United States under its forty-fifth president still fully committed to the defence of its European allies? From Estonia to Portugal, doubts prevailed.

The Trumpian moment of truth came in late May 2017, when the American president paid his first visit to Europe. After a stop in Rome for an audience with the Pope, he attended the NATO summit in Brussels. During a public speech at the new headquarters in Brussels, the American president insulted his audience – Merkel, Macron, May, Rajoy, Gentilone, Trudeau, Erdogan and 20 other presidents and prime ministers – by lecturing them on their inadequate defence spending. Fine as far as it goes, since in essence that was not unjustified in most cases. Disturbing was Trump's blunt refusal to confirm NATO solidarity, despite intense pressure from the allies beforehand. According to one commentator, the president seemed "intent on turning NATO's d'Artagnan doctrine – 'one for all and all for one' – into a mafia tough's protection racket: 'Nice territory you got here; hate to see anything happen to it'."[43]

She had swallowed a great deal, but here something snapped – and something happened. On Sunday 28 May in a Bavarian beer tent, Angela Merkel put it like this: "The times in which we can completely rely on others are to some extent over. This is what I have experienced in the last few days. And that is why I can only say that we Europeans must really take our destiny into our own hands."[44] The immediate response was a full minute of applause from 2,500 CSU supporters. Those two sentences were then discussed for days in Washington, Moscow, London and Paris. They were more than election rhetoric (although the chancellor was not averse to stealing the European cloak from her SPD challenger Martin Schulz, who in early 2017 had swapped the presidency of the Strasbourg Parliament for the Berlin political arena). Merkel's turn of phrase was more active than when she first deployed "our destiny in our own hands", in January. Then it had been a question of *having* our destiny in our own hands. Now she wanted us to "*take* our destiny *into* our own hands". To act, therefore, ourselves. Not wait and see. For that reason too, the thought was picked up broadly only now and made an impression on the public. At issue was Europe's political and geopolitical emancipation from America, with the consequences that flowed from it. This was a geopolitical uprising, by Europe in the first place, and no less so by Germany.

It requires of Germany a massive change of mentality. Since its origins in 1949, the Federal Republic has complied with American hegemony, grateful for its freedom and enjoying the opportunity to become Europe's economic superpower. When Trump blatantly pulled the rug from under this double arrangement, Merkel drew her own conclusions: we must be able to look after ourselves. No wonder her "beer tent speech" touched a chord in Washington. The emancipation of one is a loss of power for another. Both Richard Haass, dean of America's foreign policy establishment, and his opposite pole, NSA whistle-blower Edward Snowden, spoke of a "watershed"; both men tend to read world events through the lens of American power. The end of the *Pax Americana* seemed at hand.

The extent to which Merkel in Bavaria sounded like a French president was striking. "Take our destiny into our own hands", is standard rhetoric in Paris, an expression of the will to act, almost synonymous with political freedom. Even more French were the words that followed: "... of course in friendship with the United States of America, in friendship with Great Britain and wherever possible as good neighbours with other countries too, including Russia." America along with the British on one side, Russia on the other: her predecessors Konrad Adenauer or Helmut Kohl could never have brought themselves to say such a thing. By contrast it was completely in line with the European thinking of President De Gaulle (who made France an independent nuclear power and kept the British out of the European Community in 1963 as too pro-American) and President Mitterrand (who in 1991 entered the euro along with Germany, leaving Britain outside). These French politicians aimed to make Europe an independent pole in a multipolar world, not in Washington's lap but a power among powers. New man Emmanuel Macron ostentatiously placed himself within this tradition. He used the symbolism of his first greeting by Trump on 25 May by looking the American straight in the eye and giving him a handshake like a vice, producing white knuckles and tense jaws: alpha males together.* Receiving Russian President Vladimir Putin, four days later in Versailles, Macron played the card of Europe's values and press freedom. Merkel did what her predecessors since Adenauer may have wanted to do but could not. She endorsed that French paragon of self-consciousness.

The defeat of France meant that in 1945 it could win back its capacity to act as a sovereign player on the world stage only by using the lever of Europe. For Germany, which after the shame of Nazism renounced foreign policy ambition and military power and could continue to do so under the American defence umbrella, the vital moment had now dawned. *Anno Trump* the country was rudely awakened from its geopolitical coma. That was the watershed – a Machiavellian moment in Berlin, projected onto Europe as a whole.

---

* Just to make sure, Macron provided commentary on his act: "My handshake with him, it wasn't innocent. It's not the be-all and the end-all of a policy, but it was a moment of truth. [...] You have to show you won't make small concessions – not even symbolic ones. [...] Donald Trump, the Turkish president or the Russian president see relationships in terms of a balance of power. That doesn't bother me. [...] I won't let anything pass, it's how one gets respected" (Macron interviewed in *Journal du Dimanche*, 27 May 2017).

Redesigning the Union and the continent

Meanwhile, on Wednesday 29 March 2017 Prime Minister Theresa May had written the long-awaited divorce letter, starting shot of the Article 50 procedure.[45] In six pages, her government calmly set out its negotiating stance. "We are leaving the European Union, but we are not leaving Europe", May begins. "We want to remain committed partners and allies to our friends across the continent." At the same time that distinction between Union and continent – she even at one point calls it *"our* continent" – gives this congenial intention the appearance of a tactical move.

On leaving, Britain loses access to its most important market, so in the economic sphere, the heart of the negotiations, the Union is in a strong position. With regard to security, however, the British state has a great deal to offer the EU27, May suggested in her letter; the army, diplomacy and police services that London has at its disposal leave those of other states, with the exception of France, far behind. In a time of terrorism and geopolitical uncertainty, this capacity of the British state to act is an additional trump card and, as May delicately puts it, "Europe's security is more fragile today than at any time since the end of the Cold War." It therefore sounds like a barely concealed threat when she writes, "In security terms a failure to reach agreement [on trade] would mean our cooperation in the fight against crime and terrorism would be weakened." The prime minister expresses three times the UK's wish to deal simultaneously with economic and security issues in the negotiations. Unsurprisingly, the Union preferred first to settle all withdrawal aspects (mainly economic) before deciding on the future relationship (a new trade regime and security issues).

In late 2017 London caved in and accepted the Brussels sequencing. Both sides also opted for a close-to-two-year transition period following the UK's date of formal departure, then set for 29 March 2019, during which EU law would continue to apply. This would give everyone two more years to disentangle the complexities of the new situation. For London: how to become a State again, after having been a Member State for so long. And for the Union: how to conceive a relationship with a state that is no longer in the Union but is still a neighbour on the European continent, a state whose departure – although it cannot say so – simultaneously must and must *not* become a success. To deal with these intractable issues between now and 2021, the experience gained since the Brexit referendum would need to be put to good use.

The European Union has already learnt much about itself from the Brexit-&-Trump moment of truth. We have seen how it displayed a peculiar combination of frailty and firmness, resentment and determination, panic and bravura – signs of a new will to live. It is showing a new awareness of the need to protect itself and its citizens. This substantial change in policy, initiated by EU presidents Juncker and Tusk in the summer of 2016 and taken up since then by French President Macron in calls for *"une Europe qui protège"*, was in evidence in more recent decisions on border protection, foreign investment screening and defence cooperation.[46] An awareness is growing that European security and "sovereignty" are not a given.* All in all, the Union is discovering what it means to act together as a body politic in the flow of time, and the discovery is not confined to the leaders but is shared by public opinion. It is a momentous change from the Brussels rule-making factory of years past, but the sentiment is still rather thin, which may explain why the Union is not yet able to deal coolly with the United Kingdom, the first future ex-member of the club.

In maintaining a united front, the EU27 have been helped by the messy state of British politics and the weakness of Theresa May's government, made worse by her own miscalculation in calling an early general election, in which she spectacularly lost her majority, in the spring of 2017. After she failed three times to get her withdrawal agreement through Parliament, her successor Boris Johnson fared little better and called for a snap election in late 2019. For sure, the UK's internal chaos is a joy for political sketch writers and a pantomime, but it results in part from the contradictions inherent in what it means to be a member state of the European Union, a sovereign state in a sovereign union. What Whitehall civil servants already knew, the Westminster political class and the wider public are now discovering: the European Union is not a prison but a golden cage, devilishly difficult to leave.

The UK's domestic shenanigans (together with the "fire and fury" of the

---

* Although it is a good place to start, the focus on protection does not yet address another sentiment expressed in the UK referendum: voters' desire to have a say, to have a stronger grip on political decision-making (a theme discussed in Chapter 7).

Trump White House) have reassured European leaders and Brussels negotiators that there will most likely be no domino effect, but the logic remains
that Brexit must play its role of antithesis, the antidote to those who want
to harm the European Union from within. As ever, the UK must not be seen to
have its cake and eat it too.

Some in Britain have the impression that the rest of Europe wants to
"punish" the country. They have reason to imagine so. At times, the Brussels machinery seemed to be in a divorce logic: first get them out. Hence the
early focus on financial obligations and citizens' rights – the international
law equivalents of the apportionment of property plus alimony and visiting
rights. The Brussels refusal for much of 2017 to talk about the future relationship as long as there was not "sufficient progress" on withdrawal matters
looked like the vindictive reaction of an abandoned spouse.

This impression was reinforced by the set-up of the negotiations. The
Brussels side piled one demand upon another. The Commission had initially
estimated the departure bill at around €60 billion, but a few weeks later a
sum of €100 billion was doing the rounds, rumoured to be the result of Poland
and France wanting the leaving party to pay its contribution for the entire
term of the budget, ending in 2020.[47] Similarly, the citizens' rights proposal
with which the Union began negotiations implied that current EU citizens
in Britain would in future have more rights than British citizens, clearly an
unreasonable demand. The unity of the EU27 was not as solid as it appeared;
it was attainable because every member state somehow saw its own wishes
met in the internal preparatory talks. Difficult issues were avoided, with a
provocation aimed at the British as a result. On neither the British nor the
European side was the public being prepared for negotiations, for give and
take. A risky situation, since ideological confrontation with the UK is also the
path of least resistance within the 27.

Perhaps the strongest marker of this internal unity has been the Union's
support for Ireland. Although London and the Union declared their political determination to find "flexible and imaginative" solutions for Ireland as
early as April 2017, it was still very hard to imagine how a "hard" British–Irish
border could technically be avoided if the UK left the internal market and
the customs union (that is, without introducing a customs border between
Northern Ireland and the rest of the UK).[48] Rejecting Theresa May's Chequers

proposal of summer 2018 on this point, the EU27 suggested the insurance or "backstop" of a prolonged stay by the UK in an EU–UK customs union, should that be required to avoid a future hard border. In late 2018, this solution of last resort, considered a trap by radical Brexiteers, who feared it entailed the risk of permanent rule-taking and "vassalage", became the main stumbling block on the road to approval for the withdrawal agreement in the House of Commons. Although some voices warned that on the European side too, a "no deal Brexit" could have political and strategic consequences of a magnitude outweighing the risk of a hard border on the island of Ireland, patience with London had run out and the "EU26" stood firmly behind the Irish government (which had effectively been given a veto on the withdrawal process).[49] In late 2019, PM Boris Johnson broke the stalemate by reverting to the idea of an "all-island" regulatory zone for farming, food and manufacturing on Ireland. This compromise, backed by Dublin and the rest of the EU, was rejected by his Northern-Irish coalition partner, thereby adding weight to calls for a general election.

Beyond resentment and tactical considerations, however, there was another reason why European hardliners won the day internally. Leading European voices considered that the political costs of a "soft Brexit" outweighed the economic costs of a "hard Brexit"; they calculated that energizing anti-European populists at home would harm their societies' security more than diminished trade with the UK. As long as this is the case, the European side will prefer a "hard" to a "soft" Brexit. Yet this calculation will not be made by all 27 governments in the same manner – the Dutch government, for instance, will want to soften the economic blow of Brexit – so negotiations on the future relationship will see rising tensions among the EU27 as they discuss how these painful trade-offs should be made.

One final consideration. For all concerned it will be important to think beyond the hoops and hurdles of the withdrawal process and turn all thoughts to the end stage. Brexit will entail the complete reconfiguration of interstate relations in Europe. This aspect has been underestimated to the point of negligence. The Brussels machinery treats Brexit as a withdrawal from the EU institutions and frameworks, not from the Union as a club of member states on the continent. It was against this divorce logic that the UK put forward a discourse of neighbourhood. (May: "We are leaving the European Union, we are not leaving Europe".) London had a point. Withdrawing from the Brussels framework is perhaps not even the essence of Brexit. But London too has failed to digest fully how interstate relations will need to adjust. It is no coincidence that the most intractable, most explosive issues so far have been matters of bilateral relations.

Two examples stand out: Ireland of course, but also Spain. Questions concerning borders and identity politics that had been laid to rest by means of joint EU membership have flared up. In the Union's draft reply to Theresa May's letter of notification, Madrid ensured that an incidental but combustible sentence was included, placing Gibraltar on the political agenda.* Within two days it led to unprecedented war rhetoric and a nostalgia for Falklands heroism. "Thirty-five years ago this week another woman prime minister [Margaret Thatcher] sent a taskforce halfway across the world to defend the freedom of another small group of British people against another Spanish-speaking country," said former Conservative leader Michael Howard, "and I'm absolutely certain that our current prime minister will show the same resolve in standing by the people of Gibraltar". An unprecedented rhetorical escalation, concerning an internal Spanish veto on the Gilbraltan aspects, one not even applicable to the divorce itself but to a future EU–UK trade deal.[50] Unsurprisingly, the Gibraltar incident reinforced the fear, in the Republic of Ireland and Northern Ireland, of the return of a "hard" British–Irish border as a result of Brexit, putting the peace process in Northern Ireland at risk. These are vital matters. Membership of the Union has the effect of suturing; as a result of the brusque unpicking of countless stitches between governments and citizens, inserted over a period of 40 years, historical wounds might start to fester once more. "Gibraltar" and "Northern Ireland" remind us that European unification has not lost its earliest *raison d'être*: peace between European countries.

Consideration of the future relationship is not just in the interests of Britain. All member states are better off with continuing economic interaction and political cooperation with the United Kingdom – and with stability and

---

* "After the United Kingdom leaves the Union, no agreement between the EU and the United Kingdom may apply to the territory of Gibraltar without agreement between the Kingdom of Spain and the United Kingdom" (Council of the European Union, "Draft guidelines following the United Kingdom's notification under Article 50 TEU", 31 March 2017, point 22).

prosperity in the United Kingdom. The 27 member states must also think about Europe as a whole, about continental relationships between the British, the French, the Germans and Poles, and about the strategic place of Europe in the world. The Union with its institutions is an essential piece in the chess game, but not the only one.

It is striking that the European Union has been operating more convincingly in the double test of Brexit-&-Trump than in previous crises, in the thorny confrontations with the financial markets, with Putin, with streams of refugees. Why did this particular moment evoke a will to live that seemed lacking before? Earlier abysses were no less deep: the turbulence in which the euro almost collapsed (spring 2010 or autumn 2011); the threat of a Russo–American war by proxy in eastern Ukraine (winter 2015); the refugees stranded in the Macedonian snow (winter 2016). More than once not only the matter at hand but the survival of the European Union as such was at stake.

So why was it now that a desire was expressed to "take our destiny into our own hands"? Why now that the realization deepened that a capacity to act – which the Union had certainly managed to mobilize in those earlier situations under the pressure of events – is not merely indispensable when you have your back to the wall, when there is no other way, but a precondition for continued autonomous existence? The short answer: Germany. Only the double electoral blow to the international order in 2016 was able to shake the Federal Republic awake, to make the country's geopolitical vulnerability visible. What a contrast with earlier crisis management. In the euro crisis Berlin was in its own view the strong triple-A called upon to save weak brothers. In the Ukraine crisis, far from home, Chancellor Merkel was the continent's chief diplomat and peacemaker. In the refugee crisis the country stood alone with its open border policy, but it stood there in the role of Good Samaritan. Testing times, certainly, but Germany did not see its positive self-image sullied, if anything it was enhanced. By contrast the blow of Brexit-&-Trump to Germany's postwar economic and geopolitical order – its prosperity, freedom and security – was unprecedented. After Merkel's "beer tent speech" *The Economist* observed that from the mouths of the German political elite the two phenomena often sound like one word: "Brexit-and-Trump" – "however unfairly", the British magazine added, crestfallen.[51]

This experience of vulnerability, precisely at a moment of relative strength, gave Germany's political leadership the self-confidence to say: "Take our destiny into our own hands". But why "we Europeans" rather than "we Germans"? Because the European alliance, in the Trump era more than ever, remains of vital importance. Even 70 years after Auschwitz, the German government can convince its citizens that geopolitics is not evil but unavoidable only by reference to Europe. Whereas throughout the Cold War (when the Soviet Union had East Germany in its grip) West Germany needed America for its security and future unification and France for the redemption-from-sin framework of "Europe", now both those aspects coincided conceptually for the first time. It was now Germany that projected its political will to live onto the Union, and it was Merkel who time and again organized a united front.

"We Europeans", the chancellor said, not "We Germans"; European sovereignty, not German nationalism – a historic chance for all of Germany's neighbours.

Organizing a united front is not enough, however. It certainly helped the Union survive the dangerous wound inflicted on 23 June 2016. The experience of perishability has been translated into words and deeds, crystallizing around the themes of protection, sovereignty and the capacity to act; both voters and leaders confirmed their attachment to the bond of membership and a common future. And yet, in dealing with the leaving partner who triggered this new awareness of the Union's mortality in the first place, old habits of perpetuity thinking persist. There is a certain reluctance to accept in full the novelty of the situation. The British prime minister alluded to this in Munich in early 2018 when, in proposing a new "security partnership" for Europe, she warned against "rigid institutional restrictions or deep-seated ideology" jeopardising security cooperation.[52]

It takes political strength to rise above Brussels resentment and the partiality of national interests and truly place "the interests of the children" first, as a Union. To quote an authoritative European diplomat, "The lack of a long-term vision will seriously damage the whole Brexit process".[53] Is the Union capable of preserving its unity and at the same time determining its strategic interests, which include fostering relations with its most important neighbour and dealing with new unforeseeable events? That will be the true test of the Union's Machiavellian moment in the years ahead. In late 2019, the outcome of the Atlantic crisis was just as unpredictable as its beginning.

Entr'acte: acting in time

Since by his own act the innovator inhabits a delegitimized context, where *fortuna* rules and human behavior is not to be relied on, he is obliged to take the short view and continue to act – and in that sense, to innovate. In a very precise sense, then, action is *virtù*; when the world is unstabilized and the unexpected a constant threat, to act – to do things not contained within the structures of legitimacy – was to impose form upon *fortuna*.

J. G. A. Pocock[1]

Doing nothing was not an option. Wars and calamities were ravaging the Italian peninsula. The invasion by the French king in 1494 had upset the balance of power between the Italian states. Niccolò Machiavelli, a senior civil servant in the Florentine Republic in the Renaissance years 1498–1512, writes of "the great changes in affairs which have been seen, and may still be seen, every day, beyond all human conjecture".[2] When new disasters are hitting your country daily, fate has to be kept in check. For that reason, in *The Prince* and *Discourses on Livy* Machiavelli investigated the most sensible courses of political action in any number of historical and contemporary situations: dictatorship and republic, war and peace, foundation and legislation. How to get a grip on historical reality?

The mere posing of the question signified an intellectual revolution, a break with the old world, a liberation of political time from eschatology. Medieval Christianity attributed no significance to earthly intercourse between people and rulers. What counted was the salvation of the soul by God. History with its chance events was subordinated to the divine plan of salvation. Although God's plan, including the crucifixion of His son, was carried out in worldly time, God Himself stood outside it. In other words, "Secular time [...] was the theater of redemption, but not its dimension".[3] Prophets who saw the hand of God in natural disasters or political calamities – such as the sack of Rome in 410 – were regarded as heretics. The most anyone could say was that divine providence bombarded human beings with disastrous happenings to test their faith. Those unconvinced by that saw only fate, the capricious Wheel of Fortune.

Attempting to get a grip on historical reality begins with a re-evaluation of human action. In *The Prince* (1513) Machiavelli asserts "that Fortune is the arbiter of one-half of our actions, but that she still leaves us to direct the other half, or perhaps a little less".[4] In a famous image he compares fate "to one of those raging rivers, which when in flood overflows the plains, sweeping away trees and buildings". He goes on, "Yet, though its nature be such, it does not follow therefore that men, when the weather becomes fair, shall not make provision, both with defences and barriers, in such a manner that, rising again, the waters may pass away by canal, and their force be neither so unrestrained nor so dangerous". For Machiavelli, fortune is not a divine trial we have to endure but more like a partner in the world of events, a visitor, whose arrival brings difficulties but also opportunities. The Wheel of Fortune turns more quickly; the river of events swells to a flood.

Machiavelli calls the art of dealing with changing circumstances *virtù*. He uses it as a purely political concept, a combination of intelligence, bluff and decisiveness, stripped of moral and theological connotations. It is all about acting, taking the initiative, anticipating, capitalizing on the situation. Sometimes you need to wait and "play for time", but more often the Florentine – who lived in a world of wars and violence, condottieri and prophets – recommends swiftness, audacity and vigour. Risky, but Lady Fortune sometimes succumbs to chutzpah. In any case you will have no peace. Even good laws, such as those of Sparta or Rome, provide no guarantee against decline and they require continual revision. All human institutions are subject to the wear and tear of time. Whereas monarchies place themselves in an eternal, divine order, republics – mindful of the fate of Rome – recognize their own finite nature. They know that *virtù* is indispensable in the struggle against the disruptive power of *fortuna*.

It is far from simple. Anyone who acts steps onto unknown territory.

They cannot lean on custom and tradition but must set out on something new. A "new ruler" will have a tougher job winning over a populace than an heir and successor, and therefore needs to be all the more concerned about their own reputation. They need to show themselves. People will be watching them closely. Yet the fact of living in a world of ruptures and renewal offers an advantage too: "Men are attracted more by the present than by the past, and when they find the present good they enjoy it and seek no further".[5] An initiative can succeed or fail. Action introduces tension, prompts reaction; every word can be followed by a reply. Action in time turns politics into performance, which may excite the audience, bore it – or even incite it to climb onto the stage.

We have seen before how J. G. A. Pocock locates the creation of modern political thought, by Machiavelli and his contemporaries such as Francesco Guicciardini, in the recognition of the finite nature of the *polis*; we can now better understand why this entails both political emancipation and theological liberation from a history of salvation. The "Machiavellian moment", to take up Pocock's definition again, is "the moment in conceptualized time in which the republic was seen as confronting its own temporal finitude, as attempting to remain morally and politically stable in a stream of irrational events conceived as essentially destructive of all systems of secular stability".[6]

For the past ten years, the European Union has been caught up in such a moment of historical-political realization, a Machiavellian moment in Pocock's sense. Since 2008, crisis after crisis has undermined its foundations, its self-image, its existence. Although as a rule-making factory it had little experience of acting, circumstances left it with little choice. Action was required. Often the Treaty said "no" or "not permitted", but doing nothing was clearly not an option. Doing nothing was not an option when the imminent bankruptcy of a eurozone country threatened to unleash a financial shock wave. Or when behind a stream of hundreds of thousands of refugees, millions more were preparing to come. Or when after a first exit from the Union the danger of a dyke breach increased elsewhere. In these crises the Union had to let go of the holy frameworks of perpetuity thinking and act to survive. A major task: to be geared for contingency and engage in events-politics.

Such a metamorphosis takes time. It is not a sudden transformation but a gradual opening up, a transmutation by fits and starts, under the pressure of events. Sometimes the Union was empty-handed: in the euro crisis (2010–12) it lacked adequate tools; it fell back on improvisation, not without success, but only after collectively staring into the abyss. ("If the euro fails, Europe fails", was how Chancellor Merkel exorcized that early survival moment.) In other situations Europe wrestled with its self-image. The geopolitical crises surrounding Ukraine (2014–15) and the refugees (2015–16) confronted the Union, which has always found it easier to talk about universal values than about its own interests, with tragic choices: between justice and peace, between security and hospitality. It was forced to close borders, disavow principles, get its hands dirty. It did not dare say so in as many words, but action it was.

Only after the 2016 double whammy of Brexit and Trump did the words come: "We Europeans truly have to take our destiny into our own hands", said Angela Merkel in May 2017, mere days after the American president had pulled the rug out from under Europe's security guarantees. A Machiavellian statement pure and simple. Her German-European consciousness was supported by the French-European spirit of President Emmanuel Macron, who had just come to power in Paris and intended to make his presence felt on the world stage on the Union's behalf. The German chancellor had drawn the same conclusion from ten years of crisis management: increased self-confidence.

In its slow conversion into a player of *realpolitik* that takes the turbulent world for what it is, the European Union needs to emancipate itself from its own history of salvation. For Brussels ideologues – who can be heard in and around the Parliament and Commission but also in Germany, Belgium and Luxembourg, and until recently in Italy – it seems there is a great temptation to descry in every new crisis, however painful or dangerous, the promise of a United Europe.* In this sense they are like medieval prophets, able to make sense of disasters or political intrigues only as steps taken by God on the way

---

* One example: on 24 June 2016 of all days, with the Union in shock at the result of the British referendum, president of the European Parliament Martin Schulz and German vice-chancellor Sigmar Gabriel, both of the SPD, declared in a jointly written paper, "We must now work further to make the European Commission in the future into a real European government, a government that is controlled parliamentarily by the European Parliament and a second chamber of member states" (Sigmar Gabriel and Martin Schulz, 'Europa neu gründen', via *Spiegel Online*).

to the Last Judgement; for Brussels prophets too, secular time is a permanent "theatre of redemption".

So crisis-politics is governed by conflict and emotion. Resistance to action had not yet been overcome when a further theatre of war opened up. Would action now after all redeem the Promise? The touchstone for the Brussels doctrine is *who* acts: representatives of the central institutions or of the national capitals? In the euro storm, in the refugee crisis and after the Brexit shock, feelings ran high, both behind the scenes and on stage. While the Union teetered on the edge of the abyss, its rescuers sometimes fought like cat and dog. At moments of truth especially, no party wants to lose the battle. Action today places a claim on the future. In the hullaballoo between players – quite commonly between the Parliament and Commission on one side, national leaders and their governments on the other – more was at stake than a bureaucratic quarrel between departments, more than a power struggle between politicians. Straight across the visible tumult of battle, a philosophical conflict raged about the place of the Union in time: Brussels eschatology or continental contingency? Doctrinaire purity or *realpolitik*? Hence the fierce reproaches flung back and forth: betrayal of the ideal, broken promises, playing with fire, irresponsibly ideological politics. This dimension explains the impassioned racket to be heard as the Union turns itself into an active player.

It would not have surprised Niccolò Machiavelli. In an era in which the evangelical norms of charity, magnanimity and honesty forced every political leader into hypocrisy as the only way to escape ruin, the Florentine demanded a specific morality for political acts, one that put people and states in a position to take their destiny into their own hands. Christianity, which encourages people to wait for salvation after death and makes them "capable more of suffering than of doing something strong", had "rendered the world weak and given it in prey to criminal men" who "can manage it securely".[7] In defiance of theologians and priests, Machiavelli asked for room for the *vivere politico*: free public life. To be both a good person and political, one has to step into time, accept the contingency of events and take responsibility for the open future. This demands foresight, preparation, action – and an awareness that you will always be surprised.

PART II

The theatre

Courts and aristocracies have the great quality which rules the multitude, though philosophers can see nothing in it – visibility.

Walter Bagehot[1]

5

Two foundations

'Sediments of time' is a reference, like its geological paradigm, to several layers of time of varying duration and different origins, which are nevertheless present and operating simultaneously. It also presents a concept that covers the simultaneity of the nonsimultaneous, one of the most revealing of historical phenomena. [...] All conflicts, compromises and efforts to build consensus can theoretically be traced back to temporal tensions and fault lines – there is no escaping the spatial metaphors – that have been preserved in diverse sediments of time and can be released from them.

Reinhart Koselleck[2]

What have our legislators gained by culling out a hundred thousand particular cases, and by applying to these a hundred thousand laws? This number holds no manner of proportion with the infinite diversity of human actions; the multiplication of our inventions will never arrive at the variety of examples; add to these a hundred times as many more, it will still not happen that, of events to come, there shall one be found that, in this vast number of millions of events so chosen and recorded, shall so tally with any other one, and be so exactly coupled and matched with it that there will not remain some circumstance and diversity which will require a diverse judgement.

Michel de Montaigne[3]

Let justice be done, though the world perish.

Martin Luther[4]

The irony of history

In all the thrilling acceleration of the present, it is wise to keep slower things in mind: the heritage of the past, the centuries-old interplay between states and peoples, the long-term nature of identities. A historical outlook turns the Union into the totality of individual and collective answers by the member states to questions asked again and again by time. The Union's haphazard tangle then appears not as the result of political stupidity or bureaucratic short-sightedness (although these sometimes make things worse) but as the repercussion of Europe's rich and divisive history – all those clashes of states and peoples between the Atlantic and the Urals that will always require relationships with each other and with the world. There is some comfort in this realization.

Two causes of the tangle are in fact a fondly held part of the historicizing view. The first, to borrow a term from Hannah Arendt, is plurality. The Union is made up of dozens of states, each of which brings its own interests, values and experiences to the negotiating table. Since in Europe no one is in charge, or at least no single person or country, decisions always take the form of accommodation, exchange and compromise. So the choice is not between a "bad, shaky compromise" and a "good, logical decision" – for who is to judge? – but between an agreement and the lack of one. When the European currency was set up in 1991 the choice was not between a myopic euro and a perfect euro (as the smart beneficiaries of hindsight like to say), but between this euro and none.[5] The pressure to reach agreement is stronger than the demand for clarity.

A second cause of the tangle is the passage of time; social scientists, with less irony, speak of "path dependence". A choice, once made, will live a life of its own, intertwining with other interests and seeming almost impossible to change even in new circumstances. Think of EU agricultural policy, difficult to reform because of the farming lobby, or the Court, which, once established, proved able to pronounce judgments that did not suit the founding states.

Amid the hubbub of the crises afflicting the Union for the past decade, a slow but unmistakable metamorphosis has taken place. A Union that started out as a system designed for the politics of rules has shown itself ready to engage in the politics of events. To understand the importance of this metamorphosis we need to return to the essence. In its plurality the Union is the result of a Franco-German compromise, a child from a marriage of convenience between two neighbours. In its arrow of time, the Union is a product of 1945 and of 1989.

France–Germany: mutual misunderstanding

If the French and the Germans understood each other perfectly, they would no longer be French and Germans. Out of their postwar attempts to overcome the discomfort of being neighbours, "Europe" as a political project was born. The Union will always produce dissatisfactory compromises and have inscrutable institutions as long as its two protagonists remain true to themselves.

Differences in political culture between the Germans and the French show themselves tellingly in their different interpretations of the concepts "rule" and "event". In Germany a rule stands for justice, order and fairness. In France, by contrast, the semantic centre of gravity of the word shifts from protection towards obstruction, so that "rule" points to coercion and subjugation.

Given that EU politics has traditionally concentrated on the production of rules, this discrepancy consistently creates distrust between Paris and Berlin. According to a presidential adviser in 2007, "European rules are the strongest countervailing power a French political leader confronts".[6] Faced with a budgetary rule, for instance, Paris has a tendency to advocate more flexibility, both for others and for itself, responding to each violation with an appeal to "exceptional circumstances". Berlin finds this irresponsible, opportunistic and a sign of bad faith. The Germans think only of the fair application of the same budgetary rule for all, inviting the reproach that they are rigid and petty – not to say obsessed with inflation for historical reasons. During the Greek crisis surrounding the euro, there was talk of German lust for power and disciplinary diktat.

The connotations of "event" are precisely the reverse. In France an event, dramatic or otherwise, is always a sign of life, of renewal, and a demand for action. In Germany, by contrast, an event undermines the rules and brings with it the risk of destabilization and brusque changes of course, as with the abandonment of nuclear power in 2011 after the tsunami in Japan, or the zigzagging between philanthropy and border closures during the refugee crisis of summer 2015.

Emmanuel Macron once compared the Franco-German war of words over the European budgetary rules to a "religious war".[7] Five hundred years after Luther nailed his 95 theses to the door of the Schlosskirche in Wittenberg, this is not a bad comparison. Understanding for sins in 1517; flexibility in budgetary affairs in 2017 – the issue is the same: how to relate to the law? A Catholic gives the Church discretionary power and retains the chance of forgiveness. A Protestant swears by the letter and the autonomous authority of the Book, even if thereby compelled to condemn the sinner to hell.

From this arises a lack of Franco-German understanding concerning the organization of power. While rules-politics relies on supervision and balance between institutions, events-politics requires embodiment and personification by actors. France is governed in a vertical, almost pyramidal manner: the president determines the line to take, the government implements it, officialdom follows. The public, having chosen a president, wants a course, a direction, which it then approves or protests against. In Germany power is portioned out, after 1945 even more markedly so than before. The Basic Law for the Federal Republic of Germany was drawn up in 1949 by the Western Allies to prevent a concentration of power. The political executive had considerable counterforces set against it, in particular a parliament elected to a great degree by proportional representation, an authoritative Constitutional Court and a highly independent Central Bank.

A French head of state and a German head of government can therefore never engage on equivalent terms. They are not acting from the same script, as it were. All the more remarkable, then, that from time to time they have succeeded – even in the recent years of political crises – in taking decisions that profoundly alter the course of history.[8]

After the Second World War, Germany and France found an answer to their existential problem: Europe. This despite the fact that their motives differed, and each repeatedly cobbled together a response that fitted their own approach.

From 1945 onwards, France was in search of two things in Europe: a solution to the German Question and its own rebirth. France's role as a world power was played out, so it wanted to use Europe as a lever.

In 1945 Germany was a pariah among nations, occupied, divided and scarred by a boundless sense of guilt. After 1949, when Konrad Adenauer took office, it began to use Europe for its political and moral rehabilitation. In geopolitical terms, it was only from Washington that Bonn could expect real support against Russia, which had East Germany in its grip. But only from France could it be offered "Europe" as a framework within which to free itself from the burden of its past.

The first postwar efforts regarding European organization were Franco–British (including the Council of Europe in 1949), but they ran aground. The reasoning in Paris, shared by Washington, was that keeping German power in check required a European structure that went further than the British were willing or able to go. Hence the principle of "supranationality", invented by Jean Monnet. It was inconceivable that London would subordinate itself to a common, external authority. The Germans by contrast agreed immediately in May 1950 to the plan for a supranational mining organization.

On preparations for the Schuman declaration Jean Monnet writes, in his memoirs, "For a time, undoubtedly, I thought that the first step towards a European federation would be union between these two countries only [France and Germany], and that the others would join later. Finally, that evening, I wrote in on this first version that the Authority would be 'open to the participation of the other countries of Europe'."[9] These are remarkable words. Apparently the Franco-German gesture, even at the moment it was made, needed a European framework.

This decision was essential. Only the adjective "European" could confer upon the project the necessary historical-cultural legitimacy. Only with the designation "Europe" would the French public agree to share something of its own life with its hereditary enemy, Germany. Only as "Europeans" would the Germans be able, diplomatically and morally, to break free from their past.

The fall of the Berlin Wall, on 9 November 1989, was the turning point in postwar Franco-German relations. One month later, at a Summit in Strasbourg, a historic deal was made: for the Germans a united Germany, for the French a European currency. France had wanted a common currency long before the Wall fell, and the plans lay ready. It was no sudden insight as a way to anchor the reuniting Germany in Europe, as is sometimes suggested. But only now did the German chancellor commit himself to the principle and to a date for negotiations. We will never know whether the euro would have been introduced without the fall of the Wall, but it would certainly not have happened so quickly.

With German unification (1990) and an increasing number of member states from 1995 onwards, the original motives of the two neighbours to "make Europe" wore rather thin. In a Union of 15, then 25 and more, rebirth through Europe was no longer credible for France. The club is too big to be able to drag everyone along; the lever had ceased to work. The other basic theme, holding Germany in check, could no longer even be mentioned aloud. With unification Germany had achieved its political redemption, and since the euro crisis it is visibly the most powerful state on the continent again, for the first time since the war.

In the European Union, Germany's greatest challenge now is having to take the lead in events-politics despite its historical eagerness for rules. The tragic irony is that over the past 60 years it was always Paris that wanted to see the European club grow to become a major player and that gave it the capacity to act, but at the *moment suprême* it could not do it alone. Macron understands this. Now Berlin too must put leaders in play who "no longer only manage to demonstrate the cautious cultivated attitude of waiting and persevering"[10] but are able to turn decisiveness and improvisation into a fine art. Because of the burden of the past, this is an almost impossible task, which is why Germany's main interest still lies in the organizing of a European balance between power and countervailing power.

Without a clear concept of the institutional interplay of forces we cannot properly assess the potential of a new politics. Therefore, we must reread a few of what Reinhart Koselleck calls "sediments of time".

After the war: promise and taboo

As well as a judicial fact and an institutional structure, political Europe has been a promise. The promise of a new era without war. Along with the production of rules, the Brussels depoliticization machine therefore has another central task, one that has traditionally received less attention: the influencing of discourse, missionary work in which the great rhetorical power of this promise is deployed to the full. Political conflict is after all fought with words. But the language and mentality of the founding years has left an inheritance that gets in the way of Europe's understanding of itself today.

The founders discovered the key to that new era in a core idea – Monnet's axiom that the interweaving of economic interests would make warfare materially impossible – and an accompanying institutional recipe, the "Community method". Law would replace power politics. In 1950 this conviction created the courage and energy to build something unprecedented out of nothing, but as time went on it hardened into an orthodoxy that tolerated no divergence or alternative. In an uncompromising slogan used by Paul-Henri Spaak, the Belgian pacemaker of the project, *"L'Europe sera supranationale ou ne sera pas"*[11] ("Europe will be supranational or it will be nothing").

A certain tone accompanies the method. The horizon of all the squabbles in the conference room was nothing less than world peace. The practical work on the Coal and Steel Community would mean breaking with the diplomatic and power politics of before 1945. The stakes were high. Hence that remarkable, typically "Brussels" combination of technocracy and moral duress. Imagine if in the young mining Community a quarrel broke out between Paris and Bonn over an issue related to both countries' steel industry. The "European" civil servants would gravely say, "Thinking in national interests is outdated, cooperation is the watchword; ore and scrap iron must be on sale everywhere in our Community on the same terms; as experts we lay down the following objective criteria and deadlines." Inside or otherwise outside the conference room, these "Europeans" would add, with some urgency, "Watch out. Small arguments can lead to sabre rattling, a compromise is required ...".

The promise attached itself to two of the three approaches for Europe that I identified in the Prologue, the functionalist and the federalist. For some, the key to the new era lay in the civilizing effect of the depoliticized market. Commission president Walter Hallstein claimed in 1962 that the economy could actually replace politics: "The very nature of this world necessitates a redefinition of what we ordinarily mean by words like 'politics' and 'economics', and a redrawing, perhaps even the elimination, of the semantic frontier between the two".[12] Others, by contrast, linked the promise of peace with a federal future. Above all, for years there were high hopes concerning the direct elections to the European Parliament agreed on in the founding treaty. After the disappointing reality-check of those elections, from 1979 onwards, the energy behind the promise shifted to new plans. Most recently, hope was placed in Europe-wide *Spitzenkandidaten*, to create a shared public sphere and enthuse voters.

Another consequence of the promise of a new era was a permanent claim on the future. The enterprise lived, one might say, "on credit". Only then could the line between modest beginnings and grand aims be preserved. Thus, there was talk of "the European project", a future-oriented undertaking. The founders gave the promise two faces. One was the Community's intention to extend itself geographically, to bring in more states as members, perhaps one day to coincide with the continent as a whole ("enlargement"). The other was to provide the terrains already engaged upon – mining, agriculture, trade policy – with new rules and extend them into neighbouring terrains ("communitarization"). The permanent claim on the future produced the Brussels tendency to translate every "not" as "not yet". Certain powers had "not yet" been transferred, the Parliament had "not yet" gained the support of the voters, Poland is "not yet" a member of the eurozone – nothing is what it is: only *becoming* matters. Moreover, movement is presumed to be in one direction, towards more competences, more members, "more Europe". Hence the total astonishment in Brussels after the British referendum. British voters had done the unimaginable. They had put their hands in the till of today, instead of waiting for the future.

But how does this intrinsic impulse reconcile itself with the certainty and predictability of the Treaty? The fact that the founding treaty contained an invitation to its own revision is highly original. As a consequence, an institutional or substantive renovation – in international law generally regarded as a violation of the order – can be seen as confirmation of its spirit, even if it departs from the will of the parties to the Treaty. Anyone who refuses change has to provide justification. Thus, the British discovered from 1973 onwards that they had joined not just a market but a club with perpetually changing rules and functions: an "ever closer union". In the eyes of the public, those three famous words express the European forward impulse, driven by a judicial practice of teleological interpretation and justified by future-oriented aims in the preamble and opening stipulations of the Treaty.[13] The intimate connection between movement and order, between project and treaty, permeates the mentality of the Brussels inner sphere, where life is lived between vocation and law.

There was an obligation to believe in "Europe". Anyone who had doubts felt the pressure of the discourse. In Paris foreign minister Couve de Murville spoke of "supranational theology".[14] Not all the players in the Brussels arena shared this faith, yet it had an effect on everyone. At the negotiating table it was expected that all would behave according to the *esprit communautaire*, the spirit of the Community: loyal to the pact, restraining self-interest, true to the European ideal.

Striking in this connection is the ideological charge that the word "European" acquired in the 1950s and 1960s. Those who spoke of "we Europeans" were referring not to the inhabitants of the continent or the citizens of the member states but to "we who are building Europe", the crafters and forethinkers of the project, a moral vanguard of Europe-engineers. This was clear *a contrario* from the tendency in these circles to disqualify certain people as non-European. In Brussels people said, for example, "De Gaulle is not a European", suggesting that the French president did not believe in the project; he mocked the European institutions, dismissing them ironically as "utopian structures".[15] A contemporary equivalent is "Viktor Orbán is not a European".

The dream of a new beginning necessitated the banishing of the evil past. Here we encounter the obverse of the promise: the taboo. The breach between past and present had to be total.

The greatest taboo was to appeal to national interest. Those who did so were out of order. The word "taboo" is no exaggeration. When French President De Gaulle recalled his ambassador from Brussels in 1965, one Euro-commissioner called it the worst thing that had happened to Europe "since Hitler". Margaret Thatcher declared that the British wanted "our own money back".[16] Thirty years later, her words – sharpened by mythologization into "my money back" – are still engraved on the collective memory; that alone is a sign that the British premier had contravened a prohibition. It was not so much that she was counting her pennies. We can surely assume that diplomats of all member states calculated in their budgetary negotiations who was taking how much out of the collective pot or contributing to it. But you were not to mention it out loud. The affront lay in Thatcher's tone and above all in her use of the words "our own" (British money), which left little intact of the notion that it was "our shared" (European) money. She ostentatiously demonstrated that she did not believe in the promise.

What began as club feeling and a fraternal appeal to the *esprit communautaire* developed in some circles into moral superiority, inspired by the lazy equivalences European = good and national = bad (or, in the jargon, supranational = good and intergovernmental = bad). In such a phase of self-righteousness, arguments are superfluous and the weapon of anathema suffices ("he is not European"). There was a time when you needed to be of the calibre of a "General" or an "Iron Lady" not to shrink from such calumny.

Although the taboo on speaking of the national interest has been relaxed, even now, half a century after De Gaulle, interference in EU business by national leaders is still regarded with suspicion in Brussels circles. Whereas functionalism and federalism were driven by the promise, politicization through summits was taboo from the start. During the euro storm (2010–12) Jacques Delors and Jürgen Habermas denounced the involvement of Merkel, Sarkozy and other government leaders in crisis management as a "renationalization of European politics". As they saw it, the nationalism of the 1930s was not far away.[17] They left little room for a less regressive explanation, namely the possibility that this involvement by national players might be a sign of the reverse, of a "Europeanization of national politics".[18]

A second taboo concerns speaking in terms of differences between member states. The Community is a community of equals, as the name itself suggests.* The main unmentionable disparity was in the degree of power. Everyone knew that France had more power at the negotiating table than Luxembourg, but you could not say so, and still cannot. In the sphere of the law, all were equal. To the smaller member states the European legal order offered pleasing protection against dominance by the larger, principally

---

* The term "community" was introduced into the founding negotiations in Paris in 1950 by a member of the German delegation; he was seeking a connection with the classic sociological antithesis between *Gemeinschaft*, a tight, durable and identity-defining union (like village or a monastic order) and *Gesellschaft*, a group that is looser and more open (like a city or a celebration). The Germans opted for *Gemeinschaft*. Initiators Schuman and Monnet, who until then had referred to their brainchild only by using industrial terms such as "consortium", "pool" or "organization", were happy to adopt the suggestion; the name fitted their political pursuit of unification.

by France and Germany; it was indeed they who were keen to maintain the taboo on power differentials. This fiction of equality before the law is effective and useful. Even though power imbalances do not disappear in practice, the law tempers them.

The problem is that other differences between member states were also wished away – differences in economic structure, in historical experience, in geographical location, in the strength of the governmental apparatus. All were supposed to be the same or at least to become so (hence the characteristic and promising vocabulary of "harmonization" and "convergence"). As long as Europe was borne aloft on the politics of rules for a market, equality was a workable, perhaps necessary assumption. But the situation changed as soon as the member states reorganized their club after 1989 in order to engage in events-politics as well. In projects that revolve around acts rather than rules, it does matter who you are as a member state and what you want or are capable of. It becomes relevant whether you have an army, who your neighbours are and whether you are able to collect taxes. Even now, as recent crises bring such truths to light, it remains tricky even with the most circumspect choice of words to say that member states may in fact differ.

A third taboo concerns talking about a border, again understandably given the promise of a radical break with the past. The new Europe had to be open and inviting, without borders, so that boundless democratic optimism could be propagated without any limits. Borders remind us of border disputes, war, the will to power – the evil past. This taboo too is tenacious. Despite enlargement, despite the disappearance of internal borders, the issue remains thorny: what is the external border, where does political Europe stop? The prohibition is challenged, and not just by neighbours Ukraine, Russia or Turkey: the European public wants answers too.

Placing a taboo on national interests and leaders who champion those interests; curtaining off political differences between member states; refusing to define a European geographical boundary – these are three essential elements of the Brussels depoliticization machine. The taboo strategy is understandable. Initially the Community was a young hothouse plant that needed protection against forces within national governments, bureaucracies or legal systems, so the moral delegitimizing of opposition was effective.

161

Sixty years later this *raison d'être* has gone and the strategy is becoming a handicap. In the whirling events of our day the Union has to articulate and defend its own interests. The member states must draw on their own resources if they are to combine their capacities to act, and the club needs to determine its own place in space and time.

It has wrestled with such questions before. After the fall of the Berlin Wall in 1989, fascinating skirmishes took place between the old promise of peace and the new historical reality. This episode, rarely understood in its full extent, demonstrates the tenacity of Europe's understanding of itself, formed by war.

After the Wall: Union versus Community

Not one but two primal scenes lie at the origin of political Europe. The first has been described countless times: 9 May 1950, a room in the Quai d'Orsay in Paris, a speech by a French minister. The second is imprinted on the memory of millions: 9 November 1989, the Berlin Wall, the push for freedom by East German citizens. Yet its specific meaning for Europe has not been appreciated. Just as the scene in Paris led to the founding of the Community (1951), so the scene in Berlin led to the founding of the Union (1992). It was a new beginning.

The transition from Community to Union is the decisive moment in Europe's jerky transformation from rules-politics to events-politics. It was a breakthrough. As such it of course had its forerunners and portents, but earlier initiatives had always been resisted or kept outside the treaty structures. A first, anecdotal indication: on the December day in 1991 on which 12 government leaders in Maastricht signed the new Union treaty with great fanfare, Jacques Delors was, he said later, "a disappointed man".[19] Why? His beloved Community had lost its monopoly on the form Europe would take – at the very moment when the continent stood on the threshold of a new era. The second foundation of "Europe" broke the promise of the first.

This could happen only as the result of a massive impact. For Europe's events-driven metamorphosis, 9 November 1989 is the "mother shock", the start of a confusing period in which old and new forms, Community and

Union, exist alongside each other and mixed together – and which has still not led to complete peace and clarity. It is therefore time to investigate the consequences of that shock for the political system, high time to start reading the Union correctly.

THE EUROPEAN *WENDE*

The evening after the Wall fell, Spanish premier Felipe González remembered later, "history galloped riderless through the night like a runaway horse".[20] The Cold War came to an end. The continent stirred itself and a desire for freedom took hold of millions. Amid all the relief and joy there was immense uncertainty.

In Western Europe the conflict between America and Russia, the era of nuclear threat and ideological rivalry, had brought, if nothing else, a kind of stability. Only afterwards did we fully recognize the Cold War as the long tail end of the Second World War, which had ended with the division of Germany and Europe between the American-British-French and Russian occupying forces. The years 1945–89 turned out to be postwar parentheses, the "unfinished business" (as Tony Judt put it in *Postwar*) of the conflict that preceded them. So, in 1989 strategic issues from 1945 suddenly returned: security, borders, continental order. Old terms were dusted off. They resounded in the debate: "Yalta", "Oder-Neisse Line", "Helsinki Accords". The map of Europe needed to be redrawn. But at the moment itself no one had any idea of the extent of the implications.

How would the new Germany relate to its neighbours, to the national borders, to the plans for a single currency? Would the Americans continue to guarantee Western Europe's security? What would happen in Eastern Europe after a Russian withdrawal? These three uncertainties dominated thinking about Europe's political form.

You could of course seek reassurance in the existing reality. Many countries wanted to continue to shelter under the American umbrella. Some were keen to dress up the European Economic Community as "something political". Still, would American interests continue to coincide with those of Europe? And was the Brussels policymaking machine really suited to high politics? In Paris especially, there were doubts. The French found a *Pax*

Americana less than attractive and a *Lex Bruxellensis* less than credible. But what, then?

In the fascinating watershed years 1989–93, these questions came together in countless summit negotiations. The European continent assumed a new shape. In the end the German question was quickly settled. Chancellor Helmut Kohl grabbed the galloping horse of the night of the *Mauerfall* by the reins and by 3 October 1990 the country was celebrating unification. The European metamorphosis took longer and reached its conclusion in 1993. Like the German *Wende*, the European *Wende* had a geographical and an institutional side.

In Eastern Europe the Soviet Union left a vacuum that had to be filled, to prevent the collapse of economies, the loss of state authority, perhaps even civil wars or streams of refugees. Such phenomena would not stop neatly at the border. From 1991 onwards, the Yugoslav Wars demonstrated that nationalist passions given free rein could still lead to mass murder. Western Europe had to do something. Yet the 12 government leaders were hesitant about receiving into their midst a dozen or so ex-communist countries they barely knew. In June 1993, at a summit in Copenhagen, they offered the prospect of membership. It was not a desire to expand the market by a hundred million consumers that decided the matter but an awareness that Western Europe's own security would be served by continental stability. There was no timeline, but the club would shift eastwards, growing to perhaps 30 members, and Germany would end up in the geographical centre.

Just as the geographical facet of Europe's transformation is coupled to the Copenhagen Summit, so its institutional change is bound up with Maastricht. In that city the government leaders agreed a treaty in late 1991 that, after a difficult passage through the populations, came into effect on 1 November 1993, eight days short of four years after the fall of the Wall. This treaty made permanent the depoliticized market with its accompanying policy terrains, as well as marking the start of collaboration in domains of high politics. The most striking aspects were an economic and monetary union, a common foreign and security policy, and cooperation in justice and home affairs. It even became possible to discuss a common defence. In Maastricht the 12 members gave their club a new, political basis. It therefore acquired a new name: the Union.

WHY THE UNION IS NOT THE COMMUNITY

It is all too easily said of the moment of passage at Maastricht, "the Community became a Union". Not so. The Community remained the Community. It was able to throw off the label "Economic" and it gained several policy areas, but at root it remained an economic rule-making factory. The Union, which was added to it, was different. It was a formalization of relationships between the member states, relationships that had previously existed outside the treaties. The capitals created a sphere in which to do things together without immediately wanting to transfer competences to the centre – first among them foreign policy. Roughly speaking, the Community continued to concern itself with rules-politics, while the Union became a platform for events-politics, for tasks such as sending crisis missions, catching pirates or guarding borders. It did not replace the politics of rules but was added to it. Thus from 1993 onwards the Community and the Union existed side by side in law. They did not even share the same institutions. The European Council of government leaders, grown in the 20 years of its existence to become an authoritative forum, was given a key position in the Union treaty but formally kept outside the Community treaty.* This peculiar situation lasted until 2009, when the Community was formally dissolved and absorbed into the Union. To this day, old and new methods and practices exist side by side, often in a tense relationship – "sediments in time".

The strength of the Community lay in the building of a judicial area within which companies and consumers, employers and employees could enter into free transactions based on agreed rules, in other words a market. The task of the Brussels institutions consisted of the removal of obstacles and the harmonizing of standards, so that a "level playing field" was created on which supply and demand find each other all over Europe. To borrow a useful image from philosopher John Dewey, "Rules of law are [...] structures which canalize action; they are active forces only as are banks which confine the flow of

---

* With one characteristic exception, a harbinger of later tensions. At the request of the French, the European Council was given a role in monetary union, although at the request of the Germans monetary union had been made part of the Community. For the sake of the doctrine it was agreed that although the government leaders would determine the guidelines of economic policy, the Council of Ministers would take the formal decisions (Art. 103, para. 2 EC treaty, Maastricht version).

a stream, and are commands only in the sense in which the banks command the current".[21]

Action here is initiated by companies, consumers and so on, not by the public authorities. For national governments in Paris, The Hague or Warsaw, the common market is a place where they knowingly allow their hands to be tied, for example because they are not permitted to offer their industries state support at will, or because they are obliged to adhere to procurement rules. They have to sit back and experience the Community as, to overstate it a little, organized impotence.

The perspective shifts in the Union's events-politics. Here the member states themselves stand on the political stage of events. They are the players, together. They generate the action, for example by guaranteeing each country's internal or external security. They have the armies, the diplomats, the security services, the border guards. Here it is not a matter of organized impotence but of the creation of combined power.

This difference is not black-and-white, nor is it acknowledged by all the actors. Hence the battles time and again between countries and institutions as to whether the market model will also work for a new policy area. Hence the arguments when it becomes clear in retrospect that incorrect assessments were made – as when the euro turned out to be vulnerable without an improvised toolkit, or when a space without internal borders proved unable to survive impacts at the external borders. Hence too, after the shock of 1989, the deep conflict over how to give shape to forms of politics that lay beyond the grey area between rules and actions and demanded more than organized impotence, according to the dominant players, because there was a need to act jointly.

Lawyers and bureaucrats often fail to see this distinction between rules and acts. Their language is that of competences, whereas events-politics is all about responsibilities – a political notion. Those with the competences sometimes forget that they do not always have the authority to take responsibility in a given situation: there begins technocratic overreach.

The Brussels doctrine is based on a handing over of powers by the member states to the Community. Each treaty transfers competences, in competition policy or agriculture policy for example, to the central institutions. Legally watertight, this works as long as you can as it were detach bits of market or policy – steel market, beet prices – and prepare them separately. For economic life as a whole it is more problematic. Who is responsible if something goes wrong? Who faces protests by farmers because wheat prices are too low? If the market is a competence of the Community, why not the tackling of unemployment? Or the levying of taxes? Where does it stop?

The Union is a matter not of transferring powers but of agreeing to act jointly, and therefore of organizing responsibility, a word less often heard. Taking responsibility is about acting in situations for which there are no rules. You cannot lay down in a treaty how to act if a war breaks out between Russia and Ukraine, if the Greek economy collapses or if huge numbers of refugees cross the Mediterranean. So, in 1993 the central institutions were not given competences in foreign policy, defence or national security; for those each member state remained responsible. How could the Union nevertheless be meaningful? Precisely because it was not invented as a thirteenth entity alongside the 12 member states. The Union is the member states jointly. This approach leads to a system of interweaving in which "European" and "national" politics are increasingly hard to separate.

It is a revolution that places the question of authority in a different light. The Community rested on fixed rules that had legitimacy, binding force, legal authority. If member states transfer competences by treaty, they cannot afterwards complain when those powers are used. The Union, by contrast, organizes power and political authority to take decisions in unique situations. What to do if an event, a fellow government or your own population demands bold acts and decisions? Elected politicians have to organize support from the public, the voters. They should be expected to convince people, not just with laws or technical arguments but with a story about the "why?", about the importance or urgency of their choices. They can then claim political authority and ask for acceptance of it.

This naturally raises the question of how and by what route the voters were brought into play in the European Union from 1993 onwards. In the new Union treaty (and initially only there) the European Council was formally given this task – which it was already exercising – for the first time: the heads of state or government, as the highest echelon of democratically elected leaders in their own countries, could function as a source of authority for joint performance in events-politics. In the renewed Community treaty (and initially only there) the European Parliament was given more of a say, along with the Council of Ministers: in rules-politics the voters are involved both in their national capacity and in their European capacity.

Another important, rarely recognized consequence of the revolution was a qualification to the member states' equality under law. In the Brussels rules-politics of before the fall of the Wall, the taboo on inequality worked brilliantly. After the transfer of competences the member states, in the treaty sphere, remained behind "residually" as equals: each member state had the same rights, Germany no more than Luxembourg. This was at odds with their actual inequality, but as long as the member states bound their own hands with the Community rules and the tasks transferred were those of supervision, control and facilitation – those of "market superintendent" and "groundsman" – it could be made to work. But in events-politics the member states themselves are on stage. They are the actors who need to respond to unforeseen challenges. As part of the Union, in short, the member states have an army, a diplomacy, a police apparatus, a treasury, a territory and a history. These features, however, cannot be put behind a curtain to safeguard the impression of equality in law; instead they determine how much political responsibility each member separately can or will take. And it turns out that Germany can take more than Luxembourg or Greece. Therefore, the member states in the Union are unequal – large and small, rich and poor, with friendly or bad-tempered external neighbours, closed or porous borders. This determines the nature of their gathering.

The issuing of rules versus the capacity to act, power versus responsibility, anonymity or visibility, formal equality or actual equality – in the post-Wall years, 1989–91, the taboo on these dichotomies was breached, and they were ruthlessly fought over. Interests and visions clashed. It seems the main players in Paris, Brussels, Bonn, London, The Hague and Rome understood perfectly well what was at stake with the creation of a Union: a European metamorphosis. Precisely for that reason, the fiercest resistance to the breakthrough to a Union was found not just in the London of Margaret Thatcher and John Major but in the Brussels of Jacques Delors.[22]

THE OWL OF MINERVA

In his *Philosophy of Right*, Hegel writes, "The owl of Minerva takes its flight only when the shades of night are gathering". With this image, the German philosopher conveyed the tragic fact that our insight into reality comes only when dusk begins to fall. No wonder we understand the European *Wende* of 1989–93 better now than at the time; later events throw light on what went before and we learn, collectively. But there is more going on here. Countervailing forces were at work, forces that obscured the metamorphosis from view, that grabbed Minerva's owl by the feet, so to speak, and prevented it from taking wing.

Rethinking is hindered by Brussels practice and doctrine. The Commission and Parliament regarded the institutional arrangements of the Maastricht Treaty as infringements of the sacred Community method, incompatible with the pure doctrine. The specific ways of working for foreign policy and for justice and home affairs; the key role for government leaders: these were allowed – and this remains the case – only as temporary exceptions. As ever, "not" was translated as "not yet".[23]

After the Wall the confusion actually became greater than before. The Union is a political pact, which, in order to be able to control events, breaks with depoliticization. This sharpens the debate between the two approaches: politicization through Parliament or through the national leaders – a natural, scrutable conflict between two groups of politicians for executive power and authority. But one of the two groups still stresses the postwar promise of a new era of peace. On the authority of the founding treaty, supporters of parliamentarization like to translate the struggle for power into a moral conflict between the Community (good) and the Union (bad). This is a questionable move. The legitimacy of the original plan is based after all on the rules: these must be impartial, objective and binding. The institutional mechanics served purely to ensure an outcome acceptable to all. For events-politics nothing was provided. In the post-Wall situation, Brussels ideologues expertly turned things around: now the institutions have primacy. Only what passes through the hands of the Commission and Parliament is legitimate, irrespective of whether it is a normative rule (the old Community) or a decision to act (in the new Union). In a nutshell, they want to be involved and shout "betrayal of the ideal" or "contempt for democracy" whenever they are kept out. They fail to appreciate that the member states that once signed up to the depoliticized market did not by any means all look with longing at the prospect of a federal Europe – France, the Netherlands, Spain, Denmark or Poland a good deal less than Germany, Italy and Belgium (to say nothing of Britain, which shut the door partly as a result of mistrust). The parliamentary approach is not designed for Union-wide events-politics. The language is lacking, however, in which to say this. So, the government leaders, to whom in the Union the task falls of taming crises when the rules provide no usable instruments, come under fire for undermining a pure project.

Angela Merkel experienced this doctrinal pushback personally. In a speech in late 2010 in Bruges the chancellor offered her interpretation of Europe's new political and legal situation. A year earlier the Lisbon Treaty had dissolved the Community and formally made the European Council an EU institution. Merkel pointed out to her audience that the Commission and Parliament do not have a monopoly on "Europe" and that the member states also play their role in the Union through the Council of Ministers and the European Council (of which she was herself a member). "What this all adds up to is that no one of us is more European than another – depending on our place in the overall scheme – but that all of us together are Europe".[24] She advocated coordinated action in fields such as energy policy, for which the member states remain responsible; even without any transfer of powers you could set to work as "Europe".

For this intended teamwork between institutions and member states, Merkel launched, with great historical insight, the term "Union method". Although the basic constitutional shape of the Union – governmental authority concentrated in and around the European Council, legislative power for Parliament and Council of Ministers, political impetus and administrative execution by the Commission, judicial power for the Court – had in practice been defining itself for a long time, the Lisbon Treaty confirmed these relationships in a way that was visible to all. The chancellor was therefore looking for words that fitted the situation. The term "Union method", however, touched a nerve in Brussels circles. There were cries of shame; the deployment of the term was taken to be an attack.[25] Merkel had violated a taboo. Under pressure from prominent party colleagues in the European Parliament, she dropped the term. The episode is revealing. Even though the Community no longer exists, the "Community method" remains inviolable. Anyone who tries to interpret or explain in detail what is characteristic of the new Union is out of order. Taboo as a method. The old thinking restricts Europe's understanding of itself. This is counter-productive and ultimately self-destructive. In my view the rigid belief that the "true Europe" has to be built in defiance of the member states rather than with them fosters precisely the public scepticism and disruptive nationalism against which it has no defence, aside from breathless curses.

As well as this doctrinal counter-pressure, there was another force that prevented Minerva's owl from flying and hindered understanding of the political *Wende* from Community to Union. Immediately, in 1989, the idea took hold that what the new Union intended to do – guarantee security and engage in events-politics – was not urgent. The shock of the fall of the Wall, which saw the return of major issues of war and peace, was not so terrible, it seemed. So the return of History set diplomatic and institutional cogs turning – and brought about the breakthrough to the Union – but did not really penetrate Europe's self-understanding. On the contrary, that understanding anaesthetized itself with the simultaneously launched maxim "End of History", the tempting notion that the entire world was on its way to the freedom of democratic capitalism on the Western model. It is deeply ironic that at the very moment when Europe awoke geopolitically, someone called out, "History is over, you can go back to the dressing room!"

Although Francis Fukuyama thought he had accompanied History all the way to its end, it had merely been smothered. Historical acceleration reached Europe in the summer of 2008 with the banking crisis and the war between Russia and Georgia, and today it seems unstoppable. Only now, in this storm of events around the euro, Putinism, refugees, Brexit and Trumpism, does Europe actually need to call upon the authority and capacity to act that lay ready, potentially, in the Union. Only now is Europe's metamorphosis being put to the test, as events give shape to a new politics.

This indisputably leads to the development of forms of "Government". But at the same time, in this new politics the voters too can join the conversation, or voice their objections; they too are appearing onstage en masse and grabbing hold of the changed times – on occasions as a real "Opposition".

6

Directors and actors

These three powers [judiciary, legislative and executive] should naturally form a state of repose or inaction. But as there is a necessity for movement in the course of human affairs, they are forced to move, but still to move in concert.

Charles de Montesquieu[1]

It is quite obviously impossible to deal with political power and the structure of the state itself without knowing what Authority is as such.

Alexandre Kojève[2]

Most truly has the wise man said that of things future and contingent we can have no certain knowledge. Turn this over in your mind as you will, the longer you turn it the more you will be satisfied of its truth.

Francesco Guicciardini[3]

Emancipation of executive power

Anyone who visits Washington and sees the magnificence of the legislative Congress, with its majestic dome on the axis of the city, and then looks at the White House, built for the president, small by comparison and off to one side, senses what the founders of the American republic at the end of the eighteenth century believed the relationship should be between the main powers: the legislators in charge and the executive power in second place. The 13 newly united states had thrown off the British king, their colonial sovereign,

173

and did not want a citizen-king in his place. Something similar happened in France. After the revolution of 1789 and the fall of absolute monarch Louis XVI, the focus was on the impersonal and all-encompassing authority of the law. As Pierre Rosanvallon shows in *Good Government* (2018), primacy was given to parliament, as guardian of the sovereignty of the people. France went through a turbulent episode under Napoleon (and half a century later his nephew), but distrust of arbitrary leaders ultimately produced the parliamentarianism of the Third Republic.[4] Like the Americans, the French kept the executive power small.

The founders of the Community similarly drew a line under the past. Just as the young American and French republics had put aside their king, so the new European Community excluded national governments as far as possible. Ruptures and traumas of this kind can have repercussions long afterwards, affecting customs and practices, constitutional relationships, fears and passions for decades, even a century or more. Until fresh shocks shake everything up and alter the balance by force: in Paris the Great War of 1914–18; in Washington the Great Depression, triggered in 1929.

The EU now has a prominent parliament, but even after 60 years it is thought naive or taboo to ask: where is the government? The Union's doubts and uncertainties clearly lie even deeper than the initial American and French preference for a strong parliament and weak executive. Decades went by in which it was impossible to point to an EU government. Even constitutional experts were unable to decipher Europe's constitutional set-up. The *trias politica* associated with Montesquieu, the separation of legislative, executive and judicial functions, did not seem to apply to the young Community. Only the judiciary had an obvious location: the Court of Justice in Luxembourg. With its self-conscious judgments, the Court managed to extend its range from 1963 onwards.[5] By contrast the legislature and the executive were inextricably intertwined, within the Brussels rule-making factory, with the tasks of the Commission and the Council. Lawyers cheerfully concluded that the Community must therefore be *sui generis*, a peculiar creature. In due course the doctrine did identify a "European legislative power".[6] The existence of a Parliament, directly elected since 1979, accelerated this emancipation; every parliament wants to be more than just a talking shop or advisory panel and to take part in the making of laws, even if, as in Brussels, they are called "directives" or "regulations". Since 2009 the Parliament and the Council of Ministers have officially been called "co-legislators". By contrast, the third member of the *trias*, the executive power, had no uncontested, autonomous manifestation.

In modern systems of government the executive has two faces. One exists in the light, the political executive power. This is what is generally called the government: 10 or 20 politicians in the spotlight who together set out a course, in democracies vis-à-vis parliament and public. The other face, that of the administrative executive power, exists in the shadows. This is the bureaucracy, in which civil servants "execute" decisions and laws; they fall under the political authority of the government. Of course, the Union has no shortage of such bureaucratic executives, among the most important being the national ministries,[7] but at the same time this kind of power lies with the Commission, the Council of Ministers and, since the 1990s, dozens of EU agencies. We might even include the European Central Bank in Frankfurt among them, or indeed the emergency fund for the eurozone.

Where, then, does *political* executive power lie? Or rather where, after first being ousted, does it rear its head under the pressure of events? The Brussels dogmatists have a ready answer: the Commission holds the executive power and is Europe's government-in-waiting. Its first president, Walter Hallstein, described himself during a visit to Washington as "a kind of Prime Minister of Europe";[8] his distant successor Romano Prodi had a constitution drawn up that allocated as much executive power as possible to his institution.[9] In Parliamentary circles too, the smart money is understandably on the Commission, the institution it can hold to account. This is the federal model for Europe's architecture. Alongside it a line of thought developed that opted for the government leaders collectively as the source of executive authority: the confederal approach. Out of this conviction, in 1974 Giscard d'Estaing and Monnet together brought about the establishment of the European Council of heads of state and government, the latter calling it the "provisional government of Europe". In recent developments we see even more clearly how, after the judicial and legislative powers, the third of Montesquieu's *trias politica* is feeling its way towards an autonomous position.

Emancipation of the executive is of vital importance if the member states of the Union are to defend themselves against attacks from outside and offer their populations the prospect of a powerful role for Europe in the world. In light of this the correct interpretation of how a new politics is emerging in Europe is of great importance. As the political leadership of the Union prepares to strengthen its capacity to act, it is essential to choose the right path, to guide the forces in the right direction. The first step is to discern the preconditions for joint decision-making and action. In that respect, this book aims to contribute to the development of a new political sense of the future of Europe, and to reopen the debate about the Union's potential.

Leading actors

ESTABLISHMENT OF THE EUROPEAN COUNCIL

Between 1960 and 1974 there was considerable conflict over the introduction of regular summit meetings. The eventual outcome was the establishment of the European Council of heads of state and government.

Six summits had been held between 1961 and 1973. On each occasion they were a major challenge to arrange and there was no system to them. France repeatedly pressed for one to take place, while the other five countries were consistently reluctant to attend. Half a century later it is hard to comprehend how profound the resistance to regular summits was in Brussels circles, and in member states including the Netherlands and Belgium. The involvement of national leaders, so it was feared, would undermine the power of the Commission, an institution seen by the smaller member states as an ally against the larger and as guardian of the law. It is an argument still sometimes voiced.

The part played by Jean Monnet was crucial. He had invented the Community, and from 1952 onwards he was the first chair of the precursor to the Commission before becoming the champion of the European project as its top lobbyist. He was familiar with the ideological resistance of the dogmatists. Nevertheless, he had arrived at the conclusion that the member states could not withstand the economic and foreign policy storms that were gathering over Europe in the early 1970s without joint political control. The Community needed a "focus of authority", as British premier Edward Heath put it.[10]

Monnet realized that this authority could not come from the treaty-bound Brussels institutions. "The only people who might be disappointed," he wrote later, "were those who imagined that [...] one day the Government of Europe would spring fully armed from the institutions of the Economic Community".[11] He therefore became an advocate of regular meetings of presidents and prime ministers.*

Success came in 1974. After the sudden death of Georges Pompidou, Valéry Giscard d'Estaing was elected as the new French president. He came to the same conclusion as his two predecessors: "The goal I had in mind was that the European heads of state and government would come together regularly. Once that regularity was established, the scope of the power of the leaders would do the rest and the institution would consolidate of its own accord: a European executive power would begin to take shape."[12] Giscard achieved his aim at a summit in Paris. The fact that the leaders had not yet decided upon a name for the new forum did not deter the host from announcing at the concluding press conference, "*Le Sommet est mort. Vive le Conseil européen*" (The Summit is dead. Long live the European Council).[13]

Regularity had been established, the institution born and baptized. From 1975 onwards periodicity did its work and the European Council – as the best Brussels observers quickly appreciated – became an indispensable part of the "European machinery", a focus of authority.[14]

The precise frequency remained disputed. In a change to the treaty in 1986, a Dutch request to reduce the number of annual meetings from three to two was met. The Hague, traditionally suspicious of the European Council, was attempting to limit the damage. After the fall of the Wall, however, the number of "special", "extraordinary" and "informal" meetings increased. The creation of monetary union, appointment decisions, treaty changes – the

---

* In memoranda he called the forum a "Provisional European Government". The name is characteristic of the bridging function Monnet wanted to fulfil. Most public opinion would have been horrified by the implication that there was a "European government" of any kind, and for that reason the name was quickly dropped. For Brussels circles, by contrast, the term implied the rejection of the Commission as Europe's government-in-waiting, and by its own founder no less. For that audience the qualification "provisional" was intended to soften the blow, as a teleological reassurance that in the future something better, something purer would arise. But the semantic tension between the two interpretations proved too great.

leaders had more to discuss than could be fitted into an evening and a day every six months.

In the Lisbon Treaty (2007) the government leaders not only gave their summits a permanent president and the status of a fully-fledged Union institution, they made permanent the frequency of "twice every six months", while it remained the case that "When the situation so requires, the President shall convene a special meeting of the European Council".[15] When permanent president Van Rompuy opined, seemingly naively, at his first summit in early 2010, that the leaders ought to meet ten times a year – to de-dramatize their gathering – he was much criticized. Yet the actual frequency is not far below that. The acceleration began in 2008, when the economic crisis and border skirmishes with Russia (first over Georgia, later Ukraine) presented themselves. Since then the count has been six or seven summits per year, with peaks of eight (2014) and ten (2015).[16] Given the continuing turbulence, this number will not quickly decline.

FIVE SITUATIONS FOR THE HEADS

A concept, met before, that pithily expresses the character of the European Council is *Chefsache*. In German a *Chefsache* is an issue of such importance that the boss has to deal with it in person. In business this is the chief executive officer, at a ministry the permanent secretary and in German politics the federal chancellor. In the Union a problem becomes a *Chefsache* if the presidents and prime ministers gathered in the European Council – bosses in the plural, after all – decide to take it upon themselves.

Within a given organization, any matter, however trifling, can suddenly touch a nerve, become symbolic of something bigger, provoke a media storm and so demand the attention of "those at the top". Conversely, anything that can be resolved by others is not a *Chefsache*. The kernel of the *Chefsache* does not lie in the "what" but in the "when"; it is about urgency and topicality, about the sensitivity of the situation, the right moment to act.

Yet many authors discuss the European Council with their eyes on the "what". They rank by policy terrain all the things the leaders have done at summits, whether for the euro, for enlargement, or for asylum policy. Such an approach fails to grasp the political essence of the European Council. I prefer to distinguish between situations in which government leaders attend to an issue and the part therefore played by the club. Essentially there are five such situations for the heads, which make appeal to the authority of the gathered presidents and premiers.

1. *When the worst comes to the worst: the crisis tamer*

In times of crisis people look to the European Council and its most important members. The club is called upon to tame the storm. Separately and together, the members have the authority to take quick, far-reaching decisions that go beyond existing frameworks. Only they can mobilize all the Union's diplomatic and bureaucratic apparatus to achieve a specified goal. As crisis tamer and taskmaster, the club shares out the roles, among its own members and among other players in Brussels and the national capitals.

After the fall of the Wall in 1989, where but in the European Council could the unease of Thatcher, Andreotti and Lubbers, the ingenuity of Mitterrand, the drive of Kohl and all those other forces have been brought together? Who but the gathered heads of government, under the leadership of Merkel and Sarkozy, could have defended the many crisis measures after 2010 before their national tribunes, thereby saving the embattled European currency? Where but at a summit of Europe's leaders could a firm European response have been given to the Russian invasion of Crimea in 2014 that kept all the various positions in the Union, from Cyprus to Poland, in a united front?

This taming function is of vital importance to the Union. Yet it cannot be found in the texts. The Treaty laconically limits itself to the procedure: "When the situation so requires, the President shall convene a special meeting of the European Council".[17] The chapter on foreign affairs repeats this provision for use in international crises.[18]

A European concern also becomes a *Chefsache* if the political survival of a member of the club is at stake. Alexis Tsipras, who rejected an offer of credit for Greece, David Cameron, who put British membership at risk, or Theresa May, negotiating a divorce agreement: they have no appetite for doing business with a bunch of ministers or a European commissioner. They are battling for their political lives and trying to defend themselves in the face of their equals.

A crisis may unleash forces that split the Union. Then we see members each fighting their own corner at a summit, or different camps pitted against each other. This happened in 2003 over the American invasion of Iraq. During the refugee crisis of 2015–16 something similar threatened, when one country after another shut its borders. These are painful episodes. Often critics – or concerned insiders – see in such division at the highest level the "end of the Union". Up to now this has proven premature. The club comes together again each time, out of necessity. Going it alone generally does not pay; the scars heal and life goes on, until the next storm.

2. *When the game is deadlocked: the impasse-breaker*

Diagonally beneath the European Council is the regular Council of Ministers, a bureaucratic pyramid that works from the bottom up. Starting at the base, each layer manages the problems that can be handled within its mandate and pushes anything too hot to handle one level upwards. An issue therefore climbs, in many steps or singly, from the specialists from national ministries to the ambassadors, who represent every member state of the Union. Anything "too political" for even these fixers is passed to the top level, to the ministers. If they cannot resolve the matter, for example because they are not given sufficient negotiating room by their governments at home or because ministries clash (for example all the agriculture ministers against all the environment ministers), the result would once have been an impasse. The European Council was set up partly to straighten such things out. There is nowhere else to go. If the leaders cannot cut the Gordian knot, no one can: they have the final say.

It is not uncommon for the European Council to be politely requested to limit its involvement to a signature, to give the stamp of its authority to decisions made elsewhere. This does no harm to the club. "One layer of government up means one level of knowhow down", a Dutch member once joked at his own expense. The European Council can even exploit such disdain, by giving ministers the date of the next summit as the deadline for a decision. Apprehensive of the mess their ill-informed bosses are likely to make, the experts may suddenly reach a compromise after all. This was the trick used in the eurozone crisis to force through the implementation of a banking union: breakthroughs among finance ministers repeatedly occurred in the hours before a summit.

The decision-making function of summits meets with resistance in the European Parliament. This is understandable; for the making of rules, the Parliament, as "co-legislator", is on an equal footing with the Council of Ministers. Government leaders can bind their own ministers, but they exercise no formal authority over MEPs. The concept of a *Chefsache* has no grip on the Parliament, in fact it tends to make it restive. Here informal persuasion has to provide a way out, through national party channels for example (with heads of government in their role as party leaders) or through the working relationship between Commission and Parliament (as a member of the European Council, the president of the Commission needs to get "his" parliament on board). A little wrangling generally leads to an agreement between the member states and the Parliament, although not always.

3. *When the Union needs direction: the strategist*

The European Council gives the Union strategic direction. In the few sentences it devotes to this institution, the Treaty says that it "shall define the general political directions and priorities" of the Union.[19] At home the individual members determine the course to be taken by their governments; together they do so for the Union as a whole.

The same paragraph states that the European Council "shall provide the Union with the necessary impetus for its development". The development of new fields of work is a matter for the highest level. In 1972 the heads of government asked the Commission to make a start on environmental and regional policies, and these were soon in place. At the same time they set course for an economic and monetary union "before the end of the decade", an aim that was met only many years later. When in 1991 in Maastricht the leaders decided on joint engagement in foreign affairs and justice policy for their new Union, two highly sensitive areas, they tasked themselves with determining the "strategic interests and objectives" and the "strategic guidelines".[20] Give an impetus; keep a hold.

As a strategist the European Council is expected to confine itself to the broad outlines. If it puts its hands directly on the controls it will irritate the other institutions. The Treaty specifically says that it "shall not exercise legislative functions".[21] Those lie with the legislative triangle of Commission, Council of Ministers and Parliament (generally referred to as the "institutional" triangle). There are nevertheless grey areas. The strategic orientations of the heads of government often specify the deadline or parameters for new legislation. As a general rule, the more political obstacles are anticipated, the more precisely the course is mapped out. The Commission does sometimes feel stymied in the exercise of its right to "take appropriate initiatives".[22] Such friction is inevitable: who can say exactly where the "impetus" and "guidelines" end and the right to "take appropriate initiatives" begins?

A compass alone does not suffice when practical obstacles are greater than the will to reach the destination. The decision in 2000 to make the Union the world's most innovative economy within the space of ten years is one example of overconfidence. The prospect was introduced at the expense of credibility. Still, the announcement that a subject will be discussed at the highest level has an inspiring effect; it sets practical and intellectual preparations in train in all the capitals and in Brussels – even if the leaders eventually spend only half an hour on the subject. The strategist thereby reinforces a shared sense of direction.

4. *When the fundamentals have to change: the shaper*

The Union, with all its institutions, rests on a treaty. It cannot change its own fundamentals. The population has the final word on the shape Europe takes. Although every member state has a veto, and therefore stagnation might be expected, the basic rules have been changed five times since 1985. How is this possible? Anyone who looks carefully will see not merely 28 veto-holders but a single body with which they are bound up despite themselves: the club of member states, expressed in a political sense in the European Council. Here lies Europe's constituent power.*

The leaders have appointed themselves guardians of the rules of the game. In treaty negotiations the European Council, a Union institution, acts as an Intergovernmental Conference, an older form of diplomatic gathering: same club, different name.[23]

---

* To stress their fundamental position in Union law, the German constitutional court once called the member states the "masters of the Treaty", a useful notion; in light of the above analysis, this Karlsruhe self-confidence needs a slight adjustment: the club of member states is "master of the Treaty", in the singular.

As well as the rules of the game, the membership also determines the nature of the Union. Does Europe take shape with or without the British, Danes, Greeks, Poles, Bulgarians, Turks or Ukrainians? With his brusque veto on British accession in 1963, De Gaulle made a *Chefsache* out of this issue of identity. The heads of government have ever since been the gatekeeper of the club, which functions as the successor to the "Concert of Europe", the alliance that from 1648 to 1914 gave shape to the power balance and diplomatic relations between European states, and determined who could take part.

No surprise, then, that even a member state that wants to leave the Union, as Britain decided to do by referendum, reports this intention to the European Council, which draws up guidelines for the divorce.[24]

5. *When Europe needs to speak: the spokesperson*

What is the telephone number for Europe? The Kissinger Question remains pertinent. To know what "Europe" thinks about something, Kissinger's successors call leaders in Berlin, London (for now), Paris and Rome as well as the institutional EU players. National leaders speak with authority mainly in their own country's name; Brussels players cannot truly bind the member states. The best place to get everyone "on the phone" at once is the European Council. Something of the sort happened during the refugee crisis in the spring of 2016, when the complete European Council made a deal with Turkey, represented by the Turkish premier. This EU–Turkey deal, admittedly prearranged with Ankara by Berlin, The Hague and Brussels, ultimately brought 30 people, in the name of the Union, into conversation with one. At such a moment the European Council is a kind of collective head of state, not working in an Oval Office but at a Round Table.

The public at home, too, would like to know who speaks "in Europe's name". This is not just a matter of legally binding decisions, since sometimes European words are needed for public consumption. Who takes the stage when refugees drown off Europe's coasts, who offers condolences after an earthquake or a terrorist attack, who gives a speech of thanks when "Europe" goes to Oslo to receive a Nobel Prize? Gesture politics is still politics.

THE AUTHORITY OF THE MEETING

Power at home

Authority is an older, broader concept than legitimacy. The latter is familiar to academics and is generally used to analyse the democratic basis of a political system (in our case the Union). Legitimacy theories typically reduce political life to a decision-making machine. Deploying factory vocabulary, they analyse "input legitimacy", or the degree of electoral influence beforehand, "output legitimacy", or the results put out by the decision-making factory, and "throughput legitimacy", rigorously examining whether the internal process plays out as it should.[25] This pragmatic view, it struck Bagehot, ignores the fact that acceptance of decisions is often based not purely on participation, effectiveness and transparency – aspects of "legitimacy" – but on respect and trust, habit and tradition, embodiment and symbolism.[26] Theorists of legitimacy mostly find such factors inferior, primitive or "illegitimate". By contrast, the more capacious notion of "authority", familiar to historians, sociologists and philosophers of law, can give all these things a place alongside the others, in a broader perspective on society and the political order.

If we examine the workings of the European Council in this light, then we see that a precondition of a productive meeting is that each of those present brings an authority of their own. Brussels usage loosely refers to the European Council as "the heads", "*les chefs*", "the leaders", terms that usually refer to a relationship of authority. Put more formally, each member speaks at a summit in the name of one country and is expected to be able to commit his or her government and population politically to a joint decision.

At home the members of the European Council all have the same function, namely to run their countries, in which their power depends on the support of the public. They have acquired that national position as a result of personal qualities or circumstances: drive, eloquence, experience, bluff or luck. But that base is in a sense taken as read. At a summit the main thing that counts is what each contributes in the form of political power to commit. This becomes plainly visible at election time. Anybody who has recently won an election is in a strong position among colleagues; a new electoral mandate means fresh power at home. In the spring of 2012, Socialist presidential candidate

François Hollande promised his voters a "European growth pact", signifying a break with the stability pact, which focused only on discipline. At the first summit after his victory, the other leaders conceded the point. For Italian premier Matteo Renzi, not chosen at the ballot box but coming to power in a palace coup, the European elections of 2014 were a first electoral test in his own country; afterwards he declared that by number of votes his party had become "the second party of Europe", and so at the table he demanded his due. Even though this swaggering did not go down well with the other leaders, his wish was granted with the appointment of his minister Federica Mogherini to a top EU position. It works the other way too. A leader nearing the end of a term in office and behind in the polls loses influence: he or she might not be there next time. A prime minister with a substantial parliamentary majority is in a stronger position than the leader of a minority government or a shaky multi-party coalition, and can therefore more plausibly commit their government. The authority of the European Council depends partly on its members' power at home, so it is very much subject to the rhythm of national electoral cycles and the mood of voters.

For most national leaders, domestic power ultimately rests on their leadership of a political party, and they bring their political colours with them to summits. Ahead of a European Council they meet up as Conservatives, Socialists or Liberals, to coordinate their approaches or, for example, to pre-arrange the filling of posts. So, the main thrusts of party politics also enter into the forum of conflicts of interest between nations, a development that is not without consequences.

The guest list

Full-on institutional battles are fought over the question of who gets a seat at the table or a place in the summit photograph. Such incidents are to political analysis what the lapsus is to psychoanalysis. Just as Freud hoped to plumb the hidden depths of the human psyche by examining slips of the tongue and failed jokes, so a skirmish over protocol can offer a glimpse of power relationships and shifts in power that would otherwise remain invisible.

Who are the members of the European Council? In the first place the "Heads of State or Government of the Member States".[27] One person per country. Who it will be, the head of state or the head of government, is for

185

each nation to decide. Rule of thumb: you send the leader of the political executive. So Germany sends its federal chancellor, not the federal president; France sends the president of the Republic, not the prime minister; Britain sends its premier, not the queen.

The president of the European Commission is also a member of the European Council, an often neglected but crucial fact.* At the first summits in the 1960s, the holder of this office was not invited; in 1967 the president of the Commission, Jean Rey, was disappointed at being allowed to attend for just two hours. But since 1972 his successors have always participated, since 1975 as members. The president of the Commission is a good fit, as a sort of "head of the executive" not of the Union as such but of the Brussels regulatory apparatus. His or her membership creates a firm link between the gathered leaders and that apparatus. The Commission president can introduce ideas, have plans approved and, conversely, be given tasks, although institutional sensitivities mean that the latter must not be described as such ("the European Council invites the Commission to ..." is the wording used). In certain circumstances this figure raises a view expressed by the European Parliament, in that sense resembling the leaders around the table, of whom a number also bring homework set by their parliaments. The Commission president also interprets the voice of the Treaty, where necessary indicating what decisions are possible within the European legal order and where the limits lie.

Thirdly, the permanent president of the European Council is also a member. The gavel used to be passed round between the member states, with six-month terms for each. This meant that every European Council president remained the head of government in his or her own country and did the European work on top. (This rotation is still in place for the Council of Ministers.) The reform took effect in late 2009. As host the president has three tasks: to prepare the meetings and lead the debates; to draw the conclusions; and to ensure the continuity of activities. The rotating presidents had the first two of these tasks, but the third is new and a natural accompaniment to the longer

---

* Those concerned prefer not to stress the fact that they are part of the club, since in the Brussels game they, as Commission presidents, also position themselves opposite the national leaders gathered in the European Council. In reality this means they are guilty of the same double play as that for which national politicians are often reproached, in that in front of their supporters – in this case the European Parliament and Brussels circles – they distance themselves from jointly made Union decisions.

period available to the permanent, full-time president: not six months but two and a half or a maximum of five years. A term ten times as long means the president can make mid-term plans and if necessary return to matters previously discussed.

Finally, the high representative for foreign policy joins the European Council, not as a member but to "take part in its work".[28] In practice this means that he or she (the first two representatives have been women) is present when the heads of government discuss foreign policy but not other points on the agenda.

Among themselves

Essential to the success of the meetings is club feeling. Among themselves, the leaders are equals. They call each other by their first names. Even newcomers, sometimes uncomfortably, say "Angela", "Emmanuel", "Theresa", "Mark", "Viktor" and "Jean-Claude". At the table – once oval, now round – each has a fixed place: the president of the European Council sits on the axis of the room, the president of the Commission directly opposite. The seats for each nation are in the order in which they occupy the (still rotating) presidency of the Council of Ministers. Those national chairs shift round simultaneously by one place every six months, so that the country holding the ministers' gavel is always to the right of the president.

The number of civil servants in the room is kept strictly to a minimum. To the left of the president sits the secretary-general of the Council, the only non-elected figure at the table. Five more officials sit in a second row: the European Council president's chief of staff, the permanent representative of the rotating presidency of the Council of Ministers, one legal and one political Council adviser, plus the secretary-general of the Commission. More discreet, and present only at formal working sessions, are two rapporteurs who report on the gathering verbally, in relays, to the right hands (or "Anticis") of the 28 EU ambassadors, who each type out a report and send it to their national diplomatic corps. Journalists like to give chase to these Antici Group reports (although none are compiled during the exclusive dinner sessions, despite the fact that the most important decisions are made there, quite often in the middle of the night). Aside from the leaders and this handful of civil servants, no one is allowed into the room. If, for example, the French president wants to speak to his ambassador, he has to go outside. This is in marked contrast to the ordinary Council of Ministers, where there is a constant coming and going, where ministers can without embarrassment send a secretary of state or ambassador in their place, and where sometimes as many as six civil servants per delegation sit in the second row to check whether their boss is reading out accurately all the points prepared in advance. Amid such hubbub, with 150 people or more, it is hard to create the kind of mutual trust and club feeling that makes tough agreements possible. The intimate character of the European Council is indispensable to the dynamics of the meeting.

Rarely does a government leader fail to attend. Absentees are not permitted to send a substitute but have to ask a fellow leader to speak on their behalf. Members only.

For many years, government leaders were accompanied to summits by their foreign ministers. These were denied entry from 2009 onwards. Following the major enlargement of 2004 there had been at least 50 people around the table, using television monitors to see each other. This was very different from the old fireside club. The departure of the foreign ministers has a broader significance: European politics is no longer foreign policy but primarily domestic politics.

MISE-EN-SCÈNE

Visibility is a precondition of political authority. Politicians without the press, without public debate, without demonstrators are mere civil servants. Democracy demands individuals who publicly take personal responsibility for decisions and who embody institutional responsibility, if necessary attaching their own political survival to it.

The dramatic stage-setting enables summits to promote strong ties with the public. The cast is crucial. Practically all Europeans know one or more of the members: the leader of their own country, probably those of France, Germany or Britain as well, plus one or more other member states, perhaps a neighbour, and a Brussels president or one of the personalities who challenge the club rules, like Silvio Berlusconi, Alexis Tsipras or Viktor Orbán. Three, four, five famous players, unity of place – these elements give the European Council a uniquely dramatic quality. The tie with the public lends the forum a large measure of authority. Moreover, it provides the European Council with a powerful argument against the reproach that the Union is run by unelected bureaucrats, obscure ministers and parliamentarians alienated from their voters. It is the only Union institution that cannot be reduced to "Brussels" but instead presents a picture of "Europe".

For a long time the European Council was a travelling circus. Every six-month presidency organized at least one meeting in its own country, an amiable roadshow that over the years stopped at a French royal château, an Italian renaissance palace, a British stately home, a Greek island, a Belgian palace, a Portuguese monastery and countless other locations.

The membership grew and security measures – stepped up considerably around the turn of the century in response to anti-globalization demonstrations – made hosting it an increasing burden. It also became almost impossible to arrange an extra meeting at short notice. In 2000 the leaders decided to take the show off the road and since 2003 all the regular summits have been held in Brussels, for many years in a vast office block named after a humanist called Justus Lipsius, a building one permanent occupant described as "exuding a Soviet-style soberness".[29] Since early 2017 the European Council has had a new home with the official name of "Europa", also known as "the Space Egg".

Visibility requires, to put it crudely, pictures – fodder for cameras, moving or still. One of the most important visual motifs of Brussels is this: a limousine stops outside, a government leader or minister steps out and utters two or three sentences prior to the meeting, tailored to the television news. A "doorstep", the exercise is called in the journalistic jargon. It is striking how differences fall away; even speakers from small or relatively unimportant countries can emerge as media favourites for their arresting doorstep language. During the Greek crisis in the summer of 2015, hundreds of experts could hear, from the tone of the doorstep, the chances of compromise slipping away. Slovakian, Finnish, German and Dutch politicians expressed incomprehension or even anger at the behaviour of Athens, first outside the door, then inside in the room.

This threshold moment could be said to typify Europe's democratization. What happens in Brussels no longer takes place purely behind closed doors. Conflicts are increasingly discussed in public, "on the doorstep, in the transition from a national public sphere to a European sphere, which is now emerging".[30] The European Council creates a public space and thereby makes the Union more democratic. As we shall see later, in the process it can also offer a perhaps unanticipated platform for political opposition.

A second visual motif is the family photograph. The leaders, neatly arranged in two or three rows, look straight at the camera (although puerile behaviour can never be ruled out). The protocol service will have stuck little national and European flags to the floor so that they all know their place. Protocol dictates that presidents (heads of state) take precedence over prime ministers and chancellors (heads of government). Seniority and the cycle of rotation for the Council of Ministers are given due weight as well. The photograph itself has barely any news value but it does show who was there; in recent years the photo is only taken at special occasions.

This family photo provides a chance for non-members to prove to their populations they were present in powerful company. A lot can be riding on that for the leaders of candidate members. In the years before the accession of Poland and other Central and Eastern European countries, their presidents and premiers were granted this privilege. The tradition fell into disuse after 2004, to the great frustration of Turkey, a candidate at the time, as it still is, years later. After repeated urgings, Ankara attained the symbolic prize again in late 2015. Superficial nonsense? No. For domestic consumption the photograph of the Turkish premier among the European leaders gave a stronger signal that accession was possible than all the Brussels talk about "chapters" in negotiations that can or cannot be "opened". Every television viewer or newspaper reader in Istanbul or Konya saw immediately: our man is among them.

One figure who successfully fought to appear in the photograph was the president of the European Parliament. Although not a member of the European Council, this top MEP does have a brief exchange with the leaders at the start of the meeting. The family snapshot used to be taken immediately afterwards, presenting a natural opportunity to get the guest out of the room. No idle precaution this: the Parliament, in the words of a former senior civil servant in Strasbourg, has "fought a thirty-year campaign to be 'present', visibly, at the top table in the European Union". Because of its relatively low profile among its own voters, the Parliament seeks support from the media spotlight as it shines on the gathered national leaders.

190

Right from the start, meetings of the European Council have drawn more than a thousand journalists from the member states and far beyond. The press understands these summits as a "locus of power" and a story generator. Clashing personalities, historic decisions, a battle for power and money – things happen. So, summits offer what cannot easily be had from the rule-making factory: a tangible public-political moment.

When a summit ends, not just the president but all members of the European Council give a press conference. (It is as if after the Tuesday cabinet meeting at 10 Downing Street, ministers were free to speak about it to the press, and all did so.) They each give their own version, in their own language, to some of the media, largely simultaneously. Sometimes it seems as if they were all at different meetings. Nevertheless, a leader cannot tell a story that directly contradicts what the others are saying. The formal conclusions – generally published straight after the meeting – offer a reference point and bind everyone. Note that the conclusions are politically not legally binding – a significant difference. After the establishment of the European Council in 1974, Brussels lawyers and civil servants in the national capitals, fond of the tête-à-têtes between the Commission and the Council of Ministers, spent decades acting as if the newcomer did not exist, since the letter of the law stated that the leaders do not take "decisions" themselves. The press, which reported en masse on the summits, showed greater sensitivity to how things actually stood. The will of the leaders became law: their political agreements had a binding effect at the level of the Council of Ministers.[31]

Media pressure makes a decisive contribution to the dynamics of the meeting. With more than a thousand reporters at the door, it is well-nigh impossible to step out and say. "We couldn't resolve this one". The impossibility of failure, one president called it. A meeting of ministers can be adjourned – "No comment, our discussions will continue next week" – but with the circus of a summit this is impossible. If there is no agreement, the press have to be given something, if only a wafer-thin final declaration. (In four decades the leaders have gone home without giving a press conference only once, in Athens in 1983.) The media can stoke division, wreck reputations, undermine claims. Precisely because of its immense power, media attention is productive, propelling the European Council towards more unity and decisiveness than individual members think themselves capable of beforehand.

A new cast of executives

The Union has its own supreme political authority in the form of the European Council, able to give direction, cut through the knottiest of problems
and, to that end, take responsibility before the people. As a forum it therefore
meets the initial condition for engaging in events-politics. But authoritative
decision-making power alone is not sufficient. It acquires its dynamic effect
only in conjunction with other governmental functions, such as initiation
and appropriation, leadership and control, implementation and follow-up.
To avoid pinning down any train of thought in advance, I have deliberately
chosen rather loose terms; what concerns me here is the distinction between
these active characteristics typical of the profession of leaders and executives,
who benefit from energy, unity and persistence, and the representational
characteristics of lawmakers in parliaments, focused on debate, acceptance,
control and the voice of the public.[32] In this sense the bulk of government
functions should not be sought in discussions by 30 leaders around a table;
they need internal articulation, and connections with other institutions and
players.

Time to turn to the stage on which the political executive in the Union
performs – as distinct from the lawmakers opposite them and the administrative executive under them – where in the acts and scenes of the crises
we saw a motley crew at work. The members and president of the European
Council are central figures on this stage, but of course there are others; on
several occasions we encountered the president and members of the Commission, saw finance ministers in the Eurogroup labouring away, foreign
ministers on missions to Kiev, justice ministers discussing the refugee crisis
– and that is to leave aside for the time being the central bankers in Frankfurt. How best to interpret the lines of authority and the connections in this
performance? How are executive functions distributed among players and
institutions, given that it is not necessarily one-on-one? And the key question: in this combined action, how does the Union generate the indispensable
decisiveness at moments of crisis that is potentially available to it through
the summits?

What follows is not a static charting of the executive state of affairs
but a sketch of a stage full of movement, emergence, development and

displacement, an approach that better befits the turbulent interplay of events in which the executive power in the Union unfolds and emancipates itself.

EXECUTIVE COUNCILS

The Council of Ministers was always an apparently inextricable tangle of legislative and executive functions. For the rule-making factory this was an advantage, but events-politics makes different demands.

Brussels teleology sees the executive decision-making power of the Council of Ministers as "residual";[33] in the long run only legislative functions should remain. According to the federal design, in a two-chamber system the Council will eventually become a kind of European Senate (representing states) alongside the European Parliament (representing citizens), as distinct from the Commission (government), not unlike the Senate in Washington or the Bundestag in Berlin.

This vision is at odds with actual practice. Recent shifts have indeed created more constitutional clarity at the level of lawmaking, but they contradict the assumption that the executive power of the national governments collectively is a shrivelling residue. Because while the legislative power is emancipating itself, an executive function is at the same time emerging from the jumble of the original Council. The setting up of the European Council of government leaders in 1974 was an early example of this emancipation, but over the past decade it has accelerated.

The Lisbon Treaty of 2009 introduced two significant changes to the Council of Ministers. In the name of transparency it made a sharp distinction between on the one hand the Council in "legislative deliberations", when members vote (in public and viewable via livestream), and the Council when it engages in consultation, negotiation or decision-making (behind closed doors).[34] In the former case the Council of Ministers, as "co-legislator", is the partner of the European Parliament, which also meets in public. In the latter it stands alone. What happens behind closed doors remains confidential, but it cannot then be lawmaking. Potentially, therefore, there is room for the Council of Ministers to act as an executive.

The second separation of functions concerned the slicing up of the old General Affairs and External Relations Council, for years the Brussels bastion of foreign ministers, into a Council for general affairs and a Council for foreign affairs, the first with a legislative task and the second with an executive task. The intention was for the General Affairs Council to grow to become an umbrella organ for all the legislative work and legally binding decision-making. (The European Convention of 2002–03 wanted to call this body candidly the Legislative Council, a semantic move immediately overruled at the next stage by the ministers themselves.) In practice this new Council has not lived up to its promise. Legislative work therefore remains distributed among ministers in the various configurations of the Council, such as for agriculture, or for economics and finance: a failed emancipation of the legislative power.

Yet the clarity achieved by the splitting of the two councils has been preserved in the case of the Foreign Affairs Council. In this forum the foreign ministers deal with issues that are "foreign" for the Union as a whole. These rarely involve lawmaking. It produces many declarations, about countless crises in the world, so to call it an "executive power" seems overblown. Nor does it have the free range of the government leaders, although it does take decisions about sanctions against Iran, or about military and other crisis missions. For wars close by, or for issues with profound domestic consequences (security, energy), the foreign ministers act under the aegis of their presidents and premiers.[35] When in late February 2014 the Ukraine crisis changed from a popular revolt to an annexation, from "Maidan" to "Crimea", it became a matter for the leaders. For day-to-day affairs or distant crises, the foreign ministers act on their own authority. In doing so they undeniably fulfil an executive function.

EUROGROUP

What goes for the foreign ministers also holds true for the finance ministers of eurozone countries. They too have extricated themselves from a mixed body, in their case the Economic and Financial Affairs Council (ECOFIN); since the launch of the euro they have met monthly as the Eurogroup.[36] Consultation takes place behind closed doors. Participation is limited to the ministers, a commissioner and a member of the board of the European Central Bank, each with one adviser. Club feeling and a business-like style set the tone. In their own governments, finance ministers hold the purse strings and need to stand firm against colleagues in spending ministries. The informal and private setting allows the ECB to join them in political meetings without this raising doubts about its independence. Lawmaking and other binding judicial acts are not formally undertaken by the eurozone ministers. Instead, according to the Treaty, at the Union level these still lie with all the finance ministers, whether inside or outside the eurozone.[37]

Since the euro crisis the Eurogroup has engaged in more executive decision-making than ever, the main reason being that the gathering of euro finance ministers forms, as per the rules, the Board of Governors of the Stability Mechanism, the emergency fund that decides on loans to member states in need of money.[38] So this Board is therefore de facto none other than the Eurogroup. This betokens a major upgrade for the body, which in its capacity as emergency creditor takes binding and hugely far-reaching decisions.

This task in crisis management brought the executive nature of the Eurogroup into the public eye from 2010–12 onwards. The frequency of meetings increased; members sometimes came together at extremely short notice or met by video conference. The public impact of its decisions increased too, first of all in countries with aid programmes. Yet there was a determination to cling to the private and informal character of these gatherings, with relatively limited communication – especially given the intense interest among both markets and the public. (The Eurogroup does not systematically publish written conclusions of its meetings.) This way of working faced increasing criticism, which reached a peak in early 2015 when a government came into office in Greece that publicly demanded a left-wing course in EU affairs. The new Greek finance minister Yanis Varoufakis did not hold with the informal club rules of the Eurogroup. He gave his colleagues lessons in Keynesian economic policy and refused any longer to be pushed into the position of a debtor confronting the bankers. The 18 other ministers expressed their impatience. After less than three months the newcomer was ejected from the circle at a quarrelsome meeting in Riga; he spoke of an ambush and of "character assassination" with the complicity of the press.[39]

The underlying conflict concerned whether the Eurogroup as a technocratic body merely applies currency-union rules, as most of the national financial experts see it, or also takes "political" decisions, as the Greek minister contended, and whether it has the political authority to do so.* Under public pressure, the Eurogroup is now gradually putting out more accounts of its meetings.

This sequencing makes clear that executive power first has to manifest itself before it can be publicly called to account. Whoever governs needs to go out and face the opposition.

PERMANENT PRESIDENTS

The circles of foreign ministers and of eurozone finance ministers have another thing in common: not only did they both separate themselves, as executive formations of the Council, from the original array of Councils, they both gave themselves a permanent president. Since 2009 meetings of foreign ministers have been chaired by the high representative (currently Federica Mogherini), while the eurozone ministers have had a permanent president ever since 2005 (from early 2018 onwards Mário Centeno). By contrast, the gavel of the other formations of the Council, where lawmaking or policy coordination take place, continues to rotate among member states, with six-month terms. As we have seen, the European Council of government leaders, itself also an executive break-away group from the "Council family", gave itself a permanent president in the Lisbon Treaty of 2009 (since 2014 Donald Tusk).

There is a pattern to this threefold game of musical chairs. Premiers, finance ministers and foreign ministers are among the frontline players, the decision-makers, in their national governments. Permanent presidents offer continuity and a point of contact. When the world spins out of control you are better off not rotating yourself. True, since the Union is based on shared responsibility, its permanent presidents can hardly behave like presidential figures, but they do make possible a form of collective leadership and ownership of decisions. Moreover, they personify European authority. As "Mr President", "Mr euro" and "Ms EU" they are in theory the most exposed to the

---

* The same reproach was aimed at President Draghi of the European Central Bank when in February 2015 he ended emergency funding for the Greek banking system: "a hostile, deeply political move by the ECB against my own government", according to Varoufakis in *Adults in the Room*, 207.

limelight. The Council's permanent presidencies can also be seen as signifying a gradual development of executive power in the Union.

As a result of its own political authority, the European Council is the only one of the three with full executive functions and powers, and it has the fewest limitations. This is true in a political sense because all members are assumed to be "in charge" at home, and therefore able to bind their own governments and parliaments to European decisions. It is also true in an institutional sense, because the circle of presidents and premiers is accustomed to stepping outside the formal framework of the Treaty in emergencies, as an informal meeting of the leaders of the member states.[40] Not constrained by the rule-making factory, they can move onto unknown territory and, outside the Treaty if necessary, step into the future together. For engagement in events-politics this is a trump card.

CONNECTION MAN

The European Council is a political power station, generating energy from the leaders' power at home and from the dynamism of their meetings. There is a danger, however, that the power station sometimes operates in a vacuum, that the spectacle of a summit will be without consequences. The energy generated is lost if not channelled by the Brussels and national administrations.

In this energy transmission, the president has a vital role. The modest but essential remit is to lay the institutional wiring and maintain the connections, so that the Union, when things get tense, has a vehicle for events-politics. The role is rather like that of a helpful connection man between the lines. According to the first occupant of the position, the competences assigned by the Treaty are "rather vague, even meagre". The president of the European Council does not have any executive decision-making power – "no budgetary responsibility, no administration of his own and no right of appointment";[41] his or her task is to enable collective decision-making. In contrast to their rotating predecessors, who were leaders of governments at home and could therefore deploy their national administrations and governments, the permanent presidents have a limited support apparatus and no hold on the Council of Ministers. Herman Van Rompuy felt "disconnected" from the other Union institutions and his successor feels the same. From day one the Belgian tried to compensate for the lack of formal links by developing informal relationships. Council and Commission presidents Van Rompuy and Barroso arranged to have breakfast together once a week, for example, a tradition upheld by their successors, and there were monthly meetings with the president of the Parliament. As a matter of principle, the president visited all 28 members of the European Council in their own seats of government once a year, a tour of the capitals that strengthened relationships of trust and made the importance of all member states visible. This routine maintenance has been abandoned by his successor in favour of visits prompted by current events.

Before the Lisbon Treaty there was a natural chain of command between the head of state or government who led the European Council and his or her ministers, who sat in the various configurations of the Council of Ministers. This enabled a strong leader to steer the Brussels machinery from their own capital for six months, as French President Sarkozy did in the second half of 2008 (dealing with the banking crisis, the war between Russia and Georgia and the climate accord). After "Lisbon" this chain of command between leaders and ministers ceased to exist. Here too, informal coordination and consultation, along with shared administrative support by the general secretariat of the Council, has to make up for the absence of formal relationships.

Formal links were created between the forum of the leaders and the two executive ministerial councils. The high representative, in that capacity chair of the Council of Foreign Ministers, is a "participant" in the European Council. Her presence makes a connection between the leaders and the gathering of foreign ministers. A comparable formula exists for summits of leaders of the eurozone countries, where it is the president of the Eurogroup who joins in.[42] His presidency too makes an implicit hierarchical connection between two decision-making fora, as became clear in the euro crisis.

In the refugee crisis of 2015–16 the first vice-president of the Commission, Frans Timmermans, twice reported to the European Council on the negotiations with Turkey. Similarly, since March 2017 the Union's Brexit negotiator Michel Barnier has come to many summits for consultation. Such players move between technical and high politics, between the engine room and the bridge – and at moments of crisis they face into the wind.

On paper, European Council meetings are prepared by the General Affairs Council. In practice this forum does not fulfil any such role. The main reason is that not all its members – often junior ministers with the Europe portfolio, or members of a coalition party – have the ear of "their" leader in the European Council. Because personal trust is crucial in the final negotiating phase, these ministers are often unable to remove obstacles at their own level. Instead, two other bodies take on the preparations for summits. One is the formal network of the permanent representatives based in Brussels (COREPER II), a well-oiled machine but with members who in their own countries sometimes lack sufficient weight. The other is the informal network of EU advisers to the 28 members of the European Council, also known as "sherpas" (because their task is to bring their leaders "to the summit"). These are the civil servants with responsibility for the European Union in the German Federal Chancellery, the Elysée Palace, 10 Downing Street and all the other capitals, as well as in the Commission. This second organ, although informal and scattered, has gained power considerably over the past few years, as presidents and prime ministers have needed to concern themselves more and more intensively with ongoing crises. Unlike the circle of ambassadors, that of the sherpas is not led by the rotating presidency but by the chief of staff of the European Council president. The sherpa network, powerful and invisible, reinforces the executive power of Europe's system of government.

EURO SUMMITRY

Under the pressure of the financial crises, another forum of executive decision-making has made itself independent since 2008: meetings of heads of state and government of the eurozone countries, called Euro Summits.

France has for a long time wanted greater involvement by government leaders in decisions about the common currency. In July 2007 Nicolas Sarkozy, recently elected president, broke with protocol by unexpectedly inviting himself to join the ministers of the Eurogroup. This was unprecedented gate-crashing. Germany by contrast has for years resisted involvement by the national leaders in eurozone policy, fearful of politicization of the corset of rules for the currency and erosion of ECB independence. When in the autumn of 2008 the banking crisis erupted and Sarkozy happened to hold the rotating presidency of the European Council, he called a meeting of all the eurozone leaders for 12 October, after failed consultation with just the four strongest eurozone countries. Although Angela Merkel initially threatened to stay at home, in the end she came. It was wholly exceptional – "once but never again", as she repeated in January 2010 behind closed doors. Yet the Frenchman had set a precedent.

When the Greek crisis erupted, the president of the European Council cautiously built upon this precedent. In March 2010 it became clear that only the eurozone countries were willing to give financial assistance to Athens, while the sums involved and the degree of public controversy undeniably made this decision a *Chefsache*. During the scheduled European Council of 25–26 March 2010, Van Rompuy therefore announced an ad hoc meeting of eurozone leaders. The plenary session was adjourned so that the 16 could gather among themselves. (There followed a moment of hesitation: where should the meeting take place? Should the 16 eurozone members, including the German chancellor and the French president, look for a room of their own, or should the 11 non-euro countries, including the British and Polish prime ministers, absent themselves? The former remained seated.) After this discreet meeting under the cover of the ordinary summit, a separate and therefore visible summit of eurozone leaders followed on Friday 7 May. It was needed to stave off the acute threat of contagion right across the eurozone and to mobilize "the full range of means available" in the Union. Its decisions were afterwards communicated on a sheet of paper without even a proper letterhead – this too was impromptu. After another special crisis summit in the summer of 2011, plus several in the margins of regular meetings, the body acquired an official status. On 23 October 2011 it named itself the Euro Summit and three days later, in consultation with the complete European Council, it allocated itself a package of tasks, a working procedure and an administrative machinery.[43] The Fiscal Stability Treaty of early 2012, although formally external to the Union Treaty, provided for summits at least twice a year.[44] Yet resistance to the forum remained, both in Germany and in non-euro countries, such as Poland. Partly for this reason the frequency of meetings reduced as the euro crisis was brought under control. Formally there was just one Euro Summit in 2012–14, but when the Greek crisis flared up again in 2015 the number rose to four.

Like the other executive Councils, the Euro Summit gave itself a permanent president. In the spring of 2010 at least three leaders coveted the euro gavel: Spanish Prime Minister Zapatero, whose country held the six-month presidency of the Council of Ministers but was economically weak; French President Sarkozy, with good memories of his initiative in 2008; and summit chair Van Rompuy, with the argument of coherence and continuity on his side. The latter emerged the victor on 25 March 2010. He was already in position and refused to budge. He bought off the Spaniard with face-saving participation in a joint press conference afterwards. Sarkozy did not immediately give way, as evidenced by the *mise-en-scène* of his press conference after the crisis summit of 7 May 2010: from behind the flags of all the eurozone countries the Frenchman posed as the saviour of the currency. In October 2011 Van Rompuy formally acquired the presidency of the Euro Summit. The precedent of his dual role was upheld by the appointment of Donald Tusk (despite being from a non-euro country) as president of both the European Council and the Euro Summit. A useful personal union, which prevents rivalry.

Although from time to time the French express a desire for monthly meetings, as a way of forming an "economic government" for the eurozone,[45] Euro Summits have proved themselves mainly as a means of reaching decisions in times of crisis. For the daily decisions of eurozone countries, the complete European Council serves where necessary as the top of the euro decision-making pyramid (if a slightly lopsided one, since the 28 leaders have below them the Eurogroup with its 19 finance ministers and their own preparatory organs). Moreover, with the departure of Britain the relationship between member states that are part of the eurozone and those that are not will shift; it is conceivable that the pressure on members to join the monetary union will increase and the usefulness of the separate euro channel diminish.

The emergence of the Euro Summit is illustrative of a Union that institutionally renews itself under the pressure of events – first outside the treaty, then step by step within existing structures – and acquires the capacity to take quick and authoritative collective decisions. After the European Council, the Eurogroup and the Foreign Affairs Council, which gained their independence from the jumble of the original Council, it is the next executive formation to separate itself from (in its case) the European Council, and to increase the vigour of the Union partly through having a permanent presidency.

Between backstage and frontstage

THE ROLES OF THE COMMISSION

The Commission likes to call itself "the European executive" and the media are happy to echo this. It thereby cleverly exploits the ambiguity of the term "executive power", which after all embraces both administrative and political executives, both civil service and government. With the qualification "administration" the Commission feels short-changed, but it cannot demand the term "government" without prompting a revolt. By using the ambiguous "executive" it keeps its fans content, without giving its detractors ammunition. Yet this ambiguity is unsatisfactory, as is the usual academic way out of calling it one of a kind (*sui generis*).

The lens of authority creates a clearer picture of the strengths and weaknesses of the institution. The Commission is a product of the founding treaty entered into by the states. Its position therefore fundamentally rests on legal authority, which within its limitations is binding and incontestable. The Treaty assigns to it three roles: political pacesetter; supervisor and inspector; and bureaucratic operative. The precise nature of the authority that enables it to play these roles touches upon a phenomenon that is difficult to interpret and little studied. Russian philosopher Alexandre Kojève made a start by distinguishing four ideal types: the Father and the authority of tradition; the Warrior who puts his life on the line; the Leader who sets out a course; and the Judge who passes wise judgments.[46]

If we look at the Commission as Kojève would, then we see that the institution in the role of "Judge", or rather prosecutor, holds the strongest cards. It fearlessly doles out huge fines to Google or Microsoft, raids companies, rebukes member states – a formidable player, vital for the market machinery. But the Commission is proudest of its role as Leader. The Treaty gave it the glorious task of promoting "the general interest of the Union" and taking "appropriate initiatives" for that purpose.[47] Here it saw potential and began endlessly hankering, striving, angling and testing.

Why has it not succeeded? Principally because political authority cannot be derived from legal authority. While as a judge or civil servant you can get started straight away based on legal authority, the role of Leader necessitates political authority. This is not conferred in its entirety along with a task set by a treaty but must be won. So, the Commission went in search of a political authority of its own, independent of the member states, expressed in the actual recognition by the public of its power to pass final judgement and take decisions. If people listen when it speaks, then it has acquired political authority. If not, not. Compare the ECB: it likewise started from a Treaty-mandate and meanwhile indisputably also gained political authority – when Draghi speaks, the markets listen.

The Commission placed its bets on direct elections to the European Parliament, held every five years since 1979. Over time the two institutions have constructed a relationship resembling that of a government and a parliament, complete with votes of confidence, public hearings and parliamentary questions.[48] At issue, though, is whether the Commission can derive as much political authority from parliamentary elections as it hopes. Its source of authority remains twofold, with administrative appointments by the member states and political election by the Parliament: a balancing act.[49]

There remains the authority of the judge and civil servant, appropriate to the rule-making factory. This, as we have seen, is ironclad, but it does not work when the Union has to engage in events-politics. The misconception resides in the belief that the Commission can be the "government" of the Union as a whole, whereas it is more correctly seen as an essential component of the executive structures of the Union. The Commission is part of the administrative executive, where its position is strong, and it is also affiliated to the actual political executive. The president of the Commission is an important figure within Europe's political executive, that handful of politicians who face into the wind. He belongs to it both in his own right and as a member of the European Council, where his presence creates a crucial link between the inner sphere of Brussels and the intermediate sphere of the member states.

Let us look in more detail at the governmental function that the Commission finds most glorious of all: taking initiatives; playing a leadership role. The assigned task of promoting "the general interest of the Union" and taking "appropriate initiatives" gives it firm backing.[50] It even has an official monopoly on the right to take the initiative. In economic policy terrains and areas bordering on them, it alone can bring legislative proposals into play. This exclusive right, key to the "Community method", is a great asset. Moreover, the legislative procedure is such that Parliament and Council can barely diverge at all from a proposed initiative without the agreement of the Commission.

More even than in its relationship with the Parliament, the Commission sees in the task of taking initiatives its presumed destiny as a European government. In reality the Commission makes over 90 per cent of its proposals at the request of the Parliament, the Council of Ministers or the European Council. For the first two, the appropriate circumstances are formally laid down.[51] But the interplay with the European Council is essential, since as shaper, strategist or crisis tamer it is this third body that takes or approves the most important initiatives. During summits the Commission often helps to write the draft conclusions in which it is asked to expand upon an activity. It thereby writes its own "instructions", which can then be used to justify pushing a proposal through. In this way it makes use of the authority of the European Council. There is a limit: in the Union, one cannot pursue a major political initiative against the will of the gathered heads of government (as became clear in the refugee crisis with the asylum quotas). Despite this qualification, the Commission defends tooth and nail its formally exclusive right to take the initiative – even against its regular ally the Parliament, which would like to have the right of legislative initiative itself.

In events-politics, relationships change, as demonstrated by the formal division of roles in the fields of foreign policy and justice. Here the Commission has not acquired the full right to take the initiative; instead the leaders of member states keep an eye on things and determine, respectively, "strategic interests" and "guidelines".[52] Foreign policy initiatives can be proposed by "any Member State, the High Representative [...], or the High Representative with the Commission's support".[53] So the Commission comes into play here only through the high representative (who is one of its vice-presidents). It has a firmer footing in the fields of criminal law and police cooperation, but even there it has no monopoly on the right of initiative.[54] The Commission lacks the authority that would allow it to take the lead in foreign and security affairs, both with regard to the European populations and with regard to foreign powers, not only legally, because of the lack of a right of initiative, but above all in practice. In the Ukraine crisis of 2014–15, a matter of war and peace, no one disputed the relationship. This was a matter for the member states jointly and their leaders; the Commission did not step forward to negotiate a ceasefire between Moscow and Kiev. It did do important work in specifying trade sanctions against Russia and sharing out the resulting pain between the member states. Its administrative expertise and arbitration behind the scenes were indispensable in creating a united front.

Thus, the teamwork takes shape at the best moments: the Commission delivers not only initiatives but the knowhow and civil service expertise that are essential given the technical dimension of many decisions in times of crisis; it formulates the options and so, in practice, has a great deal of influence on the outcome. For its part, the gathering of heads of government (including the Commission president) delivers the political authority and the driving force that are indispensable for the difficult decisions of events-politics. In cases in which, for the implementation of crisis decisions, "normal" legislation is sufficient, as it was for the banking union, the Commission plays its cherished role and sends a proposal to legislators in the Parliament and Council of Ministers. This gives it a great deal of room for manoeuvre. If decisions made in a crisis go beyond the existing frameworks and/or the political leadership wants, or is forced, to give these decisions the gravity of a treaty change or a new treaty, as happened with the euro emergency funds, the European Council, as shaper, takes upon itself the task of finding support in the national parliaments.

In sum, the Commission plays an essential role on the executive playing field because of its right of initiative, its lead in technical expertise and its capacity to implement. But it does not embody the highest political authority; the European Council does that.[55] The division of roles is most clearly visible – in the Treaty and in the facts of the matter – at moments and in domains that by their very nature demand events-politics. Conversely, the division of roles is not visible in domains that in normal circumstances lend themselves perfectly well to rules-politics, such as the internal market. Because of its central position in the regulatory machinery, the Commission appears to its fans to be the government of the Brussels inner sphere (even if foreign observers characterize it, less deferentially, as "chief regulator"). But if the worst comes to the worst, if a crisis erupts or political innovation is required, its authority as leader turns out to be conditional and it suddenly becomes obvious that even in what are supposedly its own domains, those of rules-politics, it ultimately acts under the authority of the European Council.

Finally, a comparison, perhaps conducive to the scrutability of the European theatre. Such subtle and demanding interplay between two executives – the result of the simultaneous building of the European stage according to two rival designs – is strongly reminiscent of the two-headed executive of the French Fifth Republic. Except that the French system of government is not the product of a series of compromises like that of the Union but set up that way deliberately in 1958. At the top is the president, directly elected by French voters, who embodies the highest political authority, represents France in the world and sets a course for the government to follow. Beside and below him is the prime minister, appointed by the president and backed by a parliamentary majority in the Assemblée Nationale; in close consultation with the Elysée Palace, he leads the ministerial team and translates the broad lines of presidential policy into legislation and execution; it is therefore the prime minister, and not the president, who has the right to initiate legislation (alongside the members of parliament).[56] So in Paris a presidential system like that of the United States functions in conjunction with elements of the parliamentary system that prevails in Western Europe.

To see the analogy with the Union it is necessary to understand the European Council as a "collective president" of the Union. The gathered leaders are the highest authority for the public and the outside world. This "president" does not rely on a parliamentary majority but derives its political authority from an electorate of its own, in this case a 28-fold national electorate. From this perspective, the equivalent of the French prime minister is the president of the Commission, appointed by the European Council and relying on a majority in the Strasbourg parliament. This figure too operates within the lines marked out by Europe's collective president, does not venture into high politics, and has an authority that is partly derivative and partly his or her own.[57]

DETACHED AGENCIES

Events-politics demands not just the ability to take rapid decisions but in many cases to act on them as well. Here a new dilemma arises: who must deliver the capacity to act? Where must the border guards come from, the centre or the parts, Brussels or the national capitals? How can political authority in the Union be converted into an actual performance?

There is a strong tendency in the Union to want to derive operational clout from the tried and tested methods of the rule-making factory. Very pragmatic, of course, but it neglects the fact that action needs to be backed by political authority. The new Brussels answer to the need for executive vigour is to set up an agency: "Well then, we'll do it ourselves". With the new requirement of a capacity to act there is an increasing desire for central implementation, partly because, seen from the centre, member states look lax, unreliable, or simply too diverse.

Agencies, independent managerial bodies within the Union, have traditionally been deployed as instruments of the technical politics of rules, for the outsourcing of Commission tasks. Examples include the food safety authority in Parma and the environment agency in Copenhagen. Based on expertise, they fulfil regulatory, supervisory and sometimes supporting or coordinating roles, deliberately established at some distance from operations in Brussels. It was in this spirit that an agency for cooperation between energy regulators was set up in 2011 in Ljubljana. But in reaction to the stream of events since the fall of Lehman Brothers, and to unrest on the external borders, a new generation of agencies is seeing the light. Mandated by the governments, regulators are becoming active and taking the bull by the horns.

It began with the banking crisis of 2008–09. In the year that followed, the Union opened three financial supervisory organizations, including the European Banking Authority (allocated to London, it will move to Paris after Brexit). In the tradition of rules-politics, certainly, but all three have far-reaching powers, not just to take individual decisions but to develop regulations, which the Commission sometimes introduces into the legislative game directly: a shortcut from technocratic analysis to the political law book.

In the euro crisis this went even further. The banking union that the Union decided in 2012 to create demanded first of all a central supervisory body for all the large eurozone banks – a task given to the European Central Bank. But then a eurozone-wide resolution mechanism was required for the winding up of bankrupt banks. This Single Resolution Board, arguably at least, enabled a leap from regulation to action. Among lawyers this rightly raised the question of whether its establishment had a sufficient basis in the usual "internal market article"; after all, the winding up of a bankrupt bank is not a matter of regulation and supervision for the purpose of harmonization but of forcing action in specific emergencies, involving political choices as to where the financial losses will fall.[58] No wonder then that the first substantial decisions taken by the Resolution Board – in June 2017 a Spanish bank had to shut, whereas a week later two Italian banks were saved at public expense – were criticized as "political".

In the domain of asylum, migration and border control there was a need for a different kind of operational clout. Here, sleeves really did have to be rolled up. In February 2011, coinciding almost precisely with the start of the Arab Spring, an agency for asylum was established in Malta, a centre of expertise to support member states.[59] In its functioning it resembled the border agency Frontex, set up a few years earlier in Warsaw. During the refugee crisis both bodies were expanded considerably. After the tragedies on the Mediterranean and in the Balkans in 2015–16, Frontex was adapted to become the European Border and Coast Guard Agency, which with its customs staff at the ready helps member states to guard their land and sea borders. The modest asylum agency was given an operational role in the reception, registration and relocation (for such was the intention) of 160,000 asylum seekers from Greece and Italy to the rest of the Union. As well as countless logistical and legal obstacles, the reception of asylum seekers introduced a phenomenon previously unknown to the Union's agencies: "resistance from the local population":[60] a further unmistakable sign of a new politicization.

One detail from the staffing policy indicates the extent to which, in Brussels thinking, "regulating" is equated with "acting". The same civil servant from the Dutch finance ministry who in that famous night of 9–10 May 2010 came up with a creative legal vehicle for the eurozone emergency funds and thereby helped to save the currency, now a senior civil servant in the Commission, was sent to Athens in the summer of 2015 to address the next crisis by helping the authorities on the Greek islands to shelter and register asylum seekers – a role for which, given the chaos on the ground, you might have done better to cast a naval officer or a property developer rather than a financial whizz kid.

HUBRIS OF THE TROIKA

Another player to emerge in the euro crisis was the notorious "Troika", not a formal agency but a product of the same pivot towards "doing something". Here the lack of political backing is all the more obvious. The conditional support packages for countries in financial difficulties – from 2010 onwards provided to Greece, Ireland and Portugal – required intensive supervision of economic reforms and budgetary cuts in those countries. Based on the source of the financing, the member states allocated the task to a triumvirate or Troika (Russian тройка) consisting of the Commission, the European Central Bank and the International Monetary Fund.* It had far-reaching powers at an administrative level. Experts with the status of "heads of unit" came to tell elected ministers in detail how they were to cut pensions, or prescriptions for certain pharmaceuticals.[61] The financial relationship between creditor and debtor cut across the usual relationship between administrative and political executive authority, with intermittent short circuits as a result.

The discrepancy between this administrative power to overrule from Brussels–Frankfurt–Washington and decisions that to the Greek, Irish and Portuguese publics felt like political interference led, first in the countries visited and later in all of Europe, to fierce and fundamental criticism of the Troika. This damaged the Union as a whole. Only after years of public indignation at such technocratic arrogance, which of course had the blessing of the finance ministers of the Eurogroup in their role as bankers, did the realization dawn in the Commission that someone with political authority who could be held responsible by the European Parliament would have to be sent to Athens, Dublin or Lisbon. In 2015 the Commission under Juncker promised the newly elected Syriza government that things would change. From then on, officials-on-mission would speak only with local officials (in Athens) and politicians with politicians (in Brussels); the technical would be separated from the political. No more images of foreigners who – like "the equivalent of the nineteenth-century gunboat diplomacy used by the British

---

* Because of political disagreement between the member states, the improvised emergency financing had to be taken from three separate kitties: the Union budget administered by the Commission, the treasuries of the euro member states (in proportion to their deposits in the ECB) and the IMF.

Empire" – arrived in Athens with massive financial firepower to lay down the law. In practice little came of this, incidentally, according to the critical Greek minister Varoufakis.[62] Under the cover of an impenetrable shield of technocracy, the regulators continued to step into the political arena.

When the engineers of the politics of rules – whether from agencies or the Troika – are thrust onto the stage of events, technocratic overreach threatens. The administrative-legal logic fails to acknowledge that this is a leap from regulation to action, from creating preconditions behind the scenes for a "level playing field" for businesses or citizens to stepping into the fray. Hence the overestimation of anonymously exercised powers at the expense of political responsibility: the Troika illusion. Hence also the underestimation of practical obstacles and political emotions: the asylum-quota illusion.

The more often agencies are used to contract out politically sensitive problems – saving the shipwrecked, mapping terrorist networks, designing military drones – the more they will be the target of public criticism and the louder the call for visible political control will become.[63] It may sometimes be useful to extend the mandate of the rule-making factory a little so that the Union can act more effectively, but such a step – like decision-making in emergencies – requires explicit subordination to the political authority.

A ROBUST BANK

As the independent executor of rules-bound monetary policy, the European Central Bank – at the urging of the Germans and to the disappointment of the French – was from the start kept at a distance from politics, as a kind of super-agency. In the financial and economic storms since 2008, however, this Frankfurt-based institution has undergone a fascinating metamorphosis. Starting out as a prudent implementer of the task given it by the Treaty, that of securing price stability in the eurozone (a low and constant inflation rate), it is becoming, with its energetic behaviour on the financial markets, an enforcer of financial stability. Since January 2015 its massive purchases of billions of euros of national debt have attracted attention, but in the banking crisis and at earlier moments in the euro crisis, the ECB took decisions off its own bat that impressed the markets, known in the prudent jargon as "non-standard measures". This transformation is the monetary version of the passage to Europe's new politics. It is ironic, as a French former prime minister observed, that the result touches the sore spot of German monetary orthodoxy: "It was precisely the independence demanded by Germany that made the metamorphosis of the Bank possible".[64]

Two striking elements are involved in the transformation of the ECB into a political forum and political player. First its governing council, consisting of the six directors in Frankfurt and the 19 governors of the national banks, resorted several times in emergencies to a majority decision, a break with the mores of the earlier, stable years when Wim Duisenberg was its president (1998–2003), when all decisions were taken collectively. In May 2010, under the presidency of (former French National Bank governor) Jean-Claude Trichet, the president of the powerful German Bundesbank, Axel Weber, was voted down. Even in a dire emergency the Bank managed to break from its orthodoxy and take bold measures only by majority. The simple fact of a majority decision betrays disagreement and conflict; it shows that the ECB is not purely a committee of monetary experts that draws academic conclusions by consensus; it is also a political forum of clashing interests and values.

The ECB reached for a second instrument too from the toolkit of the political executive, one that administrative implementers do not normally have at their disposal: bluff. Well remembered are the three words used by Bank president Mario Draghi in July 2012 in the City of London, when he said his institution would do "whatever it takes" to save the euro. His words were effective primarily because he added, in his bass Roman voice, "and believe me: it will be enough". He thereby challenged the speculators besieging the currency: are you sure that you want to bet millions on the collapse of the euro? The fact that this banking bluff was introduced with the limiting, bureaucratic and orthodoxy-reassuring phrase "within our mandate" was neglected by many; it indicates the balancing act of Draghi's new Bank – on the borderline between the politics of rules and the politics of events.

The decision of summer 2012 was taken by the European Central Bank with the backing of the authority of the European Council, which had decided on a banking union in late June. As in two other memorable cases, the decision came immediately after or around a political breakthrough at the top.[65]

It enabled president of the European Council Herman Van Rompuy, looking back on the stormy years 2010–12, to write, "All along, there has been a subtle, unspoken dialogue between the political and the monetary leaders. In the European Union, monetary policy is decided independently, but not in a political or social vacuum."[66]

RUDDERLESS DIPLOMACY

The joint capacity to act does not necessarily have to be organized centrally, by the Brussels Commission and its satellites, or indeed by the ECB in Frankfurt and its branches. On the contrary, all national governments and bureaucracies have resources and manpower, with well-established lines of political authority. They too are "Europe". The task is not to transfer these to the centre but to bind them together in a coordinated effort.

The problem of political action by the Union is most clearly visible in foreign policy. Since 2010 the Union has had a European diplomatic service, under the authority of the high representative – not an agency in the strict sense, but nevertheless an extension of the bureaucratic apparatus. Of course, this does not signify the subordination or replacement, let alone dissolution, of national diplomatic services. French, Dutch or Polish diplomats work as hard as ever and in principle just as much on behalf of European interests. Over the past 40 years the member states have become used to attuning their foreign policies in bodies such as the United Nations and have experienced how their interests, ideas and practices are increasingly aligned. This is the stage on which the new European diplomatic service, with its Brussels headquarters and its 150 embassies worldwide, plays a unifying role by coordinating positions, exchanging information, or performing consular work for EU citizens. So, a stronger centre makes it easier for Europe to speak "with one voice".

But speaking with one voice does not imply that only Brussels speaks and Paris, Berlin, London and other capitals hold their peace. The Union is not a state but a union of states. The means and manpower of foreign policy are mostly in the hands of the member states. This is true of diplomats, but also of armed forces, espionage services and other resources. If we add to this the 28-fold contribution by the now several thousand EU diplomats from their

Brussels base, with considerable funding from the central EU budget, then the Union as a whole has the world's second most powerful army, its largest diplomatic service and its biggest development aid budget. On paper at least. From this perspective the greatest obstacle to readiness for the fray is not a lack of resources for "Brussels" but hesitation among member states about deploying their own resources as part of the whole. A different attitude in this respect does not require treaty change; the Treaty already requires all members to act as a Union.

Obstacles to action in the field of foreign policy are legion. To take the political obstacles first, national interests stand in the way, because governments are held responsible at national elections. Sharing the burden requires solidarity, sacrifice for the good of the whole. In the absence of centralized, immediately available resources, practical deployment faces further obstacles too; translating decisions into decisive action in the field necessitates permanent coordination and improvisation. For every mission – catching pirates off Somalia, stopping people smugglers in Libya, monitoring a ceasefire in Georgia – the generals or heads of mission responsible have to phone around for staff and equipment. They charm, nag and organize forms of peer pressure. Foreign ministers define the aims in their own Council of Ministers, but at home they do not by any means all have sufficient resources, especially if the need is great, or urgent. It is a different matter in the European Council. At the table of government leaders the capacity to set out a joint course of action comes together, as it does nowhere else, with the authority to allocate manpower and equipment, whether national or from "Brussels". Downside: the institution is crisis-driven and therefore lacks sustained attention, continuity and cohesion.

Looking ahead

When in early 2013 the French foreign minister Laurent Fabius asked his Russian colleague in the UN Security Council to support an anti-terrorism mission in Mali, Lavrov replied, "Of course, we see the terrorist danger too. But perhaps you ought to have given it rather more thought before deposing Gaddafi in Libya." "*Mais c'est la vie*", the Frenchman said. To which Lavrov promptly responded, "For Russians, *c'est la vie* is not a foreign policy".[67] Here then lies another dilemma: strategic capacity demands not only the visible support of the public but the resolute determination to oppose, when necessary, the public emotion of the moment, with a view to a broader horizon.*

There is a great desire among the political leadership of the Union to break free of the permanent state of emergency, the umpteenth "last chance" summit, the continual threat of confusion and opportunism. The heartfelt cry of Angela Merkel during the European Council meeting of June 2017 was: "Enough of crisis management! The hour of strategic choices has come; and that is exactly what we are doing in Europe along with Paris."[68] After that same summit, his first, Emmanuel Macron announced a Franco-German plan of action "for ten years", saying he wanted an end to the Union as the "curator of crisis management".[69] Such declamations had been heard since at least 2010, however. Would efforts be more successful this time?

To govern is to look ahead, as the saying goes. A Union that can be decisive only with its back against the wall is not sovereign. No one any longer doubts, after its improvisations in the euro crisis or its efforts during the refugee crisis, that the Union can surprise its critics and itself with unsuspected stamina. But a mature political body is also able to look ahead and anticipate the emergency, already prepared for the future.

In this connection "looking ahead" is not to be confused with "planning" or "prediction". To look ahead is to accept the unpredictable dynamic of history, to face upstream, discern patterns, estimate risks, take measures. To the extent that this is "planning", it is contingency planning, taking account of uncertainty or the worst-case scenario (the latter is a challenge in itself, as demonstrated by the taboo in the Union on premature discussion of a "Grexit" or "Brexit"). So, the best preparation lies not in calculating possible scenarios to ten decimal places – things always turn out differently – but in increasing resilience, decisiveness and the ability to improvise. Then, if something happens, you are able to act.

---

* The immediate reason for the Western intervention in Libya orchestrated by Sarkozy and Cameron in February 2011 lay in the advance by Gaddafi's troops towards rebel stronghold Benghazi; the fall of that city would mean the threat of "a new Srebrenica on the other side of the Mediterranean" (according to the influential media philosopher Bernard-Henri Lévy in Paris, who was in close contact with Libyan rebels at the time).

Acquiring the ability to look ahead depends on a change in mentality that the Union has started to make only since the Atlantic crisis of Brexit-&-Trump, when it allowed its historical finitude to sink in for the first time and expressed the desire to "take its destiny into its own hands". Looking ahead in this sense demands a self-image as a player among other players, living and acting in a world of conflicting interests and possible enmities, where history can turn hostile – a break, therefore, with universal perpetuity thinking, a leap into the river of time. Only such a perspective makes strategic anticipation worthwhile. After all, acting with an eye on what might or must happen presumes continuity, an identity through time. It presumes that you know who you are, that you are in fact someone, and thus can autonomously determine your own interests and values as a Union. Those interests are ultimately shaped by reasons of state, by an awareness of European sovereignty and the strength to hold your own in an ever-changing geopolitical interplay of forces. Only then will the Machiavellian moment in which the Union has been caught up through ten years of crisis be complete, namely the moment at which the awareness of your own mortality and finitude brings about a political order that can "remain morally and politically stable in a stream of irrational events conceived as essentially destructive of all systems of secular stability".[70]

A start has been made. Since 2010 the emergency funds have made the eurozone capable of absorbing financial shocks and have thereby increased its resilience. The border agency too, with its 1,500 border guards, is available for future emergencies. But both these precautionary measures came only after disaster was narrowly averted. The test is therefore whether the Union is able to make better preparations for expected and unexpected events. Strategic memorandums from central Brussels institutions or enthusiastic think tanks can help to prepare the way, but the direction and goal must be determined by binding decisions by the European Council, in its role as authoritative shaper.

The debate over the future of the eurozone is all about the switch from regulation to the capacity to act. France and Brussels are prompting contemplation of a specific "budget for the eurozone", a political tool that, like the emergency funds, would serve to absorb financial shocks and increase resilience. Although the German government has proven reluctant to go along, not least owing to pressure from other northern euro members, proposals are on the table. These do not yet reassure, however, and it looks as if the eurozone is waiting for another crisis, triggered perhaps by the Italian populist government of Di Maio and Salvini, to improve its resilience. Back to the mode of improvisation.

Whether the matter in hand is the currency, defence, or the border, there is at least a political will to escape the constraints of a decade of crisis management, to increase Europe's capacity to act, its wakefulness and flexibility. The looming end of *Pax Americana*, the growing self-confidence of the Union's political leadership, with Berlin and Paris out in front, the desire to take its destiny into its own hands and to be sovereign, mean the Union must harvest the political produce of the crisis years and further build upon the forms of government that have arisen before the eyes of those willing to see them.

One crucial element must not remain hidden any longer, however. The public, after all, tried to get the transition from rules to politics underway long ago; high time to engage the energy of public dissent. Bring on the Opposition!

7

The opposition takes the stage

I must say that it appears to me that those who condemn the distur-
bances between the nobles and the plebeians condemn those very
things that were the primary cause of Roman liberty, and that they give
more consideration to the noises and cries arising from such distur-
bances than to the good effects they produced.

Niccolò Machiavelli[1]

We cannot take politics out of politics.

Giovanni Sartori[2]

What is a rebel? A man who says no, but whose refusal does not imply
a renunciation. He is also a man who says yes, from the moment he
makes his first gesture of rebellion. [...] What does he mean by saying
'no'? He means, for example, that 'this has been going on too long,' 'up
to this point yes, beyond it no,' 'you are going too far,' or, again, 'there is
a limit beyond which you shall not go'. [...] With loss of patience – with
impatience – a reaction begins which can extend to everything that he
previously accepted.

Albert Camus[3]

Checks and balances

The fact that for decades it was impossible to point to a Brussels government of the EU had an important but hitherto neglected consequence:

no organized opposition could take shape. Oppositional forces could not be directed to an obvious forum, and so they found expression through other, uncontrollable sites.

For a governing party, the absence of a recognizable opposition – people who make your life a misery, sabotage your plans and aim to get you out of office as soon as possible – may sound attractive, but for a political system as a whole it is catastrophic. Political opposition fulfils vital functions. Here are four of them:

1. *Balance*. The presence of an opposition strengthens a political system's "checks and balances". It puts a brake on abuse of power by governments and civil servants, thereby enhancing the quality of governance and the rule of law. This works best when the opposition has a base in parliament, since from there it can make the executive aware of its potential supremacy. It is the existence of an opposition that gives Montesquieu's separation of powers its full protective and dynamic effect.

2. *Changeover*. The non-violent transfer of power has been a challenge for every political order throughout human history. Solutions range from the drawing of lots for magistrates in Athens to the appointment of a new emperor in Rome, from hereditary succession in European monarchies to self-selection by senior party members in communist China. Democracies use the ballot box, a variant that has admirable qualities, not just morally but also in a political-practical sense.* Its attributes make themselves felt, however, only when active and passive participation in the electoral contest is open and free, when the opposition can attract support in its aim of becoming a government.

3. *Vigilance*. When rulers remain in power uncontested, losing contact with the wishes or fears of the population, an opposition concentrates their minds. Just as the people's tribunes in the Roman Republic deliberately made the Senate aware of dissatisfaction or unrest among the populace, so the

---

* Machiavelli: "There is nothing that makes a republic so stable and steady as organizing it in such a way that the variability of those humours that agitate the republic has a means of release that is instituted by the laws" (*Discourses*, bk 1, ch. 7).

modern political opposition – with or without the help of the media – interprets the voice of the street to the state. Alarm bells force the government to take action, if only to deprive the opposition of its arguments during the next election campaign.

4. *Dissent*. By producing its own plans, legislative proposals, or visions of the future, the opposition shows that other political choices are conceivable. It is disastrous for a political system if people start to feel there is no other option, that "they're all the same". Of course, if the opposition comes to power one day, it will discover for itself the constraints and countervailing forces the government it so despised had to deal with. Nonetheless, oppositional dissent obliges the political leadership to justify its decisions, with a more convincing story than "There is no alternative". So, the opposition keeps open a public space for checks and balances – a vital democratic function.

From the perspective of this book, the voters' revolt of Brexit year 2016 represents, for the time being, the climax of the public's discovery of Europe, a discovery that accompanies the metamorphosis from the politics of rules to the politics of events. It is the obverse of the Union's new politics – part blustering protest, part call for democratic openness. Of course, the revolt is not limited geographically to our continent, it is spurred on by social trends and by developments in information and communications technology, and in its content touches upon far more than EU issues in the narrow sense. Nonetheless, a storm is raging in Europe. Populist parties of left and right are deploying aversion to the European machinery as a battering ram against the closed systems of the establishment. Departure from the Union is the main purpose of Britain's UK Independence Party (mission accomplished), the Dutch Partij Voor de Vrijheid, Germany's Alternative für Deutschland, as well as parts of the Italian Five Star Movement and of what used to be called the French Front National. The causes of the storm have yet to be resolved. It compels the Union to offer more space to legitimate protest. If opposition proves impossible to organize within the Union, then it will undoubtedly mobilize against the Union.

This insight forms the core of a brilliant, prescient 2006 lecture by Irish political scientist Peter Mair on the subject of "political opposition and the

European Union".[4] He was speaking a year after the firm "no" votes by France and the Netherlands against the European Constitutional Treaty. His starting point was the remarkable situation in which there is obviously a great deal of opposition to the Union and naturally also to governments within the Union, but the two are nowhere linked in such a way that a dynamic between government and opposition arises, such that, for example, those in power can be voted out.

In assessing the seriousness of the situation, Mair distinguished between three modes of opposition.[5] First there is classical opposition, the familiar mode in which parties outside government oppose it by presenting alternatives to its policies, while recognizing and respecting the right of the government to govern. Then there is "opposition of principle", in which not only the government and its policies but the legitimacy of the political order as a whole (polity) is called into question, and sometimes there may be resort to violence. Thirdly, there is "the elimination of opposition", with government by cartel, in which power is shared (as in postwar Austria between Conservatives and Social Democrats) and substantive conflict is curtailed, if not eliminated. While the first two modes concern forms of opposition, the third is a counter-concept that offers an insight into ways that opposition can disappear. The three are not separate channels. The more space there is for classical opposition, the less there will be for opposition of principle or for the elimination of opposition by assimilation. Conversely, if classical opposition is constrained, the likelihood that critics will mobilize as an opposition of principle increases. The choice is then between disappearance and revolt.

In the European Union, opportunities for classical opposition are strictly limited – a fault in the system that is not easy to repair. True, we do have the right to take part in decision-making by voting, whether for national representatives, who become members of the Council of Ministers, or for European representatives who take their seats in the Parliament in Strasbourg. But – again according to Mair – we lack the right to organize classical opposition; we also lack the capacity to do so and, above all, an arena in which opposition can take shape. His explanation for this is that there is no counterpart: there is no government.

According to Brussels ideologues, the interplay between Commission and Parliament is intended eventually to bring about a dynamic of government and opposition. A parliamentary majority, changing with every election, would lend its support to a central authority in Brussels. That was the promise. Today, however, the Commission is not the European government. The Parliament, traditionally a bulwark of consensus, has seen more conflict over the past ten years than before, but the antithesis on which these disputes rest is not currently between left and right but typically between federalists and their moderate pro-European allies on one side and Eurosceptics on the other; the fault lines are more visible in debates over polity than in arguments over policy. On the ground the "opposition of principle" is represented by the likes of Marine Le Pen (2004–17) and Nigel Farage (1999–2020), both of them longstanding Europarliamentarians.

Peter Mair's argument is nevertheless based on more than the absence of a government-opposition dynamic in the Brussels inner sphere. He claimed (again in 2006) that the development seen in the European Union "is also beginning to reach down into the domestic sphere, in that the growing weight of the EU, and its indirect impact on national politics, also helps to foster domestic democratic deficits, and hence also limits the scope for classical opposition at the national level. Here too, then, we might expect to see either the elimination of opposition or the mobilization of a new – perhaps populist – opposition of principle".[6] A decade later, we do seem to have reached this final phase.[7] The lack of a point of entry for substantial opposition feeds fundamental opposition. The fault in the system will be costly indeed if national-populist movements emerge as dragon slayers. So, the matter at issue is how to get classical opposition back, how to give it space. An existential question.

The Irish political scientist himself was gloomy. In the closing lines of his article – reprised in his posthumous *Ruling the Void* (2011) – he writes, "Political opposition gives voice. By losing opposition, we lose voice, and by losing voice, we lose control of our own political systems. It is not at all clear how that control might be regained, either in Europe or at home, or how we might eventually restore meaning to that great milestone on the road to building democratic institutions."[8] Yet we can recognize the correctness of the analysis without adopting Mair's dispirited outlook. It may be extremely difficult to give shape to a legitimate opposition, but it is not inevitably impossible, and it is of such importance that every effort needs to be made.

Moreover, developments are continuing. In the previous chapter we saw that in the Union a visible governing power is emancipating itself, with a supreme authority and a capacity to take decisions. As a result of this development of the executive, its opponents have a better idea whom or what to target, as we shall see. Now that power is working less deficiently, countervailing forces can gain a better focus and voice.

The new circumstances were met by a public that had for some time been in search of a leverage point for political opposition. As soon as European politics came onto the stage, it was happy to emerge and act as an electorate. Not, however, as an applause machine merely to say "yes", whatever the performance. Sometimes it would rather say "no", or "boo!" Gradually the audience has discovered that answering back is in fact very difficult. As a result, it became possible to talk about the lacerating option of leaving Europe's theatre altogether, for which a majority of British voters have opted.

We need to acknowledge the link between the two movements. Only if the opposition is given space can the governing power take shape. This requires of politics that it ceases to treat citizens merely as consumers of products of the rule-making factory, spoilt and looking for bargains, and instead approaches them as the embodiment of public life. This means coming up with a performance that, in the stream of events, manages to bind together actions and words – and that is prepared for a response, appreciates it even. Otherwise there is a risk that one day the audience will break down the "fourth wall" of the theatre, rejecting the show put on by self-absorbed politicians.

No leverage point

RULES AS ENTANGLEMENTS

To the public at large, "Brussels" is synonymous with bureaucratic absurdity. An endless series of bizarre examples – from compulsorily sterilized cheeses to forbidden olive-oil bottles – have been doing the rounds for years at dinner parties and in the popular press, embarrassing even the well-disposed.

Complaints about regulatory frenzy are inevitable in market Europe. The free movement of goods, services and capital across a space occupied by 28 entities, each shaped by history, requires shared norms and regulations. Naturally these can always be slimmed down. Under Jean-Claude Juncker and his right-hand man Frans Timmermans the Commission has made a start on this, labelled "better regulation". The regulatory burden is effectively lightened if 28 sets of national legislation are replaced by a single European set, but "better regulation" remains what it is: regulation. The public sees itself confronted with a vast number of rules that have come from afar and been accepted en bloc. "Because Brussels says so", is heard all too often. Few people know whether or how the rules can be changed. A starting point for protest is hard to find in the midst of the regulatory thicket.

Of course, in theory regulations generated by national or local governments are no different. On a smaller scale, rules are still rules. Yet aside from the greater distance between them and the voters, there are three features that make European rules particularly hard to access, to get a grip on, or to oppose.

The first can be called "technical depoliticization", a masking of politics by technology. In communicating with the public, Brussels likes to describe a new norm as a "solution" to a technical problem – noisy lawnmowers, health risks, inflation – rather than as a political choice or the result of the weighing of options and values. The advantage is that there are no apparent winners or losers; EU legislators attempt to prevent both jubilation and disappointment, preferring measured assent. The disadvantage of such depoliticization is that it reinforces the impression that Brussels is a technocratic rule-making machine. Seen from outside, the boundary between expertise and anonymous power is uncomfortably thin. While expertise demands trust, invisible and anonymous power arouses public suspicion, more than visible and personal power would. (Who are they? What lies behind it?).

A second strategic feature is, to use a term from Dieter Grimm, "constitutional depoliticization", the placing of policy choices outside the political battlefield.[9] Some European rules enter directly via the treaties of the European Union. Their "constitutional" inviolability means that they cannot be changed through the ordinary legislative process. Whereas most national constitutions confine themselves to the structure of the political system, the

European founding treaty has a great deal of content, or policy; its point of departure was after all the creation of the common market, with its four freedoms. This placed fundamental political choices beyond the reach of direct opposition. Something similar happens when, by treaty, certain managerial functions are transferred to wholly or partly independent institutions, such as the Commission or the European Central Bank, and when the independent Court of Justice gives a substantive twist to the Treaty or to later legislation. The rules or mandates anchored in the treaties are not impossible to change, but changing them is extremely difficult. The same goes for case law from the Court; judgments do not have a treaty-based status, but in the Union it is more difficult for the Council of Ministers or the Parliament to overrule a judgment than for legislators in a national context. As was of course the intention. At one time this set-up provided the certainty and shared confidence that agreements between countries could not be terminated at will. Constitutional depoliticization has obvious disadvantages, however, the most important being that the Union as such becomes equated with substantive choices, especially that of a liberal economic policy. In France, where the word "liberalism" can barely be used without the prefix "ultra-", awareness of this fed into the "no" to the Constitutional Treaty in 2005.

The third feature could be called "procedural depoliticization". This concerns not the nature of the rules but the way in which they come about. An ordinary citizen wanting, out of frustration or curiosity, to know who is responsible for a decision will in many cases get bogged down in the procedures. The rule-making factory is too complex. Even for those who have studied EU law, it is a full-time job to understand, say, the operations of expert committees. Typical of the intangibility of the public-political moment is that Brussels correspondents with major newspapers are often unsure when to ask their editors in Amsterdam, Rome or Prague to start paying attention. When the Commission submits a proposal? When national civil servants examine it? When ministers discuss it in their Council? When a parliamentary rapporteur delivers a report? When the Parliament votes on amendments? In the first or second round of the coordinating "trialogue"?

Of course this procedural complexity is the consequence of political balancing acts. The Brussels rule-making factory has to weave together a multitude of beliefs and interests that diverge between and within countries, parties and institutions. In a patient process of consultation and deliberation, of pushing and pulling, of compromising and deal-making, it is constructing an internal market that virtually spans a continent, a considerable feat. Nevertheless, complexity is not merely an unfortunate side-effect. Procedural depoliticization is an essential element of success, since complex procedures have the same effect as technical language: they discourage public involvement. (If no one can work out exactly what the rules of the game are, who is playing, or where the ball has got to, the stands will soon empty.) Dullness is of some importance too. The forging of compromises works best in shady corners, as the diplomats and civil servants in Brussels and the capitals, who work at it every day, are well aware. If the floodlights are turned on, if the press comes to look, then positions harden and no negotiator has further room for manoeuvre – another reason why the rule-making factory prefers to stay out of public view.

The directly elected members of the European Parliament nowadays play the same game. They generally avoid bringing cameras in their wake and are swallowed up by the technicalities of legislative work. Characteristically, the procedures are so time-consuming and complicated, even for European parliamentarians themselves, that from day one of their mandate they have to choose between gaining negotiating influence in the making of rules and building a media profile; it is almost impossible to do both. Thus, the Parliament as a player has been sucked into the Brussels inner sphere, at the expense of its role in public life.

Of course, technicalities and procedures for market rules need not in themselves be a problem. Simply put: people want to buy safe toys in the shops and most do not need to know how the safety standards were arrived at or are enforced. True, major interests, large sums of money and sometimes powerful forces are involved in the creation of market rules, but that is a matter for those directly involved, for companies, interest groups, lobbyists and "stakeholders" – of which the Brussels bubble is full – not necessarily for the public at large. To anyone well-versed in the procedures, the decision-making factory is in fact unprecedentedly transparent.[10]

The difficulties arise with decisions that make the public wonder who takes them, and there are more and more of these. Europe no longer involves itself only with the technical politics of rules. In the euro crisis, urgent joint decisions, directly or indirectly, touched upon harsh budgetary cuts and billions of euros of taxpayers' money. In the Ukraine crisis, economic sanctions against Russia placed relations with a neighbouring country under strain and thousands of jobs at risk. In the refugee crisis, "Brussels" stepped onto extremely sensitive territory with its decision on asylum quotas. During the Brexit negotiations some three million Union citizens in Britain and 1.2 million UK-born citizens in the rest of Europe were eager to know what their rights would be in the future. As we have seen, in Brussels the impact of the turn towards events-politics has been seriously underestimated.

Subjects that have traditionally belonged in the quiet sphere of rules are now unexpectedly being put under a microscope. An argument by an academic, scientist, technocrat or other expert makes less of an impression than before. Recently, trade policy – regarding the TTIP agreement with America and the CETA agreement with Canada, for instance – has met with fierce protests in many member states, spurred on by activists horrified by the prospect of chlorinated chicken, hormone-treated beef or secret tribunals. The Commission could barely believe it; such agreements are extremely technical and trade has for decades been an "exclusive competence" of the European institutions. As far as participation goes, aside from 28 democratically elected governments in the Council of Ministers and the European Parliament it has always relied on the throng of specialists, lobbyists, interest groups and social organizations that surrounds the Brussels decision-making factory, a multitude that has theoretically been promoted to the status of "European public sphere".[11] These professionals do indeed collectively form a "public policy space", a semi-public arena for experts.[12] But that is rather different from a public space in the true sense of the term, a place for protest and passion.

Contrary to suggestions often heard, what is needed most if the European public space is to work better is not in the first instance more transparency (there is no lack of that for anyone with time or money to spare) but greater scrutability of the political game. If transparency means having every single document on the internet and cameras in the meeting room, then the real debate will shift to hastily written notes or take place in the corridors, as has been the case with the Council of Ministers since 2009. No government in the world meets with the doors open. The suspicious searchlight of demands for transparency, seeking scandal, deceit and concealment, can easily destroy the place where trust grows, where an idea can be tested out, where you can jump over the shadow of your mandate. (If on 8 May 1950 Schuman had put his letter to Adenauer in the newspaper instead of sending it to Bonn by messenger, behind the backs of his fellow ministers, we would have no European Union.) Although theorists of legitimacy often imagine transparency to be the holy grail, it is not; people will drown in an excess of information. Being able to see a gaggle of players does not help to determine which of them is responsible. It is therefore more urgent to offer scrutability, a task both for the commentators on the press tribunes and for the players on the stage. Beyond the corridors of power, the players must publicly take responsibility for the decision, for the choice made, for the dilemmas and the commitment. This will create at least the beginnings of a leverage point for opposition.

Dullness, an absence of passion, was a price worth paying in order to subdue national resistance, idiosyncrasies and pretentions. Sparks had to be prevented from igniting a conflagration. But the side-effects are serious. The obstruction of protest – by means of technical, constitutional or procedural depoliticization – mobilized counterforces outside the Brussels arena. Having become more robust over time, they recently threatened to blow up the whole enterprise.

CONVICTION AS MISSIONARY ZEAL

Europe was a project that needed to be believed in. Conviction alone made the tension in 1950 bearable between the prosaic beginnings with coal and steel and the ambitious objective of peace and freedom. In the young Community, the promise of peace served to keep national politicians and civil servants on course and to strengthen their community spirit. But missionary work and attempts to influence discourse were aimed at a broader public too.

The glad tidings of Europe's foundation, told in countless brochures, schoolbooks and reference works, have an accepted cast and plot. The cast is made up of great men: Jean Monnet, grand master of depoliticization, who whispered the coal and steel plan to his minister Robert Schuman; Altiero Spinelli, who wrote a federalist manifesto while a prisoner of the fascists;

Paul-Henri Spaak, the Belgian who after setbacks found the courage needed for a new beginning. Time and again they were small groups of visionaries, with determined leaders who broke with "national egotism" for the sake of peace; "European Saints" British historian Alan Milward called them, with gentle mockery.[13] The standard plot is the erosion of national sovereignty and the development of new institutions at a European level. The process itself becomes the central character in the story: "progress" is the norm, sometimes there is "stagnation" or a "blockage", but a "relaunch" always follows and the European project once more approaches its goal. In this narrative the openness of history is lost; there is no place for conflicting perspectives or the possibility of a different outcome.[14] It might be called "teleological depoliticization", an almost intoxicating characteristic that arouses virulent countervailing forces.

Although no room was given to counter-narratives, they did not fail to appear. It has been observed that the honoured members of a visionary political class leading the ravaged continent out of barbarism had its mirror image in the Eurosceptic narrative of an elitist conspiracy against the peoples of Europe. Same cast, different rhetoric.[15] Appreciation of the plot can simply be turned back on itself. In actual debates there is no more rewarding ammunition for opponents of the Union than the federalist vision itself. The promise that the nation states will be absorbed into a European state, intended as a dream of the future, also functions as a nightmare. What to some is salvation represents the apocalypse to others.

Ironically it is precisely the imperturbable faith in Europe that elicits scepticism. The word "scepticism" implies theological or philosophical doubt. "Euroscepticism" in that sense would be a healthy and useful perspective: avoid blind faith, watch vigilantly to see whether the promise of a new era is being met, ask for facts or results. The reality is very different. The sceptics are no longer doubters and agnostics. Those who have appropriated the title "Eurosceptic" are the self-declared opponents of the Union. They stepped forward as spokespersons for the frustrated opposition; at one and the same time they were able to present themselves as down-to-earth realists, representatives of common sense, opponents of religious fervour and prickers of utopian bubbles. It gave them a rhetorical head start that should not be underestimated and that they exploited for all it was worth.

Thus, the dynamic of faith and scepticism limits the room for protest and for classical opposition. Of the varieties mentioned it is teleological depoliticization that brings about the most radical denial of politics. Whereas the rule-making factory, with its three forms of depoliticization, denies the public a leverage point for opposition and so makes people powerless in practice, religious coercion does something else. It declares opposition to be out-of-order on principle. To exaggerate a little, dogmatic faith turns the theatre of war between political supporters and opponents into a battlefield where the faithful combat unbelievers, where zealots fight heretics. No surprise then that a significant proportion of the European public has developed sympathy for the latter, to whom fell the role of heretical obstructionists who could then insouciantly become "truthsayers".

If the Union is to win out and retain the support of a majority of the public, then it will have to curb the teleological discourse and free itself from its dogmas. This means it must cease to long for a federal future that is "not yet" within reach and stop regretting that "for now" we have to make do with national governments, parliaments and identities. The time for banishing unbelievers is past. Suspicion of Brussels missionary zeal must be dispelled, preferably by means of clear signals.[16] Space for doubts and objections must be cleared and these must be given a visible and functional role – in the system of government as it has meanwhile unfolded in reality.

CRISIS AT KNIFE-POINT

The European public does not yet have as much experience with the improvisations of events-politics as with the didactic tone and form-filling coercion of the rule-making factory. All the same, experiences of the euro crisis since 2010 and the refugee crisis since 2015 have been extraordinarily intense. Suddenly the Union came inescapably close to people and they discovered what it really meant to share one currency and one border.

In a remarkable swing away from faceless bureaucracy, images drove decisions. In the euro crisis – although fought out in the technical register of spreads and rescue programmes – iconic squares full of demonstrators in Athens, photos of burning European flags and caricatures with Hitler moustaches piled on the pressure. In the refugee crisis, even more visually dramatic, the public demanded humanitarian action after seeing photographs of a drowned toddler* and streams of people crossing the Balkans. Television coverage of a march of thousands along the motorway from Budapest to the Austrian border presented Chancellor Merkel with an urgent dilemma in early September 2015: open the border or risk intolerable images of tear gas, truncheons and razor wire, of casualties, even fatalities, images she feared (unlike her Hungarian colleague Orbán). For their part the refugees chose the motorway precisely because of the open view, which afforded them the protection of cameras. They discovered how to use pictures in the media as a battering ram to open the border.[17]

So, both crises featured a public clash of interests, visions and stories. Hard-line politics was on display. Under great time pressure, leaders took far-reaching decisions. There was little opportunity for depoliticization by means of techniques or procedures (irrespective of whether that would have been desirable). The political battle was unprecedentedly visible: day after day, newspapers and news websites were full of it; several summits and Council meetings were relayed on Twitter scene by scene.

Powerlessness amplified public discontent. Again, the opposition had nowhere to go. True, the decisions of crisis-politics were unlike the output of the anonymous rule-making factory that had to be accepted with a feeble "Brussels says so". The initiative clearly lay with the government leaders in the European Council who tried to ward off the latest crisis at one "last chance summit" after another. The public could see more clearly than ever that the Union is a club of nations, with collective ownership of decisions – an instructive experience. But the political leadership rarely found a convincing story with which to defend these decisions and present them as the results of free choices. Its line of defence was, "We must; there's no other option". This meant stepping out of opaque anonymity ("we"), but responsibility was immediately diluted by the appeal to necessity, which made opposition impossible. In the euro crisis, necessity was actually built in: Germany had ensured that the club could act only if the financial stability of the entire eurozone was threatened, leaving no other option.

---

* The little boy was called Alan Kurdi and he came from Kobani, a Kurdish town in northern Syria, close to the Turkish border. On 2 September 2015 his tiny body washed ashore close to Bodrum, Turkey.

So, events-politics has a depoliticization of its own. It does not hide (or only to a limited extent) behind technicalities, treaties, procedures or plans for salvation, but ultimately it appeals to necessity. In emergencies, responsibility needs to be taken. Everyone understands that. But the claim that there is no other option is problematic. From the fact that action is needed, no "how" follows. The political leadership could have seized upon the emergency situation as an opportunity to take responsibility, to make choices with the power of conviction: politicization. A strategy of *fait accompli*, by contrast, feeds scepticism. The public hears this as "like it or lump it". The leadership thereby brings about its own "executive depoliticization". In defence of their policies, the German chancellor and her finance minister several times used the word *alternativlos* (without alternative). Its repeated use during the Greek crisis led the Germans to vote it the worst word of 2010.

As a variation on "necessity knows no law", here we are witnessing "necessity settles the argument". In response, some critics saw every executive decision-making process as unjustified; Jürgen Habermas discerned in the euro crisis traces of "executive federalism".[18]

Voting as an act of resistance

Opposition arose in three phases: the public woke up when the transition took place from the old Community to the political Union (1992), it objected to making explicit and setting down the political nature of the Union in a constitution (2005), and in the turbulence of recent crisis-politics it discovered its own essential plurality.

In the crises from 2010 onwards the public discovered how difficult it was to oppose *fait-accompli* politics. This discomfort reached the turning point that Peter Mair predicted in his 2006 article, the moment when the impact of European decisions limits the space for classical opposition at a national level as well, threatening to eliminate the opposition and mobilizing "a new – perhaps populist – opposition of principle".[19] At that point opposition parties in national arenas began to thrive on proposals to leave the Union or the eurozone; some, such as Germany's AfD in 2013, were set up specifically for that purpose.

231

THE PEOPLE'S VOICE IN THE EUROCRISIS

In the euro crisis, European electorates tried out new leverage points for classical opposition. After voters took to the floor from 1992 onwards with national referendums on treaty changes, they developed a desire to get a grip on political decisions in the here and now as well. First of all, beginning in 2010, they used national elections for this purpose. This was new. In a subsequent phase a second weapon was brought into play: national referendums on European decisions. This too had never been seen before. It started with Greece, in a euro referendum in July 2015 that was as fascinating as it was heart-stopping.

Until recently, even authoritative political scientists could claim that in half a century of integration, national elections had only once been decided by a European issue. European matters were said to be too boring or, to use the jargon, not salient enough.* That may have been the case before the transition from the politics of rules to the politics of events, but since the outbreak of the euro crisis in 2010 there has been no lack of European stimuli in national elections. Even the commotion surrounding the various referendum debates since Maastricht pales beside this new political intensity.

One indication of the scale of political difficulties is that 17 of the 20 European government leaders up for election between May 2010 and June 2012 were defeated or forced to leave the field; for at least half, their departure was a direct consequence of the euro crisis. Of course each case can be interpreted differently, but the following could be numbered among the losses: Slovakian premier Robert Fico (July 2010), Irish taoiseach Brian Cowen (March 2011), Portuguese premier José Socrates (June 2011), Finnish premier Mari Kiviniemi (June 2011), Greek premier George Papandreou (November 2011), Italian premier Silvio Berlusconi (November 2011), Spanish premier José Luis Zapatero (November 2011), Slovakian premier Iveta Radicova (April 2012) and French President Nicolas Sarkozy (May 2012).† An unprecedented

---

* Andrew Moravcsik, who adheres to this assertion, is thinking of 1965 as the exception, when President De Gaulle, because of his empty-chair policy in Brussels, lost the support of the farming electorate and was forced in the French presidential election into a – for him humiliating – second round.

† In the same period only three leaders survived a national parliamentary election: Donald Tusk, Andrus Ansip and Valdis Dombrowskis, of Poland, Estonia and Latvia respectively.

electoral massacre, and therefore a resounding victory for the opposition collectively.

When a national opposition gained power, it rapidly discovered the narrow parameters of European politics. At the negotiating table it came up against the same forcefield that in many cases had put paid to its predecessor. Each new minister or government leader, a hero at home, experienced what it was like to be one of almost 20 eurozone partners. Those who had promised their voters a European change of course – whether towards more discipline or towards more solidarity – could fulfil that promise only to a very limited degree in Brussels. Like the earlier "no" votes in national referendums on a European treaty, the swing from opposition to government could bring only short-term relief (for the winners, that is) followed by renewed frustration.

The turn towards events-politics brought more public attention to the actors onstage. Countless national elections – moments when the cast changes – were followed avidly by the entire Union. Of course the public realized during the monetary crisis the degree to which eurozone countries are economically interwoven. People were increasingly aware that debts in Italy, bubbles in Ireland and trade surpluses in Germany have a direct effect on jobs, pensions and savings in their own country. But as well as this economic involvement in each other's affairs, there was growing political involvement. We now fall under the spell of elections and referendums in Greece, Italy, Ireland, France, Germany, Austria or Spain – not out of exotic curiosity but as tremors and vibrations in a common democratic sediment of time. Those who share a currency share not just a bank account but a public realm. Yet this became obvious only when the currency needed saving.

No event in the Union has been experienced so intensely by the public as the Greek saga of the summer of 2015, with its dramatic climax in the first ever national referendum concerning an urgent European decision. The government of Alexis Tsipras that came to power in January that year made an unprecedented move. On the verge of state bankruptcy, amid complex negotiations with Greece's creditors, the prime minister deployed the referendum as a weapon on the European battlefield. In order to press other eurozone countries for more favourable terms for the rescue package, Tsipras asked Greek voters to reject the offer on the table in the negotiations. His government campaigned for a "no" vote and won it convincingly on 5 July. But the

Greeks then discovered that their political will, even when invested with the full authority of a direct pronouncement by the people, still clashed with the will of 18 other eurozone governments, who spoke in the name of their populations and were not about to give in to Athens at the expense of their own taxpayers. After a roller coaster of developments, Tsipras was eventually forced to eat humble pie.

The Greek drama of 2015 deepened public awareness of economic interconnectedness but far more still of political interconnectedness within the currency union, of ties that had become increasingly obvious to voters in eurozone countries from 2010 onwards. In this important new lesson, people saw that the Greek electorate was fighting not as a national democracy taking on "Big Europe" (as the Danes, Irish and Dutch had felt themselves to be with their referendums), but in Europe, as a democracy among democracies, as a people in the midst of other peoples. On that large and challenging battlefield, political opposition needed to take shape, as it still does. This was a historical experience.

REFERENDUMS

Other lessons too were derived from that Greek summer. Alexis Tsipras started a trend. In the refugee crisis another premier turned to the voice of the people to reinforce his own "no". In October 2016 Hungarian premier Viktor Orbán organized a referendum on the compulsory asylum quota, asking voters to reject a decision accepted in the Council of Ministers a year earlier. The "no" was overwhelming, at 98 per cent, but turnout at 43 per cent was below the validity threshold of 50 per cent. The Hungarian electorate had voted with its feet.

In the same summer week of 2015 in which the Greeks went to the polls, Dutch activists began a campaign to force an advisory referendum on the association accord with Ukraine. They succeeded. The government in The Hague was seriously embarrassed in April 2016 – during its Council presidency, too – by badly losing the referendum after a half-hearted campaign in which it avoided talking about Putin's Russia. The "no", at 61 per cent, was as loud as that against the European constitution in 2005, although at 32 per cent the turnout was only half. At the end of that year, Prime Minister Mark

Rutte obtained a clarification from his European partners designed to do justice to the "no" vote ("an instruction leaflet" he called it). On that basis, and with an eye to the geopolitical threat from Russia, he asked the Dutch parliament to ratify the Ukraine accord despite the referendum result, which it did after the general election of March 2017.

A national referendum on a European decision is a powerful weapon for the opposition, especially in a mediatized world. Fractious parties like to use freely accessible social media to challenge the politicians and demand popular ballots on subjects that until recently were the domain of governments and civil servants. Two governments, of Greece and of Hungary, put themselves temporarily outside the European order by taking a referendum with them to Brussels as heavy artillery. The vote of the people cuts across procedural depoliticization and may fan the flames of disruptive passions. Frustration is an emotion that can easily swell, especially when voters reject in a referendum something that affects all member states (such as a treaty or a deal made by the Union). It is simply misleading to promise that a direct pronouncement by your own people can trump the votes of all the other electorates in the Union as if by diktat.*[20]

Referendums are the wrong answer to a real question. They force those engaging in events-politics onto the stage to convince their own voters that they are making the right choices. This is the task of the leaders of the Union in any case, with or without the gun of the ballot box held to their heads. In that sense it is an admission of weakness to dismiss referendums as an improper instrument. How can European governments, singly or as a club, increase their capacity to act if they do not have public support? How can they make their mark on the world stage if their opponents do not feel that behind the flag is a population?

THE SIGNIFICANCE OF "TAKE BACK CONTROL"

In light of this analysis, the British vote for Brexit in 2016 can indeed be seen as the climax of the European search for a leverage point for opposition, at

---

* It is of course different with referendums on matters that mainly affect the member state concerned, such as decisions on accession, on leaving, or on participation in certain policy fields, as with the euro or Schengen.

least until now. It is a moment at which, with a referendum majority in one member state, the impossibility of classical opposition swings round into the possibility of opposition of principle or, in terms of Albert Hirschman's famous triad, the moment at which, because of a faltering voice and insufficient loyalty, the balance tips towards exit.[21]

Leaving is in itself a logical consequence of opposition of principle. A territorial separation is disruptive and destroys all kinds of connections, but in theory it is not violent, unlike a revolt or revolution to which anti-system opposition can also lead. Yet the dividing line between these variants is thin. The most radical Brexiteers are after not just the departure of their country but the end of the Union; they behave like revolutionaries, supporting their nationalist kindred spirits on the continent in their "liberation struggle". For her part, leader of the Rassemblement National (formerly the Front National) Marine Le Pen realizes that a French departure from the Union, given the country's central position, would destroy the Union as such. Her opposition of principle, which won her the support of a third of voters in May 2017, should therefore be seen as a revolt that aspired to become a revolution.

The Brexit campaign gathered momentum because it drew together all the countervailing forces that have been created over the course of time in response to the Union's depoliticization strategies. The slogan "Take back control" was the perfect trump card for mobilizing discomfort about the impossibility of gaining a grip on Brussels rules and decisions.

Technical depoliticization, the original recipe of the rule-making factory, met with British distrust from the very start ("We have not overthrown the divine right of kings to fall down before the divine right of experts", said future premier Harold Macmillan in 1950 of the Monnet plans[22]) and fed into a series of horror stories about tyrannical Brussels regulatory mania. The theme reached its peak in 2016 in a statement by Brexit leader Michael Gove: "Frankly, the people in this country have had enough of experts". As far as constitutional depoliticization is concerned, or the placing of policy choices outside the political arena, the British have always had difficulty with the position of the European Court of Justice. Of key importance in the May government's decision to read into the Brexit vote a mandate for leaving the internal market – along with the wish to limit freedom of movement – was a desire to end the tension between the jurisdiction of the Court in Luxembourg and the sovereignty of the Westminster parliament; May herself equated "Taking back control" with regaining control of Britain's own laws.[23] Procedural depoliticization, the binding of many partners and the disappearance of individual responsibilities into many-layered decision-making, runs counter to the British attachment to the personal accountability of the political leadership, underwritten by pendulum swings between a government and a political opposition that perform on the confrontational stage of the House of Commons, which is the way its system has worked for two centuries. Teleological depoliticization – the moral appeal to the ultimate goal of peace – has for a long time had a boomerang effect in a country that wants above all to be down to earth and pragmatic. Nowhere else has faith in Europe led to such virulent Euroscepticism. A particular stumbling block was the treaty formula from Rome 1957 of an "ever closer union", with its vague open-endedness; European colleagues could not understand why in the run-up to the referendum premier David Cameron expended so much diplomatic energy on hemming those three words with conditions.[24] With executive depoliticization, finally, the invocation of acute necessity for crisis decisions, the British have had little frontline contact, being outside both the currency union and Schengen. But the two major crises, surrounding the currency and refugees, nevertheless functioned in Brexit rhetoric as the perfect illustration of continental powerlessness. While the collapsing euro increased the pressure on Cameron to promise a referendum, which he did in January 2013 ("we're shackled to a corpse", said one Conservative MP), it was Europe's failure on its external border that gave Leave a decisive push three winters later.

The Leave camp would never have won had its rhetoric not resonated with long-term dissatisfaction and habits of thought. It reaped the harvest of years of distrust of a political system that may have fulfilled its continental promise of peace and prosperity but that, because of the lack of a dynamic opposition, has lost touch with a large proportion of the people of Europe.

There was a further reason why the slogan "Take back control" caught on, one that goes beyond the friction between Britain and Brussels. Voters on both sides of the Atlantic are turning against the globalization logic of open markets and open borders, as Americans showed at almost the same time by voting for Donald Trump. In the Union this market logic is still constitutionally anchored and put out of reach by the technique of constitutional depoliticization.

The absence of classical opposition means that the most elementary forms of vigilance are lacking. Brussels stresses time and again the advantages of the single market and freedom of movement, which benefit many who travel, trade, study or consume all over the continent. It has been blind, however, to the disadvantages for other groups of voters, for those who see in openness not an opportunity but a threat (such as competition in the jobs market). Their voices did not penetrate the Berlaymont building. If further exits are to be avoided, the Union will have to introduce a new balance between its support of economic freedoms and its protective role – whether in trade policy, on the external borders, or in the realm of social policy.[25]

Only by coming up with a substantial riposte to the opposition of principle can the Union withstand future voter revolts, and it must therefore permit and make use of the dynamic counterforces of opposition, in form as well as content. A direct relationship with a vigorous opposition is a precondition of survival for the Union as a whole.

Binding dissensus

Can the Union create space for protest without being untrue to itself? And if it cannot, will it survive the next voter revolt? What institutional forms lend themselves to classical opposition in the Union and which do not? Well-worn answers must be re-examined. After all, the Union has undergone a metamorphosis and it now engages in events-politics as well as rules-politics. We therefore need to know how to bring politics into both the rule-making factory and the events-Union.

To that end I will look, one by one, at the openings offered by the three institutional styles for Europe's theatre: backstage depoliticization through law and technicalities (functionalism), frontstage politicization through the Parliament (federalism), and frontstage politicization through the contributions made by national leaders (confederalism). We saw in the Prologue how these three styles were used alongside each other and in combination practically from the beginning, each with its own strategy for dealing with public expectations and each betting on specific institutional elements, and how with time they were slotted together and – for example on the executive playing field – forced to combine. The impulses from which they are derived and the interests with which they became bound up cannot simply be pushed aside. Anyone wanting opposition of principle is free to advocate a revolutionary tabula rasa. Classical opposition, by contrast, will need to take shape in conjunction with existing forms of decision-making and government in the structure that the Union has become.

Only two of the three styles have been formally investigated in the search for starting points for opposition – the depoliticized rule-making factory and the parliamentary promise – despite the fact that it is the third, the contributions made by national leaders, that provides support for events-politics, the politics that captivates the public like no other. Here lies a favourable terrain.

Political scientists have for years described the fundamental attitude of the populations towards Europe's internal market as a "permissive consensus", a benign indifference to the Brussels rule-making factory.[26] That attitude came to an abrupt end in 1992 with the Danish "no" and the French almost-"no" to the new Union treaty. With the concept that succeeded it, "constraining dissensus", political scientists expressed how national governments in the 1990s and 2000s saw their European capacity to act limited by fractious voters at home.[27] The transition is indeed unmistakable. After Maastricht the public was shaken awake; it wanted to have a say. The coded academic term for the new situation conveys not just an interpretation but a reproach: public dissent has the appearance of a barrier on the path to integration, a cause of delay. The people are putting the brakes on Europe, is the general tenor. This is to lose sight of the fact that public opposition is not just an annoying obstacle for a sitting government, it provides the oxygen for political life. Democracy is not merely a decision-making technique, it also creates an opportunity – as contemporary thinkers like Hannah Arendt and Claude Lefort have argued in the wake of Machiavelli – to stage-manage and pacify social and political conflicts symbolically, even to make them a source of freedom. Consequently, dissensus encompasses not just the power to constrain or disrupt but a binding force, one that can offer the Union the new energy that events-politics demands.

POLITICS IN THE RULE-MAKING FACTORY

After the war, depoliticization furnished the initial style of the European structure. We now need to investigate how, despite the various depoliticization techniques, space for opposition can be created, even in the backstage rule-making factory.

Technical depoliticization makes politics vanish behind technicalities. A decision appears not as a political choice or the result of deliberations but as a "solution" to a technical "problem". Consequently there are (apparently) no winners or losers, but the image of a Brussels technocracy is reinforced. This is partly a matter of communication. Press releases from the Commission currently pay less attention to procedures (how and when) than to political aims (what and why). Considerable progress. But better communication does not alter the fact that the basis for decision-making remains the same: expertise. Why, according to this model, must the public accept norms or decisions? Not because it has participated in the discussion about them but because those decisions are "good" or "useful". Legitimacy rests on expertise and objectivity, factors to which opposition is almost wholly alien.*

Nevertheless in recent years there have been proposals to introduce opposition into the sphere of expertise, for instance by Antoine Vauchez in his *Démocratiser l'Europe*. Noting the unfulfilled promise of the Parliament, this French political scientist takes aim at the Commission, the Court of Justice and the European Central Bank. He describes how all three independent institutions, which call themselves neutral and strive to remain outside the political and diplomatic battle, do in fact engage in politics, undetected, in a language of their own and according to their own protocols. Without wanting to detract from their independence, he challenges the apparently unimpeachable authority of the Commission, the Court and the Bank.

Vauchez has two targets. First there is the "sovereign interpretation of their mandate", which no longer corresponds with the changing expectations of the public.[28] He points to the degree to which jurisprudence from

---

* This is of course why Juncker, more emphatically than his predecessors, sought support from the voters as embodied by the European Parliament; this led to different tensions and the Commission president experienced how the "input" from Strasbourg did not give his institution the desired political authority.

the Court is driven by theories about the internal market, even where citizenship is concerned. In this constellation it is easier for a European lawyer to defend the right to abortion based on the free movement of services than as a fundamental right. By appealing to fundamental economic and social rights laid down in the Treaty, the direct interlocutors of the Court (lawyers, consultants, experts, activists) could take up arms against this one-sided understanding of its mandate. His second target is "the pretence of scientific objectivity", as seen in the management theories that the Commission has used since the 1990s to legitimize the setting up of agencies, or in the economic theory of monetarism on which the ECB bases its decisions. The academic community ought to mobilize criticism of these pretentions, but in doing so it requires access to "the black box of doctrines, methodologies and instruments".[29] Vauchez shows convincingly that even in the field of technocratic politics, legitimacy and desirable forms of classical opposition are conceivable.

A second form of depoliticization is constitutional, the placing of certain policy options outside the political arena. An argument against this is presented by German legal expert Dieter Grimm. As a former member of the German Constitutional Court and an authoritative academic, he makes a proposal that is radical for such circles. In *Europa ja – aber welches?* he advocates giving the section on policy in the Treaty ("primary law") the status of ordinary legislation ("secondary law").[30] Whereas in nation states the constitution regulates the form of government and the legislator makes political choices within that framework, in the Union the two levels are mixed together; the Treaty is full of policy formulations. Historically this can be explained. The founding treaty was not intended as a constitution, rather it gained its constitutional characteristics as a result of the jurisprudence of the European Court. As Grimm sees it, the Commission and the Court were thereby "made immune" to attempts by the Council of Ministers and the Parliament – both of them democratically accountable legislators – to respond to the administration of justice by making new laws. They have therefore also become immune to public pressure. The result is that "the players who have to justify themselves in the face of public opinion cannot change anything; those who can change things need take no account of public opinion".[31] Grimm therefore advocates reducing the Union Treaty to its constitutional core and reclassifying all rules of a non-constitutional nature as ordinary legislation. He claims this could be done while preserving all the rules; the operation is merely a way of "giving the treaties that have become a quasi-constitution a form that is substantively constitutional".[32] This would make it possible for the Council and Parliament to change existing case law, and thereby present a starting point for political opposition. The proposal leaves open some tricky questions, however. For example, do the "four freedoms" of the Union Treaty belong in the inviolable constitutional part?[33] This does not alter the essence of his argument, since Grimm shows how constitutional depoliticization can be resisted by creating space for legitimate protest.

Some authors argue that much can be done even without treaty change or "deconstitutionalization". Existing clauses are said to offer more space to "other", non-liberal politics than lawyers and policymakers generally recognize.[34] Freedom of interpretation is insufficiently capitalized upon; a narrow interpretation of a rule impoverishes the rule. Here too there is room for politics.

Procedural depoliticization, the third strategic characteristic of the rule-making factory that hinders opposition, removes from view those responsible for a given decision. The game is so complex that only experts among the public can keep track of who is playing and where the ball has got to; supporters of one side or the other know neither where nor when to make their voices heard. So the public would benefit first of all from better scrutability of the political game. In short, this means both the players and the commentators in the stands need to understand European decisions in terms of "government" rather than "governance": a different lens. Within our search this is an essential difference. Only when it is clear who governs can the opposition focus on something or someone.

Procedural depoliticization relies on the discourse surrounding "governance", a word in vogue in the 1990s. In that decade of overconfident globalization, the internet revolution and the End of History, complex decision-making in business and in international organizations was regarded as the pinnacle of progress.[35] In 2001 the Commission embraced the term, so that following on from "corporate governance", "global governance" and "multi-level governance" came "European governance".[36] The converse is classical constitutional government: in place of an intangible decision-making factory, the visible authority of a government. Again, only then does the opposition have something to aim at, and as a result a demonstrable place in the system.

Indeed, for ten years or so voices have been heard that violate the 60-year-old Brussels taboo on the word "government". It is no accident that they have been gaining in volume since the financial and monetary crisis, which tested to breaking point the design of the currency union, a product of rules-politics, and forced leaders and institutions to engage in events-politics. Visible decision-makers emerged out of the procedural tangles, namely the European Council, the Eurogroup and the European Central Bank, with protagonists recognized Union-wide: "Angela" and "Mario" in duet. Earlier I analysed this change, set in train by the necessity to act, as the development of an executive branch. Yet the actual emancipation of the executive is paired only to a limited degree with a semantic emancipation; the language is struggling to keep up with new relationships.

Typical is the semantic battle over the new politics of the eurozone. In the euro crisis the government in Paris and the Commission in Brussels advocated an "economic government" – a meaningful rhetorical move, even if it was to be merely "economic" and purely for the eurozone. Paris intended to give this role to the Euro Summits; the Commission wanted it for itself.[37] No less revealing is how opponents in Berlin and The Hague responded by expressing a preference for "economic governance": no visible decision-makers but instead rules and procedures. When this quarrel over the language grew heated at a crisis summit in the spring of 2010, President Van Rompuy allowed every government leader to choose their preferred version: "government" or "governance". Take your pick.* This battle of words, left undecided at the time, was between forces for and against procedural depoliticization, with differing views on political and governmental authority.

The currency union has partly freed itself from a tangle of rules. Government is happening. Can opposition to this "economic government" come from the European Parliament? Or does the new politics make other, more

---

* Those fascinated by such matters can compare the linguistic choices in the European Council conclusions of 25 March 2010. On this occasion the Germans, under pressure from the French, came round for the first time and opted for *Wirtschaftsregierung*, while Britain naturally stuck with "governance", as did the Dutch (in English, incidentally).

rigorous demands of opposition, as arguments for a eurozone parliament suggest?[38]

With these questions we will however leave, in the wake of the euro, the depoliticized rule-making factory and enter the domain of events-politics. Time now to look at the opportunities the two explicit political styles make available for classical opposition. Although the parliamentary style throws up an obstacle with the teleology of the promise of a new era and the summit style with the coercion of consensus, in both cases it seems that unexpected ways out can be, and have been, found.

THE PARLIAMENT AND THE PROMISE

Ostensibly the most effective way to create classical opposition is by means of the parliamentary style, familiar to everyone from national democracy. Following the example of a national parliament, with its internal party battles, the European Parliament was intended to create a dynamic between government and opposition. Much energy has been expended on this federal approach since 1950, by Euro-parliamentarians, by the other Union institutions and by several national governments, especially those of Belgium, Germany, Italy and Luxembourg. So why has it not happened?

To be able to interpret the voices of opposition, a parliamentary chorus needs to speak both in someone's name and to someone; it must create and sustain a meaningful relationship with both the public and the governing body. In the Union, relationships between parliament and government and between parliament and people are riddled with complications, and yet, with a bit of goodwill, it is possible to discern in both a beginning, an impulse, a prelude to something meaningful.

For a relationship with the executive, the Parliament has traditionally placed its bets on the development of the Commission into a European government. The Commission is the institution that it can formally call to account, and it would like the relationship to develop along these lines. Furthermore, Parliament and Commission have traditionally been friendly towards one another. Since they share both a perception of themselves as pioneers of Europe and a weakness in relation to the member states, it was in their mutual interest to support each other and talk each other up. This perpetuated a parliamentary culture of hopeful consensus. Division between the two institutions would only damage the European project.* To indulge in slight hyperbole: just as a parliament of a country at war generally stands united behind its government, so the Strasbourg parliamentarians closed ranks behind the Commission.

The parliamentary approach around which the Parliament and Commission united drew its strength from Europe's Promise, from the "not yet" and "one day". This produces the tension under which the Parliament labours: it wants to politicize things, to create a political arena, but it feels so fragile that it disqualifies the opposing forces by means of teleological depoliticization – not least by excommunicating unbelievers. As a result, the Parliament does not develop its own dynamic of support for and opposition to a (longed-for) government but instead leads opposition en bloc against the assembled member states. This tendency remains strong, as we see when a European Council president comes to Strasbourg to report on a summit of government leaders and in an established ritual all parties protest against the outcome. "This is the only parliament in the world where everyone belongs to the opposition", summit chair Van Rompuy (a former president of the Belgian Chamber of Representatives) let slip on one such occasion.

For its link with the population, the Parliament relies on the instrument of elections. In Community circles expectations of the direct elections promised in the founding treaty were high for many years: they would bring about a "salutary shock" to the Brussels world of offices.[39] When that shock failed to occur with the first elections in 1979, the utopian energy was transferred to other plans. So with every Treaty the Parliament gained additional powers. Nonetheless, until 2019 voter turnout was lower with every five-year term that passed. Recently hope was placed in *Spitzenkandidaten*, leading candidates for each Union-wide political grouping, as a way of arousing voter interest. Its proponents were also hoping that a classical party battle in the centre ground would develop, weakening the opposition of principle on the

---

* Of the precursors to the Parliament and Commission, one researcher wrote, "The more unanimous the Assembly was, [...] the more influence it had on the politics of the High Authority, and the better able the European executive power was to offer resistance to the undoubtedly powerful traditional particularism in the six countries" (P. J. G. Kapteyn, *L'Assemblée commune de la Communauté du Charbon et de l'Acier. Un essai de parlementarisme européen*, Leiden: Sythoff, 1962, 219).

flanks. This innovation too proved disappointing. In the 2014 elections, turn-out was stable (the hopeful could at least say that the decline had been halted for the first time), while the anti-European nationalist-populists gained more seats than before (a hundred of the 751). In 2019, although the turnout went up, the winning party's lead candidate was discarded for president of the Commission. It should come as no surprise that in federalist circles fresh ideas are doing the rounds for future elections: perhaps a pan-European con-stituency, or direct elections for a European president, or a ceremony for the newly appointed Commission president after the example of the inaugura-tion of an American president.[40] The Promise continues to feed itself.

From the side of the public there was very little response. The national referendums on Europe have all bypassed the Parliament. The crowded pub-lic squares in the euro crisis barely sought a connection with the Parliament at all. Voters clearly sense that the Strasbourg assembly has no grip on the decisions that affect them most deeply and captivate them most strongly.* Whether from disappointment at unfulfilled pledges or because of suspicion of federal pretentions, they see through the Promise. The intention was for the European Parliament to look like a parliament and act like a parliament. But all too often, behind the facade lies an inability to conduct real opposi-tion, to take part in government, to behave like a national parliament in the classical sense.

Some voters are rebelling against this model. The low turnout for Euro-pean parliamentary elections, often interpreted as signifying a lack of interest, may in fact also show that people are voting with their feet. Just as in 1992 the Danes rejected the European citizenship offered them at Maastricht and in 2005 the Dutch did not want a flag and a constitution, so there are citizens who do not want or do not recognize the Strasbourg Parliament. Dis-satisfaction with the Union can therefore, at one and the same time, lead to calls both for more power for the Parliament – the feeling being: then we can have a say – and for less, because: those people do not represent us.

The Parliament is therefore stuck. Based on the cherished "not yet" logic of the promise of a better world, it asks time and again for more powers. ("This

---

* By contrast this involvement is seen in agricultural policy, which gives a single profes-sional group its daily income – and, sure enough, an opposition that drives to Brussels, loud and visible, sounding horns and dumping dung if need be.

is not the moment for Europe to slow down further integration, but on the contrary to accelerate it", said a hundred Euro-parliamentarians in a federal manifesto at the height of the eurocrisis.)[41] At the same time, that perpetual desire for a leap forward foments public counterforces that it can itself neither understand nor control. The painful paradox is that the creation of an opportunity for classical opposition at a European level by means of the parliamentary approach leads to a strengthening of opposition of principle against the Union as such. The protest against the creation of the choir drowns out the choir.

To get out of this trap, the Strasbourg Parliament needs to adjust its view of itself. It must stop being fixated on the promise of a federal future and recognize its role in the actual Union of today. This first of all involves a mental switch from one executive to another, from the Commission to the European Council.

To this day the Parliament sees itself purely as legislator in a parliamentary system of the kind that exists in most Western European countries, where the government emerges from a parliamentary majority, indeed is almost fused with it; constitutional experts speak about a "fused powers" system. In reality, however, the Parliament could equally well see itself instead as legislator in a system of "separation of powers" of the kind that exists in the United States or Switzerland, where executive and legislature are quite distinct, each having its own voter base, for example. The position of the American president does not depend on a majority in Congress, which in turn the president cannot dissolve. Whereas in fusion systems like those of London and Berlin one government, in close association with its parliamentary majority, monopolizes decision-making power, decision-making in Washington and Bern lies with institutions that operate independently, sharing power in a permanent negotiating process. Despite European familiarity with national parliamentary systems and despite the Brussels teleology, the European Union can be regarded as a separated-powers system, with the Parliament as one of two legislative chambers (alongside the Council of Ministers) and the European Council, a collective presidency (with the Commission president among the members), as the executive. For some external observers, this reading is obvious.[42]

Such an interpretation would work to the advantage of the assembly in

Strasbourg, in that its relationship with the executive would be played out not just vis-à-vis the Commission (that eternal not-yet-government) but also vis-à-vis the highest political executive institution, the European Council (which it cannot hold to account but with which it is in a relationship of negotiation).[43]

It should also realize that the trump card it holds is not just that of elections but that of its unique visibility as a European political arena, as a place for Union-wide public debate. The very fact that it makes conflicts and fault lines visible, not just between parties but between countries, strengthens the Parliament and European political life. No other institution can do this.[*]

To steal the thunder of the opposition of principle, the time has come for plain speaking. The Union is not moving towards becoming a single state. EU countries have not merged into a single European nation, as was hoped after 1945, nor have they been absorbed into a "post-national space", as some assumed after 1989. They are, though, discovering how they can work together and alongside each other without any loss of individuality. The Union is and will remain incontrovertibly a union of states in the plural. After half a century of working through and next to each other, the creative tension between the three theatrical styles is spent; it now only produces confusion and threatens the coherence of the project.

For the European Union, federal parliamentarization is not only improbable but undesirable. Politics, as well as being a means of reaching collectively binding decisions and "solving problems", is a way of making social tensions (some of them by nature insurmountable) visible and manageable. The Union derives its *raison d'être* from this task. The parliamentary relationship of trust between Commission and Parliament can deal with party-based conflicts between, for example, left and right, while the bridging of differences between states takes place courtesy of the European Council and the Council of Ministers. Both mechanisms exist side by side; both are useful.

---

[*] For a stark recent example, take the Parliament's plenary vote, in September 2018, on whether to trigger a procedure against the Hungarian government of Viktor Orbán for undermining the rule of law at home: at that political moment of truth, leaders and parties across Europe could not hide and all had to decide how to position themselves on this decisive issue.

The simplistic view of nationalists who want to do away with the European Parliament finds its mirror image in the self-delusion of federalists who believe the European Council must be knocked off its pedestal. The nationalists want to destroy the Union; their stance is no surprise. More remarkable is the fact that the federalists, with their disruptive plans, think they are saving the Union. They forget that the main political fault lines in Europe still run between states, between North and South or East and West, not between parties. (German Christian Democrats are more likely to make an agreement concerning the euro with German Social Democrats than with Greek Conservatives; French Socialists are more likely to convince their Conservative compatriots of their views on military intervention in Syria than they are to convince Swedish Socialists.) Fault lines between countries are not a regrettable relic of history that can be swept away, they shape the identity of our continent. This fact places a limit on the introduction of classical opposition by the federal route. Those who push aside the forums for the management of conflicts between nation states by appealing to the parliamentary Promise deprive the Union of the means to keep in check its most dangerous tensions. They are playing with fire.

Opposition of principle to the federal style does not come purely from cyclical voter vexation. It also reflects the tormented longing of the European peoples to retain their individual voices in the European democratic space. The institutional style that relies on contributions by national leaders and their governments does justice to the fundamental fault lines between states (even if it underestimates the importance of law and shared institutions). At the same time it is not obvious how, in the consensual arena of summits, classical opposition can take shape, nor how it can be a *European* opposition. In defiance of expectations, opposition happens nonetheless.

DISCORD AT THE SUMMIT

The gathered governments have a firm preference for decision-making by consensus. No government wants to suffer loss of face by being forced to admit it was outvoted in Brussels. Tough battles often take place behind closed doors, certainly, but generally leaders, ministers and diplomats keep on searching for a compromise, an exemption or a transition period until they can all come together behind a decision. When there is insufficient time to iron out disagreements, as in the exhausting crisis summits of recent years, arguments about absolute urgency and survival – "necessity knows no law", "sink or swim" – force everyone into line. Such executive depoliticization, as we have seen, gives opposition little chance to organize.[*]

How can this tight governmental consensus be broken open? What forms of opposition are then possible? More than we might think. Although the Brussels doctrine traditionally sees only one crowbar, a glance at recent practice shows us four other varieties. I will look at all five, each more intense and more public in nature than the last: senatorial opposition (dividing countries up into majority and minority according to a voting procedure); Strasbourg opposition (Parliament against the club of governments); domestic opposition (one national opposition against its own government); united opposition (several national oppositions against several governments); and polemical opposition (a battle in the European public realm against the dominant discourse). Let us take each of them in turn.

Senatorial opposition

The Brussels doctrine has for many years proposed a simple way to crack open the government bloc: ministers should vote, thereby dividing member states into a majority and an opposition minority. I call this "senatorial opposition" because it is a vision that allocates to the Council of Ministers the role of an upper house or senate in a federal two-chamber system, functioning alongside the legislative Parliament and in the face of the governing Commission. This set-up flows directly from the parliamentary institutional vision, of which we have just seen the limitations and risks; after all, the abolition of national vetoes in the Council creates space for the addition of a parliamentary chorus.[†] For its advocates, therefore, senatorial opposition

---

[*] In terms of the three forms of opposition defined by Peter Mair – of which we have up to now encountered only "classical opposition" and "opposition of principle" – this resembles the third model, "assimilated opposition", a situation in which opposition is eliminated. After the example of a national party cartel, the governments in Brussels form a "consortium of countries", with all member states taking part in government.

[†] As long as all 28 member states have a veto, the Parliament is a 29th veto player; it can assert itself in the negotiations, but it is not at a level equal to that of the Council itself.

is really no more than a by-product of the main aim: to curb the power of the national capitals.

The governments have understandably resisted this approach. The breaking open of the consensus culture would come at the cost of both their individual and their collective power. France underlined the point with its empty-chair policy of 1965–66. De Gaulle turned out to be willing to destroy the Community to prevent majority decision-making in the Council. To fix the breach, the other governments, against the letter of the Treaty, gave themselves an informal veto for emergencies (known as the Luxembourg Compromise). Although as time went on countless vetoes were formally abolished and today ministers do occasionally vote, the Council of Ministers still prefers to decide by consensus.[44] For legislative work it does so on an equal footing with the Parliament, rather as if it were a senate in a bicameral system.

The European Council is different, however. Brussels doctrine incorrectly suggests that the summits of national leaders can be downgraded to senate status as well. This is to misunderstand the power and pre-eminence of the institutional vision that the national leaders bring into play as a de facto executive. For a start, consensus in the European Council is the norm according to the Treaty.[45] This makes the institution less susceptible to the "senatorial" approach of the Council of Ministers, where majority decision-making is firmly established. More essential still is that the summits, true showpieces, take place in the limelight, far more so than the Brussels machinery of which the ministers are part. The presidents and premiers make their compromises behind closed doors, true, but as figures of the highest authority in their countries they cannot avoid having to defend their positions in public, either at home or in front of the media gathered in Brussels. Yet ironically, it is the public tribune that prompts and goads these players, generally against their will, to engage in political battle in the arena.

This combination of compulsory unity and high visibility makes the rare episodes in which the leaders allow themselves to be divided by a vote thrilling to watch. Particularly memorable was the first ever vote at a European summit, in Milan in June 1985, when the government leaders, to everyone's surprise and to the anger of some, decided by seven to three to hold a conference on institutional reform. This was possible because it was a procedural decision. Under pressure from a hundred thousand pro-Europe demonstrators elsewhere in the city, the Italian host Bettino Craxi decided to break through an impasse in the meeting by means of a vote. Fault lines suddenly became visible, but the Community did not split. Those who lost the vote realized that they would have to accept the result: the epitome of a moment of passage for Europe.[46]

As well as procedural decisions, the Treaty also provides for certain appointments at the leadership level to be made by majority decision. One crucial issue concerned the nomination of former Luxembourg premier Jean-Claude Juncker for the position of Commission president by the European Council in June 2014, with votes against by Britain's David Cameron and Hungary's Viktor Orbán. In this case the gathered national leaders lost their room for manoeuvre because of an institutional coup by the Parliament. The large political groupings had declared beforehand that they would accept only the victorious Union-wide *Spitzenkandidat* as Commission president. The government leaders in the European Council grumbled about parliamentarian pretentions, but they were trapped as party leaders in the European party families (Angela Merkel as informal political leader of the Christian Democrats, François Hollande and Italy's Matteo Renzi of the Social Democrats and Dutch premier Mark Rutte for the Liberals). The British–Hungarian oppositional duo nevertheless failed to gain enough support for a countermove; an anti-Juncker offensive led publicly by Cameron, with an opinion piece in European newspapers and as its photographic climax a boat trip on a Swedish summer lake with his Swedish, German and Dutch colleagues, were to no avail.[47] The Parliament won the battle for publicity; in Germany both tabloid *Bild Zeitung* and philosopher Jürgen Habermas threw their weight behind Juncker.

True to its promise, the Parliament believed that with this appointment it had reduced the divided European Council to an upper house equivalent to the German Bundestag. It is more meaningful, however, to say that in this particular conflict the institution had shown its muscle as a legislator negotiating with the political executive, as it might in a separated-powers system like that of the United States or Switzerland.[48] (Compare this with the squabbles in Washington between president and Senate over the appointment of a judge to the Supreme Court.) Government leaders Cameron and Orbán led the opposition reluctantly, but to the last gasp; fully aware they would lose, they publicly voted against Juncker on 27 June 2014. For the British prime minister, who a year earlier had promised his voters a European referendum, the defeat was ominous.

In short, the European Council, product of the theatrical style of betting on summitry, is not becoming a senate as the parliamentary style envisages. The voting rule can sometimes, in a few special circumstances, expose division at a summit, but it is not a sufficient condition for that outcome. Among leaders, consensus remains the norm. It is a norm of collegial government, characteristic of the Swiss Federal Council, for example, an executive of colleagues in a separated-powers system. All the more striking then that unity at a summit can be broken even without allowing a vote; a few polemists contrive to do it, as we will shortly see, helped by the light of European publicity that shines in times of crisis.

Strasbourg opposition

The second version is Strasbourg opposition: European Parliament versus the club of national governments. In that role the institution functions not as an arena for a contest between governing and opposition parties (as it would prefer to regard itself), rather it is itself an opposition player. The Parliament thereby shows that even with a consensus between 28 national governments, the last word has not yet been spoken. Logically this may be for one of two reasons: either because its opponents are national, or because they are governments. Strasbourg protest comes in either a federal or a "civic" mode.

The Parliament likes to engage in opposition in the name of a promise of more Europe. From that perspective the national capitals will always fall short. Although lacking a voter mandate for federal plans and with little support among governments, the parliamentarians in Strasbourg have enough procedural power to win terrain from time to time, especially if they can affect the balance between member states divided among themselves. During the euro crisis, for example, the Parliament helped pull at the tug-of-war rope from the side of the member states that wanted the new budgetary rules to have "automatic sanctions" against those who violated them, which would increase the power of the Commission. By doing so it dragged power relations in the Council, which had shifted slightly after the Franco-German

"Deauville" deal, northwards again.* As a federal opponent, Strasbourg feels contented, even though it may alienate a segment of the public in the process.

As well as being the customary mouthpiece for federal as opposed to national plans, the Parliament can speak in the name of the totality of citizens against the totality of governments. As a "civic" opposition it actually has a firmer footing than as a federal opposition, since in this guise it represents more credibly the preferences of voters. Take privacy legislation. It is quite useful that executive powers, their investigative capacities expanding in dangerous times, are made to feel civic resistance and counter-pressure. For national legislation this pressure comes in theory from a national parliament and public opinion; in the Union, with its cooperating governments and civil servants, opposition can come only from Strasbourg. Such a voice of civic opposition was heard from the Parliament in February 2010 when it voted down an accord on the exchange of banking data with the United States (SWIFT). Three years later it rejected on similar grounds a transatlantic agreement on passenger data (PNR); only when the governments renewed the pressure to pass the legislation after the terror attacks in Paris in January 2015 was the Parliament swayed. Quite apart from any intrinsic merits, in such situations the Parliament makes the dilemma of security versus freedom visible to the European public. Hard choices must be fought over publicly.

As an institutional opponent, the Parliament likes to position itself in a heroic constitutional history. Just as the British and French parliaments once took up arms against an absolute monarch and little by little won civic freedoms – or so the reasoning in Strasbourg goes – the European Parliament fights against the European Council, whose members are accountable to their 28-fold voting publics at home but not to a single democratic forum, while collectively, from a parliamentary perspective, they behave like an absolute monarch. What such a comparison tellingly shows is that, because of the absence of classical opposition, even true believers crank up their rejoinders such that classical opposition becomes opposition to the system.

---

* It was striking that in the summer of 2011 ECB president Jean-Claude Trichet came to Strasbourg to whip up the parliamentarians; the ECB was using the public nature of the Parliament for purposes of institutional opposition.

Domestic opposition

The third version is domestic opposition, in which classical national opposition puts pressure on its own government to play a tough game in Brussels. This dynamic has been present time and again in recent years. Its voters demand that government A must get more money, B must pay less, C must not cross a specific red line while D must win on a certain point, all on pain of no-confidence motions at home. This politicization hampers the work of forging compromises in the Council of Ministers and at summits. Whereas national governments in Brussels used to work away patiently in private at building a market, convinced that their national interests would be served in the long term by the give-and-take of shared interests, they now feel forced to announce the benefits of a decision promptly and loudly to avoid coming under fire at home as traitors to the national interest.

But amid this new European openness, other governments and public opinions watch and listen. German political scientist Herfried Münkler speaks of the "politicization paradox": what is good from a joint perspective requires from each government a strong national narrative and rhetorical focus to counter criticism.[49] The consequence is that ministers who in their own countries brandish their own fabulous negotiating skills in Brussels will be less able to defend their interests the next time round, since they have apparently got away with too much.[50] In this dynamic, the preparedness to compromise declines and the gap increases between the language used in Brussels and at home. Münkler – who pursues the political-science postulate of "constraining dissensus" to its logical extreme – believes it is "not improbable" that the Union will succumb to this paradox.[51]

National opposition therefore puts the system under strain, even though it may initially appear to have no European expression because by its very nature it stays at home. All the same, the image of 28 governmental puppets unable to move any longer in Brussels because of the 28 home crowds breathing down their necks is too static. There is real dynamism. In part this is generated by the slowly turning cogs of the national election mechanisms all over the Union. If an opposition party wins, its representatives take up their country's seats in Brussels. As a government, they experience the European forcefield and have to accept responsibility for joint decisions. In many cases

255

fellow governments will accommodate the newcomer in order to demonstrate that election results "make a difference". By this route alone, a single national opposition is rendered visible in the Union.

But national forces of opposition can do something else, too, to put the consensus of the gathered national governments to the test: they can collaborate.

United opposition

United opposition, the fourth variant, arises when several national oppositions in the Union join forces. This is far from easy. If even governments, despite the regulatory efforts that bind them and despite events that affect them all, have immense difficulty reaching agreements in Brussels, what must it be like for opposition parties, spread out across the member states, barely bound to shared frameworks at all, and not corralled by the responsibilities of government?

The joint task of the national oppositions would be clearer if there was among governments a classic pendulum motion. Imagine if all across the Union the right was in power and the left in opposition. In election after election the seats in the European Council and Council of Ministers would change party colour. Given that every member state has its own parliamentary cycle, generally lasting four or five years, this would not happen overnight but instead take several years. (This makes it comparable to the American Senate, where every two years a third of senators are elected for six years, a rhythm that dampens large electoral shocks but nevertheless results in leaps from one majority to another.) Such electoral movements do occur in the European Union; in the mid-1990s a highly visible wave brought Social Democrats to power in London, Paris and Bonn, led by Blair (1997), Jospin (1997) and Schröder (1998). During the euro crisis a wave in the other direction occurred in the countries affected. Beginning in the spring of 2011, Ireland, Portugal, Spain and Greece replaced left-wing governments with right-wing governments. These, however, are incidental swings. Because of their diverse voting systems, party landscapes and political situations, the Union rarely exhibits a clear electoral pattern.

From capital to capital, different parties or coalitions rule. The 28 government representatives encountered at summits or at the Council of Ministers form a kind of grand coalition of Conservatives, Christian Democrats, Social Democrats and Liberals. The balance of power changes, but all the major parties are at the table. By the same token, the large families of parties – most prominent among them the conservative European People's Party and the Party of European Socialists – are always in opposition somewhere. It is therefore difficult for the 28-fold opposition at home to unite Union-wide in order to manifest itself as a classical opposition, as an alternative governing power.

Into this vacuum leap the parties on the flanks, from the far right and the far left. They can react against the compromises of the governing centre. They do this both nationally and as Europeans, but with an essential difference. Take the French Front National in the spring of 2017. In France the party engaged in classical opposition; Marine Le Pen wanted to become president, not to abolish the Republic. By contrast, in Europe her party engaged in opposition of principle, wanting to destroy the Union by bringing about a French exit. To this day only the parties of the far right and far left, which hold power hardly anywhere, have managed to organize themselves explicitly as a united opposition, and in many cases it takes the form of opposition to the system.

On 21 January 2017 the heads of the European extreme and nationalist right appeared in public in Koblenz. For the first time, Front National leader Marine Le Pen and Alternative für Deutschland leader Frauke Petry shared a stage. Geert Wilders of the Dutch Partij Voor de Vrijheid and Matteo Salvini of Italy's Lega Nord put in an appearance as well. A day after the inauguration of Donald Trump in Washington, the mood in Koblenz was expectant; with their kindred spirit occupying the White House, the European opposition could hardly wait to bring the revolutionary Brexit-&-Trump movement to the continent. When the Dutch leader failed to make his party the largest in the Dutch parliament in elections two months later, and then Le Pen was defeated by Macron, the entire movement experienced the setback. Those who combine forces in the Union in hope of victory have had to endure each other's losses.

Opposition parties of the extreme left likewise formed a European alliance. The euro crisis created a bond between southern European critics of Brussels austerity politics. Syriza in Greece and Podemos in Spain discovered each other as radical start-ups opposing a decaying domestic political class: the parties drew strength from each other's success; their leaders spoke during each other's campaigns. Syriza leader Alixis Tsipras, in 2014 the pan-European candidate of his party's family for the Commission presidency, even set himself up as the ideological leader of a continental anti-Merkel movement. Rhetorically these parties engage in classical opposition, both at home and in the European arena. In theory they advocate not departure from the Union or the euro but a different economic and monetary policy. The changes they press for are sometimes so radical, however, that the boundary between classical opposition and opposition of principle becomes blurred. In practice the French extreme-left candidate for the presidency Jean-Luc Mélenchon was on the same anti-Europe wavelength in spring 2017 as Front National leader Marine Le Pen.

Polemical opposition

It fell to Greece's Syriza to experiment with a fifth and final variety of opposition: on coming to power in Athens, it brought the opposition to Brussels. Its strategy could be called "polemical" opposition, in the sense of a battle (Gk. *polemos*, war) against the dominant discourse.

For a proper understanding of this episode we need to go back to the double Greek election of the spring of 2012. In May the voters punished both the traditional parties of government, making short work of past misrule. The impossibility of forming a government made a second round unavoidable. By this point the Greeks had a clear view of what was at stake; the choice was between euro plus reforms (moderate right and left) and leaving the euro (the preference of both the nationalist right and Syriza on the extreme left). In June the Greeks opted by a narrow majority for parties that wanted to keep the euro, to the immense relief of the eurozone.

The 2015 sequence began with a snap election in January. This time Syriza campaigned for a reduction in austerity but also for continued membership of the eurozone. With this twofold promise it won convincingly. It was going to do things differently. The Tsipras government refused to settle for the narrow parameters of European politics and went further than any other party in its attack on the depoliticized consensus. It did so with a formula no one had yet tried: govern at home and engage in opposition in Brussels. Fireworks guaranteed.

But opposition against what or whom? Rhetorically the Tsipras government was fighting against the world of high finance and Brussels austerity policies. Even foreign correspondents from Europe and America rejoiced that a people had staged a revolt at the ballot box against the technocratic consensus. It was as if democracy was demanding its due – in the land of its birth, no less – and rejecting the "There is no alternative" argument of the recipes for reform prescribed by Brussels and the IMF in Washington. Yet the Greek government gradually discovered that rather than fighting on behalf of democracy against international capital, it was locking horns as one democracy with 18 others (each with its own enfranchised taxpayers). It was people against people.

This quickly became obvious in the isolation of Greek minister Yanis Varoufakis amid the eurozone finance ministers. The other governments had no desire to make good the election promises of Athens at their own expense. They included the Eastern European eurozone countries where pensions were lower than in Greece (Slovakia, Slovenia, the Baltic states), several northern creditor countries (Germany, the Netherlands, Finland), and countries that had themselves resolutely adhered to an EU programme (Spain, Ireland, Portugal). Moreover, with a negotiating style consisting of economics lessons, game theory and blackmail by means of the Putin connection, Athens alienated its best friends, including France. At meeting after meeting the will of the Greek people came up against 18 others. Jürgen Habermas may have wanted to dispose of this somewhat denunciatorily – "Both sides bragged like parrots that they were empowered by their own 'people'"[52] – but in the eurozone it is the 19 governments, existing alongside the Brussels institutions but also as part of them, that are the democratically mandated players who take the decisions. Europe means democracy in the plural.

Opposition against whom is one question, opposition how is another. The Tsipras government quickly concluded that it had nothing to gain on the usual terrain of compromise politics. It found itself in an unfavourable forcefield. The Greek government did not want to engage in governmental compromise. Understandably, Athens longed to break loose from the position of debtor state, in which capacity the country had been humiliated for years by banker-minsters in the Eurogroup. It wanted once more to engage in politics on equal terms with other eurozone nations.

The flamboyant Varoufakis was reproached for an excess of interviews and publicity; he should get on with reforming the economy at home, was the message. But with his torrent of words the minister, rationally enough, was attempting to overturn the discourse, to change the rules of the game. Immediately after Syriza's victory he left on a European tour to visit colleagues in Paris, London, Rome and Berlin. A cunning encircling manoeuvre: two left-wing governments, to pick up political sympathy, with a stop in between at the City, where bankers gave the thumbs-up to debt relief, before an attack on the German fortress of disciplinary rhetoric. Rarely had we witnessed such a clash of views as was seen at the Berlin press conference held by Schäuble and Varoufakis. "We did not even agree to disagree", said the Greek, brushing aside the usual platitude for diplomatic emergency landings.[53] Going along with the austerity logic of his creditors would mean defeat from the start. So the Syriza government resorted to outsider tactics to turn the situation around: against Greek financial debt it set the German war debt; against aid-post Brussels it briefly sought help from Moscow. The partners in Brussels, Berlin and Paris consequently recognized that this was not merely an opponent ready to play the political game fiercely and recklessly; the suspicion arose that Athens was prepared to destroy the European playing field quite deliberately. The impasse was complete.

The moment of truth came on Friday 26 June 2015, after five months of fruitless consultation between Athens and its creditors about an extension to the support package. Shortly after midnight the Greek premier appeared on television and announced a referendum within eight days on the final formal offer by the creditors. His advice was to vote "no". With this gesture Tsipras blew the bridges between him and his European partners. It was not so much the referendum itself – the idea had been hanging over the markets since 2011 – as the unprecedented advice to vote against the offer. A government freely deciding to hold a referendum is a different matter from its being forced to do so by a constitution, a parliamentary majority or a citizens' initiative. In theory the purpose is to give difficult decisions more solid support than can be had from the parliament alone. In any case you have to stand by your principles. (If David Cameron had recommended that British voters should vote "leave" in the 2016 referendum, his European colleagues would have turned their backs on him.) With his advice on how to vote,

Tsipras transformed himself that Friday evening from a colleague in need – Merkel and Hollande spent many hours with him – into the leader of the opposition. It was as if he had taken the ball out of the game and dramatically laid it in front of Greek voters. He was deploying his people's vote as a weapon.

Banks had to shut, capital controls were introduced, yet the prospect of chaos did not have an intimidatory effect. The outcome of the referendum on Sunday 5 July 2015 was a convincing "no" (by 61 per cent). Greek voters had followed their political leader in his reckless negotiating strategy. Many voted "no" fully aware that this strategy could end in failure. The feeling was: it cannot get any worse; better dignified poverty than a future as Europe's penal colony. The departure of Greece from the eurozone seemed imminent.

The referendum was followed, however, by another roller coaster of surprises, ending with an agreement on 13 July after an all-night Euro Summit. The leadership of the eurozone – a private consultation at dawn between Tusk, Tsipras, Merkel and Hollande proved decisive – cleared the way for a new rescue package, a "last chance" for Athens to stay in the monetary union. The deteriorating financial position of his country meant that Tsipras had to swallow more stringent conditions on several points than those proposed to him three weeks earlier. He realized that refusing and therefore leaving the eurozone would be a catastrophe for his country, for pensions and for employment; the Greek prime minister did not believe that the plan for a parallel currency advocated by his finance minister Varoufakis would avert disaster. Within a week the Greek and German parliaments agreed to the deal. The Syriza leader choked off a revolt by the left by resigning as prime minister, announcing new elections and winning them convincingly on 20 September. He maintained the confidence of the voting public, which appreciated the fact that he had done his utmost and apparently accepted that nothing more could be achieved. His role as European opposition had a financial price but a political benefit: self-esteem.

Only one government leader came out of the exhausting Euro Summit of 12–13 July 2015 in high spirits. This was the conservative Mariano Rajoy; the normally dour Galician even stuck his thumbs in the air.[54] For the past four years he had loyally implemented the prescribed policy of austerity, "because there is no alternative"; the last thing he wanted was a message to his voters that it had been unnecessary. Tsipras' capitulation robbed Rajoy's domestic rivals, Syriza's sister party Podemos, of their key argument in the Spanish election campaign that autumn. The polemical opposition, highly visible at the summit, had been halted and forced to regroup.

By this route, unexpectedly, a new pan-European arena, with a visible opposition, formed itself out of events-politics and the public tribune that comes with it. Because of the media spotlight that falls on summits and on other crisis forums, dissident national politicians become recognizable right across the Union, not just as bearers of their national flags but as European opposition figures. The polemical opposition shows in word and deed that clashes in the Union can take place not just between different countries but between different discourses, without investing the hope for its institutional expression in a federal future – an important difference between polemical opposition and the parliamentary style of engagement.

Just as the Tsipras government joined battle with the dominant discourse in the erupting euro crisis, Prime Minister Orbán did so in the refugee crisis that grabbed the headlines at practically the same time. The Hungarian too showed no hesitation in putting into words a coherent alternative to the line laid down by the Union, in this case opposing Merkel's culture of welcome. Against the Christian motif of the Good Samaritan he set the image of the crusader defending the West. This dissident too, regarded by many as dangerously and mercilessly nationalistic, sought public support on the terrain of opposition. Particularly memorable was Orbán's visit to Bavarian CSU leader Horst Seehofer on 23 September 2015. Seehofer was no less critical of Merkel's open door policy than his guest and, although the leader of a governing party, he wanted to engage in opposition on the issue. Delighted German anti-Merkel demonstrators welcomed the Hungarian as a defender of European culture.[55] Six months later Orbán struck a symbolic blow as a guest of former German Chancellor Helmut Kohl, honorary citizen of Europe.[56] After the dramatic winter with refugees in the snow, the ethic of conviction professed by Merkel and Juncker finally confronted the primacy of self-preservation advocated by Orbán in the responsibility-politics choices made by the Union and its member states (such as the Turkey deal of March 2016), which worked out well for many leaders who had not dared to contradict the chancellor openly. In that sense the Hungarian premier was a more successful opposition player than his Greek colleague.

Regarding both the currency and the border, the polemical opposition fired its sharpest arrows at Berlin – combatting, from within, the strongest governing power in the Union.

Epilogue

[T]he theatre is the political art par excellence; only there is the political sphere of life transposed into art.

Hannah Arendt[1]

The fundamental, long neglected matters of Government and Opposition in the Union are not easily resolved. Nor was that my intention; this book is not a manifesto. I did, however, after a decade of improvisation, want to offer a new perspective on ways of addressing these issues. The events-politics that the Union is learning to engage in under the pressure of crises takes it a long way from its origins in rules-politics. The realization has dawned that the new Europe needs to be in a position to act. Only then can it step into the future with self-confidence and show itself on the world stage. As long as executive power in the Union is continuing to develop – and in light of historical necessity and political determination there is every sign that it is – the Opposition too will find new and, we can hope, better ways of effectively making its voice heard. We have seen an unexpectedly large number of lines of thought along which public dissent can be ascertained and organized. Opposition can contribute to the Union's set-up of the vital functions of balance, changeover, vigilance and dissent, with the result that the public experiences "Europe" not just as driven by technocratic necessity but ultimately as an outcome of choices freely made.

After ten years of events-politics, the wider public clearly sees the stakes. The May 2019 European Parliament elections signalled a resounding rebuttal of the rule-makers' strategy of anesthesia. For the first time in four decades, voter turnout went up, and massively: in the EU as a whole from 42 to 51 per cent – in Germany from 48 to 61 per cent, in France from 42 to 50, in Poland from 24 to 46. Even if people voted in national constituencies for national candidates that were only loosely united in pan-European parties, the overall election was more than the sum of 28 national ones. Three phenomena stand out in this respect. First, pan-European electoral trends were at work. Traditional governmental parties lost everywhere: in the UK, the Conservatives and Labour Party garnered less than 25 per cent of the vote between them; in France, *Les Republicains* and the Socialist Party were likewise squeezed between Macron's upstart centrists and Le Pen nationalists. In Germany, the SPD was dealt a massive blow, for the first time surpassed by the Greens, who also did well elsewhere in northern and western Europe. All across Europe, the old left/right cleavage no longer structured the debate. Secondly, more than ever voter choices were driven by EU-related issues. Voters want a say over decisions that they now know affect their lives, their interests, their values. Climate worriers expect European action. Migration remains a top issue for seven out of ten EU voters, according to a French poll.[2] Brexit also left its mark: having witnessed the UK chaos, voters on the continent no longer consider an EU exit credible; Salvini in Rome and Le Pen in Paris could only win by dropping their euro exit plans (in the Netherlands, Wilders stuck to them and went home empty-handed). Thirdly, the election itself set in motion events affecting the Europe-wide arena. Two prime-ministers resigned: for the tenacious Theresa May in London the vote proved one too many, while Alexis Tsipras in Athens, humiliated by his right-wing rivals, called for a snap general election (which he would lose). Aftershocks reached Rome, where later in the summer a power-drunk Salvini blew up his populist coalition in an act of hubris. Likewise it was only *after* the voters had spoken that the EU leadership positions for the 2019–24 cycle could be decided, in a fascinating interplay between national leaders and the new Parliament. A new set of actors enters the stage, new voices of opposition have yet to make themselves heard.

This new European politics cannot exist without new openness. The contrary voices and loud mouths of recent years have an important part to play: they make tough political choices and dilemmas visible to the European public that has poured in en masse, to all those people who to their own surprise suddenly find themselves in the public gallery of the political theatre. In doing so they break through the sometimes dispiriting logic of depoliticization. The public battle of words enables viewers and voters to see the present-day freedom in which we are creating our future.

Here lies a special task for the media, too, indispensable as they are in giving shape to that public realm, in connecting politics and people. With stories and images they can unite and encompass the public spaces of the Union – by shining national spotlights on the European stage, by conveying the best aspects of neighbouring countries, by digging away distrustfully behind the scenes of politics old and new. Over recent years they have brought home to us that Europe, because of its currency, border and neighbours, is part of the fibre of all national political bodies and, conversely, that all national elections resonate throughout the Union. True, it is walls and laws that give a *polis* solidity but, as Hannah Arendt wrote, even walls and laws cannot ultimately survive without stories, without speakers, dissenters and listeners who preserve memories and share expectations of the future. A political community is a community of storytellers.[3]

While a place for opposition in the Union needs to be shaped and consolidated, its place in the individual member states must remain open. The separation of powers continues to come under pressure in Hungary and Poland. There is a risk that space for free media and social organizations in the Union will become restricted. For a long time, the governments were reticent about criticizing each other; they too would rather not have anyone looking over their shoulders at home. It fell to the European Commission to press the Hungarian and Polish governments for an explanation, and to reprimand them. In doing so it has the authority of the Treaty on its side. Yet it is no surprise that the deeply conservative government in Warsaw has accused the Commission of bias and of being in cahoots with the local opposition. The rejoinder from the Commission and from the Union as a whole must be: no, we do not support the local opposition but the principle of Opposition as such.

The return of History that we have been experiencing since 1989, which has clearly gained momentum since 2008, carries within it the rebirth of politics. Democracy is a way of making social and political conflicts visible. Opposition, protest and dissent can give Europe once again the dynamism without which events-politics cannot continue to unfold.

This change will result in a Union with more commotion and noise, more drama and conflict – a development not without risk. But the cherished rules-politics consensus of the past, which fewer and fewer voters feel to be credible, is inadequate for a Union that needs to act. The binding effect of dissensus presumes two things: confidence that the Union can withstand a buffeting and – in the spirit of its earliest architects – the conviction that what unites us as Europeans on this continent is bigger and stronger than anything that divides us.

Notes

PREFACE

1. "Remarks by President of the European Council Donald Tusk at the handover ceremony with the outgoing President Herman Van Rompuy", 1 December 2014.

2. After Herman Van Rompuy's term of office ended on 30 November 2014, I worked for his successor Donald Tusk for a transition period of three months, until 28 February 2015.

PROLOGUE: RAISING THE CURTAIN

1. Hannah Arendt, *The Human Condition* (Chicago, IL: University of Chicago Press, 1998 [1958]), 198.

2. Marcel Gauchet, *Le nouveau monde. L'avènement de la démocratie*, part 4 (Paris: Gallimard, 2017), 262.

3. A random sample of statements by three Grexiteers, Buiter, Roubini and Krugman. Willem Buiter, 16 November 2011, Bloomberg interview: "I think we maybe have a few months – it could be weeks, it could be days – before there is a material risk of a fundamentally unnecessary default by a country like Spain or Italy which would be a financial catastrophe dragging down the European banking system and North America with it". In July 2012 Buiter named 1 January 2013 as D-Day for a "Grexit" (a term he invented). Nouriel Roubini, 25 January 2012 (pronouncements at the 2012 World Economic Forum): "The eurozone is a slow-motion train-wreck. Countries – and not just Greece – are insolvent. I think Greece will leave the eurozone in the next 12 months, and Portugal after. [...] There is a 50pc chance that the eurozone will break up in the next three to five years." Paul Krugman, "Apocalypse fairly soon", *New York Times*, 17 May 2012: "Suddenly, it has become easy to see how the euro – that grand, flawed experiment in monetary union without political union – could come apart at the seams. We're not talking about a distant prospect, either. Things could fall apart with stunning speed, in a matter of months, not years." (From Francesco Papadia's blog moneymatters-monetarypolicy.eu and Noah Barker, "Euro doomsayers adjust predictions after 2012 collapse averted", Reuters, 28 December 2012).

4. Julien Benda, *Discours à la nation européenne* (Paris: Folio, 1979 [1933]), 124.

5. Officially the Council of Ministers is called the "Council of the European Union"; in order to distinguish it more clearly from the "European Council" where EU heads of state or government gather, I prefer the informal name Council of Ministers. It

goes without saying that both these EU institutions are to be distinguished from the "Council of Europe", the Strasbourg-based body for human rights and democracy whose 47 member states include Russia and Turkey and which is best known in the UK for its (European) Court of Human Rights.

6. In the "Fouchet plans" of 1961–62, the French president proposed summits of the European Community's six heads of state or government that would de facto supervise the Brussels institutions. The plans met with fierce resistance, the Dutch and Belgian governments fearing summitry would end in Franco-German power-play, and left a bitter aftertaste.

7. Unparalleled among contemporaries on this triptych remains Altiero Spinelli, *The Eurocrats: Conflict and Crisis in the European Community* (Baltimore, MD: Johns Hopkins University Press, 1966), 1–25; see also Luuk van Middelaar, *The Passage to Europe: How a Continent Became a Union* (London & New Haven: Yale University Press, 2013), 1–11 ("Three European Discourses"). In his book *Which European Union? Europe After the Euro Crisis* (Cambridge: Cambridge University Press, 2015), Sergio Fabbrini is on the track of a similar threefold division (although he creates confusion by speaking of "three unions", whereas it is all about three conflicting visions of and within one and the same Union).

8. Similarly, the tasks and powers of a late-medieval European ruler are usually ranked on a scale that runs from *jurisdictio* (literally, the saying of the law) to *gubernaculum* (being at the helm), or from the appeal to common law or an advisory council to the lonely, rapid decision. John Pocock describes the spectrum as follows:

> At one end [*jurisdictio*, LvM] the decisions of experience had already been made and the monarch had only to say what they had been to exercise memory to the exclusion of other aspects of prudence; his own experience need make no contribution to custom and he took no initiative of his own. At the various intermediate stages, as unfamiliarity and the required speed of response concurrently increased, more was demanded of prudence by way of inputs to the customs-forming process; the king took advice of fewer counselors, relied more upon his own prudence but made decisions whose generality, permanence and binding force as laws correspondingly decreased. Finally, the point was reached where unfamiliarity was total, response must be instantaneous, and there could only be one hand at the tiller; the monarch was absolute in the sense that his decisions were bound neither by custom nor by counsel, but they did not, because they could not, instantly become general laws of conduct. Only repetition and further experience could make them that. (J. G. A. Pocock, *The Machiavellian Moment: Florentine Political Thought and the Atlantic Tradition* (Princeton, NJ: Princeton University Press, 1975), 26.)

In our context it is intriguing that this relates to the range of tasks of a single ruler, whereas over the course of modern European history the ruler's functions have been divided up between various figures and holders of political, bureaucratic and judicial authority.

9. The example of the scrap metal market is drawn from a lecture by the man who, as a young civil servant, established it: E. P. Wellenstein, "Dankrede bij aanvaarding van de Von der Gablentzprijs", The Hague, 29 November 2007.

10. "Rede des Bundesministers der Finanzen Dr. Wolfgang Schäuble an der Université Paris-Sorbonne, 2 November 2010". Available at: https://www.bundesfinanzministerium.de/Content/DE/Reden/2010/2010-11-02-sorbonne.html (accessed 20 December 2018).

11. Think of the "historical semantics" of O. Brunner, W. Conze and R. Koselleck, or what is known as the "Cambridge school" of political thinking, represented by Quentin Skinner and J. G. A. Pocock, or the "linguistic turn" in American philosophy of language associated with Richard Rorty and others.

12. Michel Foucault, *L'Ordre du discours* (Paris: Gallimard, 1971), 12.

13. Van Middelaar, *Passage to Europe*, 280–2.

14. "Remarks by President Donald Tusk before his meeting with French President Emmanuel Macron", 17 May 2017.

PART I: *ACTS AND SCENES*

1 IMPROVISING: THE EURO CRISIS

1. Arendt, *Human Condition*, 177.

2. Quintilian, *Institutio Oratoria*, book X, ch. 7, trans. H. E. Butler (Cambridge, MA: Harvard University Press, 1920).

3. Nicolas Sarkozy, via *Le Canard enchaîné*, cited in Jean Quatremer, "L'Allemagne est-elle encore européenne?", *Libération* blog, *Les Coulisses de Bruxelles*, 2 February 2009.

4. J. W. Goethe: "Ein jeder kehr' vor seiner Tür, und rein ist jedes Stadtquartier", cited in Cerstin Gammelin and Raimund Löw, *Europas Strippenzieher. Wer in Brüssel wirklich regiert* (Munich: Econ, 2014), 62.

5. Luuk van Middelaar, "Het sprookje is voorbij, red de euro!" in *NRC Handelsblad*, 29 December 2009.

6. European Council president Herman Van Rompuy formally took office on 1 December 2009, the day the EU Lisbon Treaty (providing a stable summit presidency) entered into force, but he graciously let the last "rotating president", Swedish Prime Minister Fredrik Reinfeldt, finish his six-month term and effectively started work on 1 January 2010. He offered a short account of his time in office in Herman Van Rompuy, *Europe in the Storm: Promise and Prejudice* (Louvain: Davidsfonds, 2014).

7. Peter Garner *et al.*, "Traders make \$8 billion bet against euro", *Financial Times* (Alphaville), 9 February 2010.

8. Art. 125 Treaty on the Functioning of the European Union (TFEU).

9. "Statement by the Heads of State or Government of the European Union", 11 February 2010.

10. The "intermediate sphere" is a concept developed in Van Middelaar, *Passage to Europe*, 11–33.

11. On this subject compare the Humboldt speech delivered by Herman Van Rompuy two years later: "The discovery of co-responsibility: Europe in the debt crisis. Speech at the Humboldt University Berlin", 6 February 2012.

12. Jean-Claude Juncker cited in Carlo Bastasin, *Saving Europe: How National Politics Nearly Destroyed Europe* (Washington, DC: Brookings Institution Press, 2012), 204.

13. For this, at the Summit of 25 March 2010, under pressure from Merkel, the term "ultima ratio" caught on.

14. "Statement of the Heads of State or Government of the Euro Area", 7 May 2010, point 2.

15. "Statement of the Heads of State or Government of the Euro Area", 7 May 2010, point 1.

16. Angela Merkel cited in Carlo Bastasin, *Saving Europe*, 213.

17. José Luis Zapatero in *El País*, 25 July 2010, "He pasado noches sin dormir".

18. ECB press release, 10 May 2010, "ECB decides on measures to address severe tensions in financial markets".

19. The 7 May 2010 emergency meeting constituted a key moment in the emancipation of the "Euro Summit" from the full European Council; more on this institutional evolution in Chapter 6.

20. In its landmark Maastricht Judgment of 12 October 1993, the German Constitutional Court green-lighted ratification of the EU Maastricht Treaty but placed firm limitations on the future development of the Economic and Monetary Union, which would have to remain a "stability community" and not erode national parliamentary budgetary rights. In safeguarding this fundamental stability concept, as a measure of last resort, the German Court did not exclude "solutions outside the Community". (BVerfG 89, 155 C II 5(e)).

21. Speech by Angela Merkel at the presentation of the Charlemagne Prize to Donald Tusk, 13 May 2010. Available at: https://www.karlspreis.de/de/preistraeger/donald-tusk-2010/laudatio-der-bundeskanzlerin (accessed 20 December 2018): "Warum also Griechenland retten, warum den Euro retten, warum unzählige Tage und Nächte, um nach harten, manchmal zähen Verhandlungen ein gemeinsames Ergebnis zu erzielen? Weil wir spüren: Scheitert der Euro, dann scheitert nicht nur das Geld [...] Dann scheitert Europa, dann scheitert die Idee der europäischen Einigung."

22. Angela Merkel, Government statement to the Bundestag, 19 May 2010.

23. Vestert Borger, "The Transformation of the Euro: Law, Contract, Solidarity" (unpublished dissertation, Leiden University, 2018), esp. ch. 2 and Conclusion.

24. Jean-Claude Trichet cited in Bastasin, *Saving Europe*, 239. For an atmospheric Dutch perspective on "Deauville", see the relevant chapter in Martin Visser, *De eurocrisis. Onthullend verslag van politiek falen* (Amsterdam: Business Contact, 2012).

25. Nicolas Sarkozy cited in Jean Quatremer, "Oublier Deauville", *Libération*, 6 December 2011.

26. Conclusions of the European Council, 28–29 October 2010, point 2. The abbreviation "i.a." for *inter alia*, which Van Rompuy's Latin-trained chief-of-staff came up with, put an end to a heated debate in the meeting and served to ensure the "private sector involvement" would be looked at without prejudging any outcome, thereby more or less satisfying all sides.

27. Neil Hume, "The Merkel crash", *Financial Times* (Alphaville), 20 November 2010.

28. For this powerful narrative and its effects, see Martin Wolf, "The grasshoppers and the ants – a modern fable", *Financial Times*, 25 May 2010. Dutch author Geert Mak later blamed the harsh austerity measures on German "ant morality".

29. The comparison of private equity and hedge fund investors to "locust swarms" was first made on the campaign trail by German SPD leader Franz Müntefering in 2005.

30. "Statement by the Heads of State or Government of the Euro Area and EU Institutions", 21 July 2011, point 6.

31. "Statement by the Heads of State or Government of the Euro Area and EU Institutions", 21 July 2011, point 7.

32. Bastasin, *Saving Europe*, 302.

33. *Corriere della Sera*, 29 September 2011.

34. Daniel Schneiderman, "Berlusconi, le cancre et ses profs", 26 October 2011. Available at: https://www.arretsurimages.net/chroniques/le-matinaute/ berlusconi-le-cancre-et-ses-profs (accessed 20 December 2018).

35. Reconstruction in Peter Spiegel, "It was the point where the eurozone could have exploded", *Financial Times*, 12 May 2014.

36. José Manuel Barroso, as cited in Spiegel, *Financial Times*, 12 May 2014.

37. Alan Friedman, "Monti's secret summer", *Financial Times*, 10 February 2014.

38. Machiavelli, *Discourses on Livy*, I.7., trans. Julia Conaway Bondanella & Peter Bondanella (Oxford: Oxford Univeristy Press, 2003 [1517/18]).

39. "Regierungserklärung von Bundeskanzlerin Dr. Angela Merkel zum Europäischen Rat am 9. Dezember 2011 in Brüssel vor dem Deutschen Bundestag am 2. Dezember in Berlin". Available at: https://www.bundesregierung.de/breg-de/service/bulletin/ regierungserklaerung-von-bundeskanzlerin-dr-angela-merkel-800684 (accessed 20 December 2018).

40. Nicolas Sarkozy, "Discours à Toulon", 1 December 2010. Available at: http://www. lefigaro.fr/politique/le-scan/2014/03/27/25001-20140327ARTFIG00086-le- discours-de-nicolas-sarkozy-a-toulon-en-2011.php (accessed 20 December 2018).

41. "Nicolas Sarkozy and Angela Merkel, letter to the President of the European Council, 7 December 2011".

42. Protocol 12 of the EU treaty, "On the excessive deficit procedure".

43. "Statement by the Euro Area Heads of State or Government", 9 December 2011, unnumbered final paragraph.

44. Government of the Czech Republic, "The main arguments of Prime Minister Petr Nečas regarding why the Czech Republic has not committed to ratification of the fiscal compact", press release 6 February 2012. Available at: https://www.vlada.cz/en/ media-centrum/tiskove-zpravy/the-main-arguments-of-prime-minister- petr-necas-regarding-why-the-czech-republic-has-not-committed-to- ratification-of-the-fiscal-compact-92710/ (accessed 20 December 2018).

45. This argument was first developed in Jacques Keller-Noëllet and Luuk van Middelaar, "Une Europe 'gothique'? Comment refonder l'Union", *Le Monde*, 27 December 2011.

46. As disclosed in the remarkable speech by Ivan Rogers, David Cameron's EU adviser from late 2011 (first in London and then as the UK's permanent representative to the EU), who also served under Theresa May before resigning in January 2017, in his "Lecture at Hertford College, Oxford", delivered on 24 November 2017.

47. Herman Van Rompuy, 21 May 2012, "Invitation letter to the informal European Council of 23 May 2012".

48. José Luis Zapatero, *El Dilema*, as cited in Paul Taylor, "Merkel tried to bounce Spain into IMF bailout – ex PM", *Reuters*, 25 November 2013.

49. "Euro area summit statement", 29 June 2012. The draft version requested the legisla- tors to look at this as "a matter of urgent importance".

50. Van Rompuy, *Europe in the Storm*, 21.

51. The decisive meeting on Cyprus took place on Sunday 24 March. Van Rompuy had not wanted to call a full-blown EU summit for a relatively minor issue (the €10 billion bailout package would be considered peanuts by the markets); however, since the

banking system represented a fifth of the island's economy, the final deal needed to be done with newly elected Cypriot President Nicos Anastasiades and could not be dealt with at ministerial level (quite apart from the fact that the finance ministers had messed up in a first attempt). In agreement with Chancellor Merkel and President Hollande, Van Rompuy invited the Cypriot leader to Brussels and even sent a Belgian air force plane to Nicosia to fetch him. Tough negotiations ensued between Anastasiades on the one hand and ECB president Draghi, Commission president Barroso, IMF managing director Lagarde, Eurogroup chair Dijsselbloem and Van Rompuy as chair on the other – with Draghi playing bad cop and Van Rompuy good cop. The meeting lasted 12 hours, while the finance ministers (who had been summoned to finalize the deal) were waiting elsewhere in the Council building. Only a few news outlets understood what had happened behind the scenes (see, e.g., Nikolas Busse, "Feuer und Flamme. Verhandlungen über Zypern-Hilfe", *Frankfurter Allgemeine Zeitung*, 25 March 2014). It made sense to bring in all the institutional EU actors plus the political heads of the three creditor institutions working together in the "Troika", with the European Council president himself acting as a lynchpin between national leaders (Merkel was on the phone with him), yet even experienced observers spoke of a "Byzantine plot of bewildering complexity" (David Marsh, *Europe's Deadlock: How the Euro Crisis Could be Solved and Why it Won't Happen* (London & New Haven: Yale University Press, 2013), 60).

52. Peter Spiegel, "Greece: Donald Tusk warns of extremist political contagion", *Financial Times*, 16 July 2015.

53. Arendt, *Human Condition*, 245.

54. Jean Pisani-Ferry, *La crise de l'euro et comment en sortir* (Paris: Fayard/Pluriel, 2013), 138.

55. Herman Van Rompuy, "Speech during the signing ceremony of the Treaty on Stability, Coordination and Governance", 2 March 2012.

56. On 29 June 2012 the German Bundestag ratified both treaties plus the changes to Art. 136 of the Treaty on the Functioning of the EU by a two-thirds majority; the Italian Chamber of Deputies did the same on 19 June 2012. In Ireland the parliament debated both treaties together, although the Fiscal Compact Treaty came into force only after a positive referendum result on 31 May 2012; voter surveys show that Irish voters were well aware of the political and legal link with the ESM Treaty.

2 NEGOTIATING: THE UKRAINE CRISIS

1. Arendt, *Human Condition*, 186.

2. Joseph Nye, *Bound to Lead: The Changing Nature of American Power* (New York: Basic Books, 1990).

3. Romano Prodi, "A wider Europe: A proximity policy as the key to stability", speech at the Sixth ECSA Word Conference, 5–6 December 2002.

4. European Commission, "Wider Europe – Neighbourhood: A New Framework for Relations with our Eastern and Southern Neighbours", COM (2003) 104, 11 March 2003.

5. George W. Bush, cited in "History of an Idea", *The Economist*, 30 December 2003.

6. Art. 49 Treaty on European Union (TEU): "Any European State which respects the values referred to in Article 2 and is committed to promoting them may apply to become a member of the Union".

7. Ian Manners, "Normative Power Europe: A Contradiction in Terms?", *Journal of Common Market Studies* 40 (2002), 252.

8. European Union treaty, Maastricht version, Art. J.1, para. 2.

9. Federica Mogherini, "Shared Vision, Common Action: A stronger Europe. A Global Strategy for the European Union's Foreign and Security Policy", 28 June 2016.

10. Pierre Vimont, "Les intérêts stratégiques de l'Union européenne", in *Le Rapport Schuman sur l'Europe, l'état de l'Union* 2016 (Paris), English translation adapted from the text available via the Carnegie Europe website; see http://carnegieeurope.eu/2016/04/20/strategic-interests-of-european-union-pub-63448 (accessed 20 April 2016). Vimont was the first secretary general of the European diplomatic service, from 2010 to 2015.

11. Nicolas Sarkozy, 12 August 2008, press conference in Moscow. Available at: http://en.kremlin.ru/events/president/transcripts/1072 (accessed 20 December 2018).

12. Nicolas Sarkozy, 23 September 2008, speech to the General Assembly of the United Nations. Available at: http://discours.vie-publique.fr/notices/087002941.html (accessed 20 December 2018). Nicolas Sarkozy, 16 December 2008, speech to the European Parliament. Available at: http://discours.vie-publique.fr/notices/087004026.html (accessed 20 December 2018).

13. Van Middelaar, *Passage to Europe*, 210.

14. Štefan Füle, speech to the European Parliament, 26 October 2010.

15. Sergey Glazyev, in *Vedomosti*, 19 August 2013, cited in Anders Åslund, "Ukraine's choice: European Association Agreement or Eurasian Union", Peterson Institute for International Economics Policy Brief, 13-22, September 2013.

16. In retrospect Europe's top diplomat Pierre Vimont said of the refusal to hold trilateral talks between the EU, Ukraine and Russia, "What strikes me is when we ask is this really incompatible as it's really said, we discover, discussing with our experts, that maybe it's not exactly that, and we can find a common ground. [...] What strikes me is that we had our whole bureaucracy saying we should not do things that way." (Vimont, cited in Georgi Gotev, "EU shunned from US–Russia meeting on Ukraine", https://www.euractiv.com/, 14 March 2014).

17. José Manuel Barroso, press conference in Vilnius, 29 November 2013. Available at: https://tvnewsroom.consilium.europa.eu/event/eastern-partnership-summit-2013 (press conference – part 6) (accessed 20 December 2018).

18. José Manuel Barroso, press conference in Vilnius, 29 November 2013. Available at: https://tvnewsroom.consilium.europa.eu/event/eastern-partnership-summit-2013 (press conference – part 4) (accessed 20 December 2018).

19. "Pressestatement von Bundeskanzlerin Merkel auf dem Gipfeltreffen der Östlichen Partnerschaft 29 November 2013". Available at: https://archiv.bundesregierung.de/archiv-de/pressestatement-von-bundeskanzlerin-merkel-auf-dem-gipfeltreffen-der-oestlichen-partnerschaft-843282 (accessed 20 December 2018).

20. Council of the European Union, "Council conclusions on Ukraine", pt. 5, 10 February 2014. The extraordinary meeting of EU heads of state and government on Ukraine of 6 March 2014 did not adopt this wording.

21. See http://www.itv.com/news/update/2014-02-21/polish-minister-tells-protest-leader-you-will-all-be-dead/ (accessed 20 December 2018).

22. See www.auswaertiges-amt.de/cae/servlet/contentblob/671350/publication-File/190051/140221-UKR_Erklaerung.pdf (accessed 20 July 2017). The Russian ambassador Lukin, incidentally, did not in the end sign the document.

23. "Statement by the President of the European Council Herman Van Rompuy and the President of the European Commission in the name of the European Union on the agreed additional restrictive measures against Russia", 29 July 2014.

24. See www.sputniknews.com/voiceofrussia/news/2014_03_18/EUs-Van-Rompuy-to-visit-Moscow-on-Wednesday-diplomatic-sources-3596/ (accessed 20 July 2017).

25. *Spiegel Online*, 10 February 2015, "Amerikas Krawall-Diplomatin. Victoria Nuland". Available at: http://www.spiegel.de/politik/ausland/victoria-nuland-barack-obamas-problem-diplomatin-a-1017614.html (accessed 20 December 2018).

26. "Rede von Bundeskanzlerin Angela Merkel anlässlich der 51. Münchner Sicherheitskonferenz", 7 February 2015. Available at: https://www.bundesregierung.de/breg-de/service/bulletin/rede-von-bundeskanzlerin-dr-angela-merkel-792392 (accessed 20 December 2018); question and answer session with interpreter available at: https://www.securityconference.de/en/media-library/munich-security-conference-2015/video/statement-and-discussion-with-dr-angela-merkel-1/ starting 46.46 minutes in.

27. Reconstruction in *Der Spiegel*, "Die längste Nacht", issue 8 (14 February 2015), 22–8.

28. "Package of measures for the Implementation of the Minsk Agreements", 12 February 2015, Art. 11 & 12.

29. For example, by Germany's former foreign minister Joschka Fischer, "Goodbye to the West", Project Syndicate, 5 December 2016. Available at: https://www.project-syndicate.org/commentary/goodbye-to-american-global-leadership-by-joschka-fischer-2016-12 (accessed 20 December 2018).

30. See Barack Obama's defence of his foreign policy legacy in Jeffrey Goldberg, "The Obama Doctrine", *The Atlantic*, April 2016. Available at: https://www.theatlantic.com/magazine/archive/2016/04/the-obama-doctrine/471525/ (accessed 20 December 2018).

31. George F. Kennan (8 September 1952), "The Soviet-Union and the Atlantic Pact", in G. F. Kennan, *Memoirs, 1950–1963* (New York: Pantheon, 1972), 342.

3 SETTING BOUNDARIES: THE REFUGEE CRISIS

1. Angela Merkel, Berlin, press conference of 15 September 2015, during a visit by Austrian Chancellor Werner Faymann. Available at: https://www.bundesregierung.de/breg-de/aktuelles/pressekonferenzen/pressekonferenz-von-bundeskanzlerin-merkel-und-dem-oesterreichischen-bundeskanzler-faymann-844442 (accessed 20 December 2018).

2. Régis Debray, *Eloge des frontières*, (Paris: Gallimard, 2010), 57.

3. See https://ec.europa.eu/eurostat/statistics-explained/index.php/File:Asylum_applications_(non-EU)_in_the_EU_28_Member_States_2005-15_(1)_(thousands)_YB16.png (accessed 20 December 2018).

4. Max Weber, "Politics as a Vocation", in *"Politik als Beruf", Gesammelte Politische Schriften*, Munich 1921, 396–450; lecture originally pronounced in 1919. Available in English in *Max Weber: Essays in Sociology*, (trans. & ed. by H. H. Gerth & C. Wright Mills), 77–128 (Oxford: Oxford University Press, 1946). The German terms are

"*Gesinnungsethik*" (ethic of conviction) and "*Verantwortungsethik*" (ethic of responsibility), although the OUP edition opts for a translation of the former as "ethic of ultimate ends".

5. Pope Francis, "Omelia Lampedusa", 8 July 2013. Available at: http://w2.vatican.va/content/francesco/en/homilies/2013/documents/papa-francesco_20130708_omelia-lampedusa.html (accessed 20 December 2018).

6. *The Independent*, 20 April 2015.

7. "Frontex is a small agency and cannot take over Mare Nostrum tomorrow", said EU commissioner Cecilia Malmström after an informal meeting of interior ministers in Milan. Quoted in Steve Scherer and Ilaria Polleschi, "Italy in talks with EU to share responsibility for boat migrations", Reuters, 8 July 2014.

8. Frontex director Gil Arias in the European Parliament, 4 September 2014, cited in Sergio Carrera and Leonard den Hertog, "Whose *Mare*? Rule of law challenges in the field of European border surveillance in the Mediterranean", CEPS Papers in Liberty and Security No. 79, January 2015.

9. "Mediterranean migrant deaths: UK sends just five workers to assist EU", *The Guardian*, 20 April 2015; the quote is from Labour MP, Yvette Cooper.

10. "Outcome of the Council meeting, Foreign Affairs and Home Affairs", 20 April 2015; "Special meeting of the European Council, 23 April 2015 – statement".

11. Donald Tusk, cited in Matthew Dalton and Valentina Pop, "EU to triple funding for sea patrols in migration crisis", *Wall Street Journal*, 23 April 2015.

12. "Special meeting of the European Council, 23 April 2015 – statement", point 3(c).

13. Mohamed El-Ghirani, foreign minister in the Libyan Government of National Salvation, cited in *The Guardian*, 24 April 2015.

14. Jean-Claude Juncker, "State of the Union 2015. Time for Honesty, Unity and Solidarity: Speech to the European Parliament", 9 September 2015.

15. Juncker, "State of the Union 2015".

16. Peter Ludlow, *Eurocomment, Preliminary Evaluation* 2015/8, 23 September 2015, "The Refugee Crisis".

17. François Hollande, cited on Lexpress.fr, 22 September 2015. Available at: https://www.lexpress.fr/actualite/monde/europe/accord-sur-les-refugies-pour-hollande-l-europe-a-pris-ses-responsabilites_1718447.html (accessed 20 December 2018).

18. European Commission, "Communication from the Commission to the European Parliament, the European Council and the Council. Managing the refugee crisis: State of Play of the Implementation of the Priority Actions under the European Agenda on Migration", COM (2015) 510, of 14 October 2015.

19. From 22 September 2015 to 6 December 2016, according to the Commission, 8,162 asylum seekers were relocated: 6,212 from Greece and 1,950 from Italy. After a hesitant start, the numbers grew to some 1,400 per month, meaning that the planned relocation of 160,000 would take around ten years. See following sources: European Commission, "Relocation and resettlement: state of play", 6 December 2016; figures for 31 April 2018, Factsheet International Organization for Migration, "IOM's activities for the EU relocation scheme". Available at: http://eea.iom.int/sites/default/files/publication/document/EU_Relocation_Info_Sheet_-_April_2018.pdf (accessed 20 December 2018).

20. Jean-Claude Juncker in his New Year press conference, 15 January 2016.

21. Jean-Claude Juncker, "In mijn Europa klopt ook een hart", opinion piece in *NRC Handelsblad*, 27 August 2015.

22. Interview with Jean Asselborn, "Wir sind doch nicht in der Afrikanischen Union", *Süddeutsche Zeitung*, 15 September 2015.

23. Nicolas Sarkozy, "Déclaration devant le Parlement européen sur le bilan de la présidence française du Conseil de l'Union européenne", Strasbourg, 16 December 2008.

24. "Remarks by President Donald Tusk after the informal meeting of heads of state or government", 23 September 2015.

25. Notes of an EU delegate on a conversation between Tusk, Juncker and Erdogan after the G20 in Antalya, 16 November 2015, leaked via the Greek website www.euro2day.gr, February 2016.

26. Juncker, New Year press conference, 15 January 2016.

27. The confidential letter was leaked, for example, via Independent.mk, a Macedonian news site.

28. Press conference by Czech premier Bohuslav Sobotka and Slovak premier Robert Fico, 26 January 2016, at which they announced the forthcoming summit of the "Visegrád 4" to be held on 15 February 2016.

29. Statement of the EU Heads of State or Government of 7 March 2016. The draft of 6 March did not yet say it in so many words. See the reconstruction in Peter Ludlow, "February and March 2016: Migration Policy, the British Question and Economic Policy", European Council Briefing Note 2016/1–3, 44–7.

30. Figures from UN refugee organization UNHCR. Available at: https://data.unhcr.org/mediterranean/regional.php (accessed 18 September 2016).

31. Alex Barker, "Brussels Briefing: Beached in Italy", *Financial Times*, 5 April 2016.

32. "Report by President Donald Tusk to the European Parliament on the March European Council Meeting", 13 April 2016.

33. European Commission, unpublished "Factsheet", December 2016.

34. Council of the European Union, "Factsheet", November 2016. The top ten countries of origin of "irregular migrants" in Italy in the years 2014–16 were Nigeria, Eritrea, Guinea, Ivory Coast, Gambia, Senegal, Mali, Sudan, Bangladesh and Somalia.

35. Duncan Robinson, "EU border force accuses charities of collusion with smugglers", *Financial Times*, 14 December 2016.

36. Slovak Presidency, "Solidarity and responsibility in the Common European Asylum System: Progress report of the Slovak Presidency", 1 December 2016: "On the basis of consultations, the Presidency doubts whether any attempt to establish, in a manner considered as fair, quantitative equivalence between the various strands of action that are necessary to face a crisis would be productive". In 2018, comparable ideas were circulated by the Austrian presidency, with the watchword "obligatory solidarity".

37. As laid down in the treaty: "The policies of the Union set out in this Chapter and their implementation [including policies relating to border control, asylum and immigration; LvM] shall be governed by the principle of solidarity and fair sharing of responsibility, including its financial implications, between the Member States. Whenever necessary, the Union acts adopted pursuant to this Chapter shall contain appropriate measures to give effect to this principle" (Art. 80 TFEU).

38. "Souverän ist, wer über den Ausnahmezustand entscheidet." Carl Schmitt, *Politische Theologie* (Berlin: Duncker & Humblot, 1922), first sentence.

39. "Regulation (EU) 2016/1624 of the European Parliament and of the Council of 14 September 2016 on the European Border and Coast Guard", Art. 28.

40. "Speech by President Donald Tusk at the award ceremony of the International Charlemagne Prize to Pope Francis", Rome, 6 May 2016.

4 UPRISING: THE ATLANTIC CRISIS

1. Pocock, *Machiavellian Moment*, 53–4.

2. Emmanuel Macron, "Europe holds its destiny in its own hands", *Financial Times*, 24 January 2017.

3. Jean-François Deniau, *L'Europe interdite* (Paris: Seuil, 1977), 74 *n*.1; the author was a member of the French delegation in the treaty negotiations.

4. European Convention, sitting of 25 April 2003, verbatim (speakers Haenel, De Vries, Meyer; for a dissenting opinion: Stuart).

5. Art. 50, section 1, TEU.

6. Pocock, *Machiavellian Moment*, viii.

7. Martin Schulz, 24 June 2016, quoted in Klaus Brinkbäumer *et al.*, "Tödlich für Europa. Martin Schulz und Jean-Claude Juncker über Brexit, EU und Freundschaft", *Der Spiegel*, 9 July 2016.

8. Jean-Pierre Stroobants *et al.*, "Brexit: 'Les déserteurs ne seront pas accueillis à bras ouverts', prévient M. Juncker", *Le Monde*, 20 May 2016. In that same interview, Juncker had warned that "le Royaume-Uni devra accepter d'être considéré comme un Etat tiers, que l'on ne caressera pas dans le sens du poil" [the UK will have to accept being seen as a third state, one that will not be coddled].

9. "Statement by President Tusk on the outcome of the UK referendum", 24 June 2016. Available at: https://tvnewsroom.consilium.europa.eu/videos?keywords=tusk%20 outcome%20uk%20referendum (accessed 20 December 2018).

10. "Joint statement by Donald Tusk, President of the European Council, Martin Schulz, President of the European Parliament, Mark Rutte, holder of the rotating Presidency of the Council of the EU, and Jean-Claude Juncker, President of the European Commission, on the outcome of the United Kingdom referendum", 24 June 2016 (EUCO/381/16) (12h57).

11. Martin Schulz on *Tagesthemen*, 24 June 2016, and Jean-Claude Juncker on *ARD Brennpunkt*, 24 June 2016.

12. "Pressestatement von Bundeskanzlerin Merkel zum Ausgang des Referendums über den Verbleib Großbritanniens in der Europäischen Union am 24. Juni 2016". Available at: https://www.bundesregierung.de/breg-de/aktuelles/pressekonferenzen/ pressestatement-von-bundeskanzlerin-merkel-zum-ausgang-des-referendums-ueber-den-verbleib-grossbritanniens-in-der-europaeischen-union-am-24-juni-2016-844796 (accessed 20 December 2018).

13. "Brexit: déclaration du Président de la République, François Hollande (24 June 2016)".

14. Council of the European Union, "Outcome of the Council meeting: General Affairs", 24 June 2016, 4.

15. "Gemeinsame Erklärung der Außenminister Belgiens, Deutschlands, Frankreichs, Italiens, Luxemburgs und der Niederlande am 25. Juni 2016." The next day, Sunday 26 June 2016, Frank-Walter Steinmeier and Jean-Marc Ayrault, the German and French

foreign ministers, jointly publish a nine-page report entitled "A strong Europe in a world of uncertainties", which included an appeal for a security pact.

16. Art. 50, para. 1, TEU.

17. "Conclusions of the European Council", 28 June 2016, pt 23.

18. David Cameron, "European Council meeting 28 June 2016: PM press conference", 28 June 2016. Available at: https://www.gov.uk/government/speeches/european-council-meeting-28-june-2016-pm-press-conference--2 (accessed 20 December 2018).

19. "Remarks by President Donald Tusk after the informal meeting of 27 EU heads of state or government", 29 June 2017; "Informal meeting at 27 – Brussels, 29 June 2016 – Statement", pt 4.

20. "Remarks by President Donald Tusk", 29 June 2016.

21. Later, debate arose on this point; see Harold Clarke, Matthew Goodwin & Paul Whiteley, *Brexit: Why Britain Voted to Leave the European Union* (Cambridge: Cambridge University Press, 2017).

22. Art. 50 TEU, para. 2 (emphasis added).

23. "Statement after the informal meeting of the heads of state or government of 27 member states and the presidents of the European Council and of the European Commission; Annex, point 1", 15 December 2016. It was repeated in the European Council's Brexit Guidelines of 29 April 2017.

24. Note the unprecedented precision in the declaration of that same summit of December 2016: "To ensure transparency and build trust, the Union negotiator's team will be ready to integrate a representative of the rotating Presidency of the Council. Representatives of the President of the European Council will be present and participate, in a supporting role, in all negotiation sessions, alongside the European Commission representatives".

25. A British legal analyst called the preparations on the Union side "methodical, firm and consistent; its stated views have also corresponded with its actions", David Allen Green, "Brexit by timetable: The evolution of the EU's position", *Financial Times*, 25 April 2017.

26. Donald Tusk, "The Bratislava Letter", 13 September 2016, part II.

27. Tusk, "Bratislava Letter", part II.

28. Jean-Claude Juncker, "State of the Union 2016. Towards a better Europe – a Europe that protects, empowers and defends", 14 September 2016.

29. "The Bratislava Roadmap", 16 September 2016, part II(c).

30. Press conference by Angela Merkel after the informal summit in Malta, 4 February 2017; Benelux paper, 3 February 2017. Available at: http://www.benelux.int/nl/nieuws/visie-van-de-benelux-op-de-toekomst-van-europa (accessed 20 December 2018).

31. "Déclaration de M. François Hollande, Président de la République, sur les défis et priorités de la construction européenne, à Versailles le 6 mars 2017"; European Commission, "White Paper on the Future of Europe", COM (2017) 2025, 1 March 2017.

32. The biggest diplomatic hurdle was resolved as follows: "We will act together, at different paces and intensity where necessary, while moving in the same direction, as we have done in the past, in line with the Treaties and keeping the door open to those who want to join later. Our Union is undivided and indivisible." ("Rome Declaration

of the Leaders of 27 Member States and of the European Council, the European Parliament and the European Commission: The Rome Declaration", 25 March 2017).

33. Donald J. Trump, 7 November 2016 (campaign speech in Raleigh, North Carolina) quoted in George Fuller, "Trump: US vote will be Brexit-plus-plus-plus". Available at: https://www.telegraph.co.uk/news/2016/11/07/trump-us-vote-will-be-brexit-plus-plus-plus/ (accessed 20 December 2018).

34. "Full transcript of Donald Trump's interview with Michael Gove and Kai Diekman, former chief editor of the German newspaper *Bild*". Available at: https://www.thetimes.co.uk/article/full-transcript-of-interview-with-donald-trump-5d39sr09d (accessed 20 December 2018).

35. *Ibid.*

36. *Ibid.*

37. Angela Merkel, press conference 16 January 2017, quoted in Almut Möller *et al.*, "Germany votes: European dilemmas in the federal elections", in ECFR Policy Brief No. 4 (30 May 2017).

38. Jean-Claude Juncker, speech in Trier, 18 January 2017, quoted in Alistair Macdonald, "Hands off EU, Trump; we don't back Ohio secession: Juncker", Reuters, 18 January 2017. Two months later Juncker repeated the point at the EPP congress as a (jocular?) threat, saying that if Trump carried on promoting Brexit among other member states "I'm going to promote the independence of Ohio" (quoted in Krishnadev Calamur, "An EU Official Lets Loose on Trump", *The Atlantic*, 30 March 2017).

39. Emmanuel Macron, "Humboldt speech", Berlin, 10 January 2017, main points in *Financial Times*, 24 January 2017. Macron advocated speaking of a "Europe of sovereignty" rather than the classic French "l'Europe de la puissance".

40. "Letter by President Donald Tusk to the 27 EU heads of state or government on the future of the EU before the Malta summit", 31 January 2017.

41. Theresa May, speech at Lancaster House ("The government's negotiating objectives for exiting the EU"), 17 January 2017.

42. James Dean and Bruno Waterfield, "Trump puts EU ahead of Britain in trade queue: Merkel lands Brexit victory for Brussels", *The Times*, 22 April 2017.

43. Paul Taylor, "Merkel's thunderbolt is starting gun for European defense drive", *Politico*, 30 May 2017. Available at: https://www.politico.eu/article/angela-merkel-nato-g7-donald-trump-germany-us-thunderbolt-is-starting-gun-for-european-defense-drive/ (accessed 20 December 2018).

44. Angela Merkel, campaign speech in Trudering, 28 May 2017.

45. Facsimile available at: www.gov.uk/government/uploads/system/uploads/attachment_data/file/604079/Prime_Ministers_letter_to_European_Council_President_Donald_Tusk.pdf (accessed 20 December 2018).

46. "Council Decision (CFSP) 2017/2315 of 11 December 2017 establishing permanent structured cooperation (PESCO) and determining the list of participating Member States".

47. For detailed analysis, see Alex Barker, "FT Breakdown, the €100 bn. Brexit bill", *Financial Times*, 3 May 2017.

48. Special European Council meeting, 29 April 2017, "Guidelines", pt 11.

49. "If the UK offer is unacceptable for Ireland, it will also be unacceptable for the EU", Tusk on 1 December 2017, cited in David M. Herszenhorn, "Donald Tusk: EU will back Ireland's Brexit progress decision". Available at: https://www.politico.eu/article/

brexit-ireland-border-negotiation-donald-tusk-eu-will-back-progress-decision/ (accessed 20 December 2018).

50. On the agreement on a future relationship, at least if it is, as expected, a "mixed agreement" that requires national ratifications, Spain would have a veto in any case. But perhaps Spain has in mind the preservation of an informal veto for emergency cases, the "Luxembourg Compromise" – used by Madrid in 1999 in another Gibraltar matter, which concerned the use of Gibraltar's airport – in a new form, for the situation after the British departure, when the "Club of Luxembourg", made up of countries that support each other in such cases for reasons of principle, will no longer have a blocking minority.

51. J. C., "What's brewing in Germany? How to understand Angela Merkel's comments about America and Britain", blog on *Economist.com*, 28 May 2017. Available at: https://www.economist.com/kaffeeklatsch/2017/05/28/how-to-understand-angela-merkels-comments-about-america-and-britain (accessed 20 December 2018).

52. "Prime Minister Theresa May's speech at the 2018 Munich Security Conference", 17 February 2018. Available at: https://www.gov.uk/government/speeches/pm-speech-at-munich-security-conference-17-february-2018 (accessed 20 December 2018).

53. Pierre Vimont, "Bringing Brexit back to reality", Carnegie Europe, 15 June 2017; http://carnegieeurope.eu/2017/06/15/bringing-brexit-back-to-reality-pub-71262 (accessed 20 December 2018).

ENTR'ACTE: ACTING IN TIME

1. Pocock, *Machiavellian Moment*, 177–8.
2. Machiavelli, *The Prince*, ch. 25, trans. W. K. Marriott (London, 1908).
3. Pocock, *Machiavellian Moment*, 8.
4. Machiavelli, *The Prince*, ch. 25.
5. *Ibid.*, ch. 24.
6. Pocock, *Machiavellian Moment*, viii.
7. Machiavelli, *Discourses on Livy*, II.2.

PART II: *THE THEATRE*

5 TWO FOUNDATIONS

1. Walter Bagehot, *The English Constitution*, R. H. S. Crossman (ed.) (London: Collins, 1963 [1867]), 248.
2. Reinhart Koselleck, *Zeitschichten. Studien zur Historik* (Frankfurt: Suhrkamp, 2000), 9–10. Published in English as *Sediments of Time: On Possible Histories* (Redwood City, CA: Stanford University Press, 2018), although without the Preface from which this quotation is taken.
3. Michel de Montaigne, "De l'expérience", in *Les Essais*, ed. Claude Pinganaud (Paris: Arlea, 1992 [1580]), 815. This English translation from Michel de Montaigne, "Of experience", trans. Charles Cotton, ed. Patrick Madden. Available at: http://essays.quotidiana.org/montaigne/experience/.

4. Martin Luther, *Werke* (Weimar, 1910), part 41 (sermon delivered on 10 May 1535), 138.

5. A point made on several occasions by former Dutch central banker André Szász, for example in André Szász, "Een Duits dilemma: de euro van geloofwaardigheids- naar vertrouwenscrisis", *Internationale Spectator* 66 (2012) 3, 137.

6. Henri Guaino, interview in *Le Monde*, 21 July 2007.

7. "Macron: Pas de 'guerre de religion' économique", *Le Figaro*, 29 January 2015.

8. For an extensive historical analysis of Franco-German misunderstanding, see Luuk van Middelaar, "France-Allemagne: une incompréhension permanente", *Le Débat* no. 187 (Nov–Dec 2015), 4–20.

9. Jean Monnet, *Memoirs*, trans. Richard Mayne (New York: Doubleday, 1978), 76. Originally published as Jean Monnet, *Mémoires* (Paris: Fayard, 1976).

10. Herfried Münkler, *Macht in der Mitte. Die neuen Aufgaben Deutschlands in Europa* (Hamburg: Korber, 2015), 184–5.

11. Paul-Henri Spaak, January 1962, cited in Anthony Teasdale, "The Fouchet Plan: De Gaulle's Intergovernmental Design for Europe", LSE Europe in Question Discussion Paper Series no. 117, 1.

12. Walter Hallstein, *United Europe: Challenge and Opportunity* (Cambridge, MA: Harvard University Press, 1962), 58.

13. This is why the decision of the heads of state or government in favour of a "New Settlement for the United Kingdom within the European Union" of 18–19 February 2016 (which lapsed as a result of Britain's negative referendum result) contains the following reassurance to the British in section C: "The references in the Treaties and their preambles to the process of creating an ever closer union among the peoples of Europe do not offer a legal basis for extending the scope of any provision of the Treaties or of EU secondary legislation. They should not be used either to support an extensive interpretation of the competences of the Union or of the powers of its institutions as set out in the Treaties."

14. Maurice Couve de Murville, *Une politique étrangère, 1958–1969* (Paris: Plon, 1971), 310.

15. Charles de Gaulle, press conference, 5 May 1962.

16. Margaret Thatcher, 30 November 1979, press conference after the European Council in Dublin.

17. See, for example, Jacques Delors, "Discours lors de la remise de la médaille de la Paix de Nimègue", 15 March 2010. Available at: https://institutdelors.eu/wp-content/uploads/2018/01/2010_discours_jd_prix_de_nim_gue_fr.pdf (accessed 20 December 2018); Jürgen Habermas, *Zur Verfassung Europas. Ein Essay* (Frankfurt: Suhrkamp, 2011).

18. Herman Van Rompuy, "Discours à Sciences-Po Paris", 20 September 2010.

19. Éric Bussière and Vincent Dujardin, "Entretien avec Jacques Delors", recorded on 13 January 2016 in Paris as part of the project *HistCom3: Histoire de la Commission européenne, 1986–2000*, 23 (unpublished).

20. Felipe González, "Europa am Scheideweg", *Frankfurter Allgemeine Zeitung*, 17 October 2001, cited in Tilo Schabert, *Wie Weltgeschichte gemacht wird. Frankreich und die Deutsche Einheit* (Stuttgart: Klett-Cotta, 2002), 533.

21. John Dewey, *The Public and its Problems* (Athens, OH: Ohio University Press, 1954 [1927]), 54.

22. On this Brussels resistance to the breakthrough to the Union, see Van Middelaar, *Passage to Europe*, 186–92.

23. This specific kind of Brussels teleology borrowed self-confidence from several later developments. The most important was that some of the justice and home affairs policy was poured into the Community mould in 1999; the subjects of asylum, visas, immigration and free movement of people were moved within the Union Treaty from the "third" to the "first pillar". This tidied up vetoes and made decision-making easier, or so it was claimed (and indeed, in the refugee crisis of 2015–16 it was possible to vote on a controversial asylum decision); perhaps it was merely a matter of time before the rest would follow.

24. Angela Merkel, "Rede der Bundeskanzlerin anlässlich der Eröffnung des. 61. Akademischen Jahres des Europakollegs Brügge", 2 November 2010.

25. Manuel Sarrazin and Sven-Christian Kindler, "'Brügge sehen und sterben': Gemeinschaftsmethode versus Unionsmethode", in *integration* 35 (2012) 3, 214–23. Both Bundestag members for the Green Party concluded (p. 223) "Der Weg über die Methode Brügge hingegen könnte für die Europäische Union – wie im Film der Aufenthalt in Brügge für manchen Protagonisten – tödlich sein." (The route via the Bruges method could – as in the film of the sojourn in Bruges for many of the protagonists – be fatal for the European Union).

6 DIRECTORS AND ACTORS

1. Charles de Montesquieu, *The Spirit of Laws: A Compendium of the First English Edition*, bk. XI, ch. 6, 211 (Oakland, CA: University of California Press, 1977). Originally published as *De l'esprit des lois* (Paris, 1758).

2. Alexandre Kojève, *La notion de l'autorité* (Paris: Gallimard, 2004), 49.

3. Francesco Guicciardini, *Counsels and Reflections*, trans. Ninian Hill Thomson (London: Kegan Paul, Trench & Trobner, 1890), 58. Originally known as the *Ricordi*, written in 1530, published Florence 1857–66.

4. Pierre Rosanvallon, *Good Government* (Cambridge, MA: Harvard University Press, 2018). Originally published as *Le bon gouvernement* (Paris: Seuil, 2015).

5. For a political interpretation of the judgments Van Gend & Loos (1963) and Costa/ENEL (1964) see Van Middelaar, *Passage to Europe*, 48–54.

6. Pierre Pescatore, *Le droit de l'intégration. Émergence d'un phénomène nouveau dans les relations internationales selon l'expérience des Communautés européennes* (Leiden: Aspen, 1972).

7. Art. 291, para. 1, TFEU : "Member States shall adopt all measures of national law necessary to implement legally binding Union acts".

8. Walter Hallstein, cited in Van Middelaar, *Passage to Europe*, 56.

9. A. Mattera (ed.), *"Pénélope". Projet de Constitution de l'Union européenne* (Paris: Editions Clement Juglar, 2003), 11–34.

10. Edward Heath, 16 September 1973, cited in Jean Monnet, *Memoirs*, 504.

11. Monnet, *Memoirs*, 509.

12. Valéry Giscard d'Estaing, *Le Pouvoir et la vie*, Vol. I (Paris: Compagnie 12, 1988), 119.

13. For a more detailed account of this "summit to end all summits" and its preparation, see Pierre de Boissieu *et al.*, *National Leaders and the Making of Europe: Key Episodes in the Life of the European Council* (London: John Harper Publishing, 2015), 19–38.

14. Émile Noël, *Les rouages de l'Europe: comment fonctionnent les institutions de la*

Communauté européenne (Paris: Nathan, 1977), 43–54 (the author was the secretary-general of the Commission from 1958 until 1987).

15. Art. 15, para. 3, TEU.

16. Counted here are the actual trips by the leaders, so if a European Council meeting and a European summit occur on the same day – formally two separate meetings – they are counted as one.

17. Art. 15, para. 3, TEU.

18. Art. 26, para. 1, TEU: "If international developments so require, the President of the European Council shall convene an extraordinary meeting of the European Council in order to define the strategic lines of the Union's policy in the face of such developments".

19. Art. 15, para. 1, TEU.

20. Art. 22, para. 1, TEU (foreign affairs); Art. 68, TFEU (justice).

21. Art. 15, para. 1, TEU.

22. Art. 17, para. 1, TEU.

23. Analysed more broadly in Van Middelaar, *Passage to Europe*, "Coup in Milan", 100–11.

24. Art. 50, TEU.

25. Fritz W. Scharpf, *Governing in Europe: Effective and Democratic?* (Oxford: Oxford University Press, 1991) ("input" and "output"); Vivien A. Schmidt, *Democracy in Europe: The EU and National Polities* (Oxford: Oxford University Press, 2006) ("through-put").

26. Bagehot (*English Constitution*, 61) observed how pragmatists tempted by engineering metaphors misunderstand precisely the function of authority, separating off the "dignified parts" of a constitution from the "efficient parts" that are more like a machine: "There are indeed practical men who reject the dignified parts of Government. They say, we only want to attain results, to do business: a constitution is a collection of political means for political ends, and if you admit that any part of the constitution does no business, or that a simpler *machine* does equally well what it does, you admit that this part of the constitution, however dignified or awful it may be, is nevertheless in truth useless" (emphasis added).

27. Art. 15, para. 2, TEU.

28. Art. 15, para. 2, TEU.

29. Van Rompuy, *Europe in the Storm*, 108.

30. Matthias Krupa, "Wie hat die Krise Europa verändert?", *Die Zeit*, no. 29 (16 July 2015).

31. Since 2009, when it became a fully-fledged Union institution with the signing of the Lisbon Treaty, the European Council has been able to take binding "decisions", concerning appointments, for instance. Nevertheless, the "conclusions" remain its appropriate instrument.

32. Stimulating for the analysis of the relationship executive-lawmaker remains, T. Koopmans, *Vergelijkend publiekrecht*, second edition (Deventer: Kluwer, 1986), 143–207.

33. A. Mattera (ed.), "*Pénélope*", 11–34: 19.

34. Council of the EU, "Rules of Procedure of the Council", Art. 7.

35. Stefan Lehne, "Are Prime Ministers Taking Over EU Foreign Policy?", Carnegie Europe, 16 February 2015. Available at: https://carnegieendowment.org/files/prime_min_for_policy.pdf (accessed 20 December 2018).

36. The classic study from before the euro crisis is Uwe Puetter, *The Eurogroup: How a Secretive Circle of Finance Ministers Shape European Economic Governance* (Manchester: Manchester University Press, 2006); for an update by the same author see, *The European Council and the Council: New Intergovernmentalism and Institutional Change* (Oxford: Oxford University Press, 2014), 155–70.

37. The Treaty does enable the ECOFIN Council to vote without the member states from outside the eurozone (Art. 139, para. 4, TFEU), whereby the Eurogroup de facto takes legally binding decisions.

38. Treaty Establishing the European Stability Mechanism, Art. 5, para. 1.

39. Yanis Varoufakis, *Adults in the Room: My Battle with Europe's Deep Establishment* (London: Bodley Head, 2017), 383–8; the Eurogroup meeting concerned took place on Sunday 24 April 2015.

40. Ministers can also use this formula, but it is less common and currently happens only with the authority of the European Council (as on 9 May 2010 with the setting up of the ad hoc rescue funds).

41. Van Rompuy, *Europe in the Storm*, 114–5.

42. This provision was superfluous in the case of the first president of the Eurogroup, Jean-Claude Juncker (2005–13), since as both prime minister and finance minister of Luxembourg he was a member of both circles and was able officially to act as a natural link between the two.

43. "European Council 23 October 2011, conclusions", pt 7; "Statement by the Heads of State or Government of the euro area", 26 October 2011; "Statement by the Heads of State or Government of the European Union", 26 October 2011.

44. Treaty on Stability, Coordination and Governance in the Economic and Monetary Union, Art. 12.

45. For example François Hollande, interview in *Le Monde*, 17 October 2012. His successor Emmanuel Macron, by contrast, favours instead a "finance minister" for the eurozone.

46. Kojève, *Notion de l'autorité*, 67–9. The French terms are *le Père, le Maître, le Chef, le Juge* (I have translated "*Maître*" as "Warrior" because Kojève means the Hegelian "master" who is prepared to put his life on the line in a battle of life and death).

47. Art. 17, para. 1, TEU.

48. An essential element that is lacking here is the political relationship between the term in office of the Parliament and Commission that characterizes parliamentary systems. In a conflict between them, the Commission cannot dissolve Parliament to gain support from voters for its view of the matter. The Parliament can send the Commission home, but the Commission that replaces it can only sit out the rest of its five-year "term of office" (Art. 17, para. 3, TEU), a procedure that reflects its civil service origins.

49. To this day the president and members of a new Commission are not just, respectively, "elected" or "subject as a body to a vote of consent" by parliamentary majority, they are also, respectively, "proposed" or "appointed" by the European Council (Art. 17, para. 7, TEU).

50. Art. 17, para. 1, TEU.

51. Art. 225, TFEU (Parliament); Art. 241, TFEU (Council).

52. Art. 22, para. 1, TEU (foreign policy); Art. 68, TFEU (justice).

53. Art. 30, para. 1, TEU.

54. Art. 76, TFEU.

55. In other words, what is unusual about the Union compared to national systems is that "right of initiative" and "government" do not coincide.

56. Art. 39 of the Constitution of the French Fifth Republic.

57. The comparison with the French Fifth Republic is not unknown in the French literature, and it has popped up occasionally in Dutch reference works too, for example, in W. T. Eijsbouts *et al.*, *Europees Recht, algemeen deel*, second revised edition (Groningen: Europa Law, 2006), 365.

58. This concerns Art. 114, TFEU. See, for example, Stefano Micossi *et al.*, "The New European Framework for Managing Bank Crises", in CEPS Policy Brief no. 304, 21 November 2013, 16–19.

59. Report by its first director: Robert K. Visser, "Naissance d'une agence. Le cas EASO", in *Revue du Droit de l'Union européenne* 3/2003, 1–14; he writes (p. 6), "Constructing a European agency means having to start from zero. There is a situation of tabula rasa, of zero, there is nothing. Zero, which is to say no agents, no internal regulations, no premises, no equipment, nothing at all."

60. Frans Timmermans, first vice-president of the Commission, in his opinion piece "Turkije-deal werkt, nu ook nieuwe samenwerking zoeken met Afrika", *de Volkskrant*, 15 June 2017: "Before 20 March 2016 [the date of the deal with Turkey] there was no functioning asylum service and professional authority on the Greek islands, insufficient reception capacity, a lack of organized accommodation and no functioning return scheme. Even in the best organized country it would take time to get all this in place, taking into account that the setting up of reception capacity can sometimes encounter resistance from the local population."

61. European Commission, "The economic adjustment programme for Greece", 26 May 2010.

62. Varoufakis, *Adults in the Room*, 339–45. One example: in March 2015 an Irish official at the Commission sent an email to the Greek head of the expert group in which, on behalf of the Troika, he insisted that a bill aimed at easing the humanitarian crisis in Greece must be taken off the parliamentary agenda. Varoufakis leaked the email and Greek indignation resulted. See also *The Irish Times*, 20 March 2015, "EU mandarin Declan Costello faces Greek 'wrath' over ultimatums letter".

63. The problem with these new tasks is their distance from political authority; it is not essentially any different from the problem with which the Commission struggles when it operates off its own bat in events-politics. In this sense the legal debate on the subject, generally conducted based on the so-called Meroni doctrine produced by the Court of Justice, is largely beside the point. In the Meroni judgment (1958) the Court proposed limiting the powers of the legislator to delegate powers to agencies, logically calling for restraint in the delegation of discretionary powers that include a certain margin for political judgement and go beyond strict administrative implementation. The new tasks of agencies obviously create tension with this doctrine, which is still in force. But the preliminary question is whether the Commission itself has the political authority to implement certain powers without a relationship with the Union's supreme political authority. (Does it make very much difference to the public whether a Commission official or a Border Agency customs inspector decides which boat will be rescued and which will not?) The delegation of powers makes the problem a little greater but does not cause it.

64. Dominique de Villepin, *Mémoires de paix pour temps de guerre* (Paris: Grasset, 2016), 551.

65. Think for example of the purchase of debt securities under the Securities Markets Programme, announced on 10 May 2010 (after the political decision of 7–9 May 2010 to set up the emergency funds), or of the Long-Term Refinancing Operations programme that made cheap credit available to commercial banks, announced on 8 December 2011 (within sight of the political accord at the summit of 8–9 December 2011 on the "Fiscal Compact" – a name suggested by Draghi himself). As we have seen, it was Draghi who spotted the opening for the Outright Monetary Transactions programme for massive conditional purchasing of national debt of 6 September 2012 – to which he alluded in his speech in London of July 2012 – in the night-time decision of the euro summit of 28–29 June to set up a banking union, after which, in the early morning, he said to Herman Van Rompuy, "Do you realise what you all did last night? This is the game-changer we need." See also Chapter 1.

66. Van Rompuy, *Europe in the Storm*, 21–2.

67. Sergei Lavrov, "Speech and answers to questions at the meeting with representatives of the Association of European Businesses (AEB), Moscow, October 25, 2016", available on the website of the Russian ministry of foreign affairs (http://www.mid.ru/en/vistupleniya_ministra/-/asset_publisher/MCZ7HQuMdqBY/content/id/2506106); the Lavrov quote used here is as rendered by the director of Clingendael, Monika Sie, in an interview with *de Volkskrant*, 16 June 2017.

68. Anonymous German diplomat cited in *Le Figaro*, 24–25 June 2017, "Macron veut un pacte pour dix ans avec Berlin" (Macron wants a ten-year pact with Berlin).

69. Emmanuel Macron cited in *Le Figaro*, 24–25 June ("ten years"); Emmanuel Macron, "Discours du Président devant le Parlement réuni en congrès", 3 July 2017 ("curators"). Available at: http://discours.vie-publique.fr/notices/177001264.html (accessed 20 December 2018).

70. Pocock, *Machiavellian Moment*, viii.

7 THE OPPOSITION TAKES THE STAGE

1. Machiavelli, *Discourses on Livy*, I. 4.

2. Giovanni Sartori, "Constitutionalism: A Preliminary Discussion", *American Political Science Review* 56 (1962) 4: 864 (cited in Turkuler Isiksel, "The dream of commercial peace", in Van Middelaar and Van Parijs (eds), *After the Storm*, 38).

3. Albert Camus, *The Rebel*, trans. Anthony Bower (New York: Vintage, 1956), 13–14. Originally published as *L'Homme révolté* (Paris: Gallimard, 1951).

4. Peter Mair, "Political Opposition and the European Union", *Government and Opposition* 42 (2007) 1, 1–17. Revised version of the "Government and Opposition/Leonard Schapiro Annual Lecture", delivered on 5 April 2006 at Reading University.

5. In making this threefold distinction, Mair refers to a well-known article by Otto Kirchheimer, "The Waning of Opposition in Parliamentary Regimes", *Social Research* 24 (1957) 129–56. Another classic text is Robert A. Dahl (ed.), *Political Oppositions in Western Democracies* (New Haven, CT: Yale University Press, 1966).

6. Mair, "Political Opposition", 15.

7. At the same time, American political scientist Vivien A. Schmidt, in *Democracy in Europe*, warned of "the twin problems of growing voter dissatisfaction and political extremism in response to Europeanization" (156).

8. Peter Mair, *Ruling the Void: The Hollowing Out of Western Democracy* (London: Verso, 2011), 142; slightly adapted from Mair, "Political Opposition", 17. The term "milestone" in the final sentence is a reference to Robert Dahl's three milestones on the way to democratic politics in Dahl, *Political Oppositions*, "Preface".

9. Dieter Grimm, *Europa ja – aber welches? Zur Verfassung der europäischen Demokratie* (Munich: Beck, 2016).

10. For this reason many political scientists claimed until recently that the European Union, defined as a "regulatory state" (Giandomenico Majone in an oft-quoted article from 1994), need not let itself be talked into having a guilt complex about insufficient democratic participation. This was systematically argued in 2002 by Andrew Moravcsik in "In defence of the democratic deficit: reassessing legitimacy in the European Union", *Journal of Common Market Studies* 40 (2002) 4: 603–24. He writes (p. 603): "The EU's appearance of exception insulation reflects the subset of functions it performs – central banking, constitutional adjudication, civil prosecution, economic diplomacy and technical administration. These are matters of low electoral salience commonly delegated in national systems, for justifiable reasons." Words from a bygone age.

11. The Commission's Directorate-General for Trade proudly declares on its website that over the past few years it has received a total of 2,866 representatives of 771 civil society organizations; http://trade.ec.europa.eu/civilsoc/statistics.cfm (accessed on 28 August 2018).

12. Jos de Beus, "The European Union as a Community: An argument about the public sphere in international society and politics", in Paul van Seters (ed.), *Communitarianism in Law and Society*, 71–108, (Lanham, MD: Rowman & Littlefield, 2006), 76.

13. See the chapter "The lives and teachings of the European saints", in Alan Milward, *The European Rescue of the Nation-State*, 318–44 (London: Routledge, 1992).

14. For this last point see Mark Gilbert, "Narrating the process: questioning the progressive story of European integration", *Journal of Common Market Studies* 46 (2008) 3, 641–62.

15. Gilbert, "Narrating the process".

16. See for example the proposal that government leaders issue a solemn declaration that for two years they will make no moves towards "more Europe", expressed a week before the Brexit vote by former French foreign minister Hubert Védrine in "Radikaler Wandel oder Untergang", *Frankfurter Allgemeine Zeitung*, 17 June 2016.

17. So concluded a detailed reconstruction of that weekend in Georg Blume *et al.*, "Die Nacht, in der Deutschland die Kontrolle verlor", *Die Zeit*, no. 35, 22 August 2016.

18. Habermas, *Zur Verfassung Europas*, 48 ("postdemokratischer Exekutivföderalismus"). Another school of authors appealed to Carl Schmitt's concept of *Ausnahmezustand*, usually translated as "state of emergency", in analysing crisis-politics; for an overview see Christian Kroeder-Sonnen, "Beyond integration theory: the (anti-)constitutional dimension of European crisis governance", *Journal of Common Market Studies* 54 (2016) 6: 1350–66; the author endorses (p. 1359) "the assessment that European exceptionalism has blended into a more permanent structural configuration of authority that bears authoritarian traits of executive discretion and autocratic decision-making".

19. Mair, "Political Opposition", 15.

20. Compare Yves Bertoncini, "Les référendums nationaux sur l'Europe: de la clarification à la frustration", in *Rapport Schuman sur l'Europe: l'Etat de l'Union 2017* (Paris: Lignes de Repères, 2017), 183–90.

21. Albert O. Hirschman, *Exit, Voice, and Loyalty: Responses to Decline in Firms, Organizations, and States* (Cambridge MA: Harvard University Press, 1972).

22. Harold Macmillan, cited in Nora Beloff, *The General Says No: Britain's Exclusion from Europe* (London: Penguin, 1963), 59. He was speaking in the Parliamentary Assembly of the Council of Europe. The full quotation runs: "Fearing the weakness of democracy, men have often sought safety in technocrats. There is nothing new in this. It is as old as Plato. But frankly the idea is not attractive to the British. We have not overthrown the divine right of kings to fall down before the divine right of experts."

23. Theresa May, "Global Britain", speech at Lancaster House, 17 January 2017.

24. European Council meeting (18 and 19 February 2016) – Conclusions, Annex I.

25. This, along with how the post-Brexit Union can and must do more to protect citizens, is examined in more detail in Luuk van Middelaar, "Protect and Survive", *Europe's World* 33 (Autumn 2016, published 19 October 2016), 10–12.

26. The term "permissive consensus" was coined in 1970 (Leon N. Lindberg and Stuart A. Scheingold, *Europe's Would-Be Polity: Patterns of Change in the European Community* (Upper Saddle River, NJ: Prentice Hall, 1970), 242 ff.) but it has been on everyone's lips since 1992.

27. Liesbet Hooghe and Gary Marks, "A postfunctionalist theory of European integration: from permissive consensus to constraining dissensus", *British Journal of Political Science* 39 (2008), 1–23.

28. Antoine Vauchez, *Démocratiser l'Europe* (Paris: Seuil, 2014), 82.

29. *Ibid.*, 87.

30. Grimm, *Europa ja*, 26.

31. *Ibid.*, 115.

32. *Ibid.*, 120.

33. For a critical, rather defensive discussion of this see "Editorial comments: A way to win back support for the European project?", *Common Market Law Review* 54 (2017), 1–10.

34. See, for example, the young German legal expert Clemens Kaupa in his *The Pluralist Character of the European Economic Constitution* (London: Hart, 2016).

35. For an early critique see Philippe Moreau Defarges, "Gouvernance: une mutation du pouvoir?", *Le Débat* (May–Aug 2001) 115, 165–72; he writes: "In the flux of governance, the choice is no longer a clearly defined decision but the product of endless interactions. [...] But politics, power relations, have they disappeared or have they instead merely been obscured?" (167, 172).

36. European Commission, "European Governance: a white paper", COM (2001) 428, 25 July 2001.

37. On the Paris side, Nicolas Sarkozy said, in a speech to the European Parliament on 21 October 2008 during the banking crisis, "The eurozone cannot continue without a clearly identified economic government". Sarkozy believed that with the formalizing of the Euro Summit in the eurocrisis, October 2011, the argument had been settled: "It is the *raison d'être* of the government of the eurozone that France has wanted and that will bring together the heads of state or government to make joint decisions" (speech in Toulon, 1 December 2011). His successor François Hollande said something along the same lines at a press conference on 16 May 2013: "Establish among the eurozone countries an economic government that comes together every month around a president who will be assigned this one task". Not so Emmanuel Macron, who places his

bets on a eurozone "finance minister" instead. As for Brussels, see José Manuel Barroso, "European Renewal: State of the Union Address 2011", Strasbourg, 28 September 2011: "Indeed, within the Community competences, the Commission is the economic government of the Union; we certainly do not need more institutions for this" (note the bureaucratic qualification "within the Community competences").

38. Stéphanie Hennette, Thomas Piketty, Guillaume Sacriste and Antoine Vauchez, *Pour un traité de démocratisation de l'Europe* (Paris: Seuil, 2017). English translation published as *How to Democratize Europe* (Cambridge, MA: Harvard University Press, 2019).

39. "Rapport général de Fernand Dehousse, président du groupe de travail pour les élections européennes, relatif au Projet de convention sur l'élection de l'Assemblée parlementaire européenne au suffrage universel direct, soumis à l'Assemblée le 30 avril 1960, part. 24". In full: "Direct elections should therefore serve to administer a salutary shock to the peoples of the Six. Only from their conscious participation can we expect a sense of purpose capable of bearing up the Community structure despite the accidents, disputes and sectarian attitudes of the moment." Translation taken from European Parliament, Directorate-General for Parliamentary Documentation and Information, *The Case for Elections to the European Parliament by Direct Universal Suffrage*, selected documents (Luxembourg, 1969).

40. For this latter plan, drawn up by the secretary-general of the Parliament Klaus Welle, see Florian Eder, "Anything Trump can do. EU plans presidential inauguration", Politico, 10 March 2017. Available at: https://www.politico.eu/article/who-wants-to-have-the-greatest-inaugurial-crowd-ever/ (accessed 20 December 2018).

41. Manifesto, Spinelli group, 15 September 2010. Available at: http://www.spinelligroup.eu/2018manifesto (accessed 20 December 2018).

42. Amie Kreppel, "Looking 'Up', 'Down' and 'Sideways': Understanding EU Institutions in Context", *West European Politics* 34 (2011) 1: 167–79. The American political scientist writes:

> The nature of the executive-legislative relationship within the EU is the source of much confusion and misinformation. Partially this is a result of the gradual evolution of the various institutions, and partially it is the result of improper comparisons based on familiarity rather than an examination of the institutions themselves and the functional relationships between them. Despite the fact that almost all of the member states have very clear fused powers (parliamentary) systems, the EU as a whole is organised on the basis of the separation of powers (p. 169).

The European Union as a separation-of-powers system is also the perspective in Fabbrini's *Which European Union?*; see 172–84 for his criticism of complete parliamentarization, because of interstate fault lines.

43. It is also possible to say that the European Union is "mixed" and contains elements of both a "separation of powers" and a "fused powers" system, much like the French constitutional system (for this comparison in the executive field, see Chapter 6).

44. For the empty-chair crisis and its consequences see Van Middelaar, *Passage to Europe*, 54–80. The Luxembourg Compromise allowed (de facto if not de jure) a national government to veto a decision for which it could otherwise have been outvoted, on the basis of an appeal to "vital interests". For successive UK governments it constituted an important element in the "unwritten constitution" of the club's life. Although most lawyers consider that the "Luxembourg veto" was abolished with the Single European

Act of 1987, a number of governments (including those of France, Spain and Denmark) still uphold its existence. As late as June 2014, David Cameron appealed to it behind the scenes in his desperate attempt to block the nomination of Jean-Claude Juncker as Commission president. In an equivocal but telling response, French president François Hollande said he certainly did not wish to abolish an agreement of which his own government had been at the origin, but that in this particular case "it was a matter of personnel policy, not a vital interest". The British PM begged to differ, but he was duly outvoted in the European Council meeting of 27 June 2014.

45. Art. 15, para. 4, TEU: "Except where the Treaties provide otherwise, decisions of the European Council shall be taken by consensus".

46. Episode examined in detail in Van Middelaar, *Passage to Europe*, 100–111 ("Coup in Milan").

47. David Cameron, 13 June 2014, published in many member states, original available at: www.gov.uk/government/news/presidency-of-the-european-commission-article-by-david-cameron (accessed 20 December 2018).

48. For a refined account of an earlier battle between Parliament and government leaders, concerning the appointment of the first Barroso Commission, see Thomas Beukers, "The Invisible Elephant: Member states' collective involvement in the appointment of the Barroso Commission", *European Constitutional Law Review* 1 (2004) 2, 217–25.

49. Münkler, *Macht in der Mitte*, 143.

50. This point was made by Dr Thomas Bagger, head of planning at the German ministry of foreign affairs, in a public conversation with the author on 21 June 2016 at the Dutch embassy in Berlin.

51. Münkler, *Macht in der Mitte*, 143.

52. Jürgen Habermas, "Warum Merkels Griechenland-Politik ein Fehler ist", *Süddeutsche Zeitung*, 22 June 2015.

53. Yanis Varoufakis, press conference in Berlin with Wolfgang Schäuble, 5 February 2015.

54. Matthias Krupa, "Wie hat die Krise Europa verändert?", *Die Zeit* no. 29, 16 July 2015.

55. Ferdinand Otto, "Horst Seehofer: Mit Orbán gegen Merkel", *Zeit Online*, 23 September 2015.

56. *Spiegel Online*, "Orbán 80 Minuten Gast von Kohl. Besuch beim Altkanzler", 19 April 2016.

EPILOGUE

1. Arendt, *Human Condition*, 188.

2. Dominique Reynié (ed.), *Démocraties sous tension: une enquête planétaire*, vol. 1 (Paris: Fondapol, 2019), 56.

3. Arendt, *Human Condition*, 192–7.

Index